LIFE IN A TROUBLED LAND

Also by author

Music You Will Never Hear
A Modern Greek Tragedy
iUniverse, Inc.
2005

Of Bear, Mice, and Nails
Outhouse Chronicles
iUniverse, Inc.
2010

Too Good Cooking
Morris Press Cookbooks
2008

Cover and photograph credits - Angelo J Kaltsos

LIFE IN A TROUBLED LAND

MIRUPAFSHIM
(Good-bye)

Angelo J. Kaltsos

iUniverse LLC
Bloomington

Life In A Troubled Land
Mirupafshim (Good-bye)

iUniverse books may be ordered through booksellers or by contacting:

iUniverse LLC
1663 Liberty Drive
Bloomington, IN 47403
www.iuniverse.com
1-800-Authors (1-800-288-4677)

ISBN: 978-1-4759-3557-8 (sc)
ISBN: 978-1-4759-3556-1 (hc)
ISBN: 978-1-4759-3555-4 (ebk)

Library of Congress Control Number: 2012912075

Printed in the United States of America

iUniverse rev. date: 08/14/2013

DEDICATION

In memory of my ancestors, my mother and father, their families, and all those citizens that resided during the period of this novel that endured the difficulties and tragedies of living in Albania and what was and still referred to as Northern Epirus, Albania.

CONTENTS

PART TWO

This story is based on actual incidents and historical facts about Albania and an American of Greek descent traveling to Albania after the fall of communism and the recognition of embassies between Albania and the United States of America. The two countries closed their embassies from November 1946 to October 1991: forty-five years. The story's years of travel are accurate.

Some of the village's names are fictitious and in order to protect the privacy of all individuals, names have been fictionalized and any similarity to the name, character, or history of any person, living or dead, is entirely coincidental and unintentional.

ACKNOWLEDGMENTS

To my family in Albania I want to thank you for being as loving as you were, for sharing when some foods were rationed and other food items were not in great supply, and for helping me to travel within the country. Because of all of the problems you endured it made this story possible. I also want to say that the courage I witnessed made me proud to write these words.

I want to thank Rebecca Orr for all her printouts and for assisting me in all my computer difficulties. Without her aid I would still be writing with a pencil. I have to thank Carol Melzar and Tina Warren on reading the rough drafts and their generous encouragements to complete this manuscript. To my two English language editors, Doug Mawhinney and Bruce Kurland, many thanks for helping me finish this project, and many thanks to my dearest Greek friend, Margarita Kaltsa for editing the Greek language written in the text.

I need to thank the September, 1994, issue of the Greek Helsinki Monitor report when doing my research on the political problems between Greece and Albania because of the killing of two Albanian soldiers. Last but not least, I want to thank Maine Press of Rumford, Maine for their many printings.

PREFACE

The following is a brief history of a specific area in the Balkans which was part of ancient Illyria; this specific area is now called Albania. Illyria has a rich and interesting history.

Illyria comprised part of the Roman Province of Dalmatia. It remained under Roman control until the 7th century. This section of Illyria (Albania) was conquered in the 16th century (1546) by the Ottoman Empire and remained under its control until the war of 1912. This area is also referred to as Epirus and by the Greek populace and Greek government as Northern Epirus.

War broke out on May 1912 when Greece, Serbia, Montenegro, and Bulgaria invaded the last of the Balkan Ottoman Empire in Europe. European ambassadors from Russia, Germany, Britain, Austria-Hungary, Italy and France, finalized a peace between the warring nations. On November 28, 1912 Albania declared its independence. The European ambassadors set up a monarchy, replaced by a Republic, and then another monarchy.

The Europeans' settlement ignored the population demographics, especially the Greek settlements in southern Albania (Northern Epirus). The population of 35,000 to 40,000 Greeks were now included within the southern area. Because of the large Greek Orthodox population in Northern Epirus, Greece claimed it to be their territory. This became a source of friction between Albania and Greece beginning in1913.

During the Paris Peace Conference after World War I, President Woodrow Wilson, largely through his personal efforts, averted the partitioning of Albania to bordering nations. The League of Nations finally recognized Albania as a sovereign nation in 1920.

During the early years of the 1920s, Albania was led by Ahmed Bey Zogu, a chieftain from north central Albania, and between 1921 and 1924 the country enjoyed political freedom, but Zogu fled to Yugoslavia in 1924 because of his unsuccessful governmental programs. The new leader, Bishop Fan S. Noli, a bishop of the Orthodox Church became Albania's prime minister.

With the assistance of Yugoslavia, Ahmed Bey Zogu returned and became president (1925-28) then he ruled as King Zog I (1928-39). Under King Zog, Italy and Albania signed a twenty year economy and defense pact. The first formation of communist groups appeared in Albania because of the King's failure to improve conditions. Under the defense pact Italy took control of the Albanian military and foreign affairs. Dissatisfied with indirect control, Italy invaded Albania on April 7, 1939 and occupied and annexed the country; King Zog fled to Greece.

Communist groups merged and formed the Albanian Communist Party on November 1941. The so-called Partisans began to fight the occupiers (Italians). Germany took control of Albania after Italy surrendered to the Allies in 1943. The Germans set up a fascist government, and the Partisans battled the Germans. When Germany evacuated Albania on October 1944 the communist groups seized power.

On November 29, 1944, Enver Hoxha became the leader of Albania. He was a college instructor and also secretary of the communist party. Albania changed its name to the People's Republic of Albania, and in 1976 the People's Socialist Republic of Albania.

Under Enver Hoxha, the government nationalized banks, industry, and all commercial and foreign properties. It began agrarian reform and finally established collectivized agriculture. The communist government then turned to Yugoslavia for military support, economic aid, and military security (1944-47). When problems developed between the two governments Albania turned to the Soviet Union (1948-61), and finally it turned to China (1961-78). With what was the country's backwardness, and with this new modernization and aid, Albania entered the 20th century.

The government of Yugoslavia tried to overthrow Enver Hoxha in 1948, but the political differences between Yugoslavia and the Soviets saved Hoxha from being removed. Yugoslavia and Albanian relations were strained from that time on. Both countries placed soldiers on their border.

The Soviet government tried to solve the problems between Yugoslavia and Albanian, but the relationship between Albania and the Soviet Union became strained during 1955. In June 1960, Albania turned to China; China at that time was at odds with the Soviet Union. At the end of 1960 Hoxha denounced Khrushchev, and in 1961 Albania closed the Soviet submarine base in Vlora, a base on the Adriatic Sea, and this caused the Soviets to break relations in December 1961.

In 1978 when the governments of the United States and China started to become closer China ended aid to Albania. Because of this action by the Chinese, Albanian and Chinese relations ended. When Enver Hoxha saw Marxist and Leninist ideologues abandoned and rapprochement to western capitalism become a reality he had nowhere to turn for aid or security; Albania became isolated from nations.

To eliminate all dissent and opposition during Hoxha's forty-one year rule (1944-1985), he removed opponents by imprisonment or execution. Government officials were allowed to travel, but regular citizens were forbidden, even within their country. Owning property was banned, freedom of speech was banned, all mail was censored, and telephone calls were monitored. In 1967 all religions were officially banned, Albania became the only country to officially ban all religions, and all Christian and Muslim houses were closed; some to become warehouses or animal enclosures, others were completely destroyed. Hoxha became a dictator.

Hoxha died in 1985, he had hand-picked Ramiz Alia as his replacement. Alia wanted to keep communism in force, but he expanded diplomatic relations and legalized some foreign investments. Albania only had embassies in Rome, Paris, and Switzerland. In 1987 Greece and Albania ended their state of war, in effect since the end of World War II. In 1989, with the fall of communism in some nations, Albanians became anti-communistic and politically active against the government. Trying to keep the government in force Alia restored travel, allowed religious freedom, and established some free market reform. Ramiz Alia allowed independent political parties to form during the end of 1990. With all these reforms the government weakened and in March 1992 an election removed the communist leaders. Thus Albania became democratic again, the last democratic leader being Fan S. Noli in 1924.

The American embassy opened in Tirana, Albania on October 1, 1991. On December 21, 1991, the American ambassador to Albania presented its credentials to the government of Albania.

The author's parents and many past generations were born under the rule of the Ottoman Empire, but during those times, the Northern Epirus villages were still considered a part of Greece. His mother was born in 1910, his father in 1906. The Northern Epirus villages were incorporated into Albania in 1912. This became a conflict for the Greek villages and for Greece and Albania.

During the Enver Hoxha's regime Greek-Albanian men had to do military service in the Albanian armed forces, but they could not become officers, and they were not allowed to become police officers. The Greek populace resented this position.

This story begins on September 1992.

PART ONE

PART ONE

Chapter I

George Stamos arrived at the northwest Greek border where surprisingly he found Greek soldiers about the complex fully armed with automatic weapons. It is September 2, 1992, and he is the only American there, and he sees no one else in civilian clothes. This Greek custom's modern cement building is located on the Greek and Albanian border in an area that is called Kakavia,

With his passport in his hand George approached a counter and a Greek uniformed custom official, seeing that his passport is American, he checked his passport and gave George a document to fill out, reporting his nationality, his destination in Albania, and other personal official questions. Glancing at the filled out form, the official informed George that there is a Greek-Albanian man, who lived in one of the Greek villages in Albania with an automobile who will take you to your destination for two thousand drachmas ($13.33).

"You will find him parked beyond the guarded Greek border crossing gate."

George informed the official, "Thank you. My aunt is to meet me on the Albanian side. Why are there so many soldiers about?"

"We are protecting the border from Albanians entering the country illegally."

The official stamped his passport to exit and gave him permission to enter the border crossing through the doorway in the rear of the building.

George exited the building, going down a few stairs and onto a cement pathway, leading to a tall chain-link fence and gate. A junior Greek official, after checking his passport, unlocked a padlock on a metal chain securing the chain-link gate, opened the gate and allowed George to pass into the no-man's tall chain link fenced-in graveled passageway.

The walkway is about two hundred feet long and about twenty feet wide. George struggled to carry all his baggage while holding his passport in his hand; at that time large suitcases didn't have wheels. He passed a small faded light blue automobile parked near the Greek side of the fence. George could not recognize the make or year of the car; it looked old and in very poor condition. He assumed it belonged to the Greek-Albanian driver that the custom official told him about, who could drive him to the village. George and the driver nodded at each other. As it was, George was the only person walking in either direction. The sun was high and the weather was hot and dry. George could feel perspiration accumulating under his shirt. It seemed to George that he was in a prison yard with no way to escape; there were guards at both ends.

Reaching the far end of the deserted walkway, George approached two metal chain-link gates and an unkempt small unpainted one-room building on the other side of the first gate. There were Albanian soldiers at the gates talking. They stopped and stared at George, then one nodded his head at George and another extended his arm to look at his passport. The soldier with the extended arm said something in Albanian, but because George didn't understand, George looked him in the eyes with a blank expression. The soldier glanced at the passport and opened the unlocked gate and pointed to the small building.

George entered the small one-room building where there were two men in civilian clothes. One man was sitting behind an old wooden desk; the other man was sitting on an old soiled and sagging living room chair. Other than that, the building was empty. There were no windows, only the open doorway emitted light. George saw no electric light fixtures. George stood in front of the desk, said, "Hello," in English, and the man behind the desk said in English, "Passport." No greeting or smile. The other man just looked at George with wide opened eyes. The two officials were thin with straight jet black hair and dark eyes, dressed in white shirts, no ties, dark pants, and well-worn suit jackets. They had pleasant faces and looked to be in their late thirties or early forties.

The man behind the desk went through George's entire passport slowly, page by page, and on the last page he stamped it and handed the passport back. There was not the usual inspection of baggage or questions about his personal luggage. George said, "Thanks," and went out the opened doorway and without hearing a word from them.

He had to show his passport to an Albanian soldier at the second fenced-in gate, which were only a few steps beyond the small building. This soldier checked the entry stamp and then opened the second gate. Again no words were passed. George was now officially in Albania. The Greek side was paved and had a modern cement building with electricity, and the custom officials were friendly and wore uniforms. The Albanian side was quite different, to say the least.

Crossing the border it seemed to George that he had stepped into another era. The surroundings seemed alien and unfriendly. George had traveled to many third world countries, but something felt very different. For the moment he felt very alone and stranded. He couldn't say he felt at ease, but he didn't feel threatened either.

Nothing was paved and there were no visible facilities other than the small building he had entered and a tiny ramshackle makeshift structure on the far side of the open area; there were a few individuals standing near it. To his left he could see an unpaved road leading down a gradual grade and then disappearing out of sight. Both countries had built their border crossings on a hillside. George assumed it was to enable them to look in both directions. As it was, there was still some tension between the two countries but no military conflict. He could see tall mountains in every direction. The only visible comfort was the fact that the countryside was beautiful.

George looked for his aunt, but there was no female in sight. There were young men alone or in groups mingling about, sitting on the ground or standing, talking or being quiet. There was no indication of jovial conversations. The areas atmosphere was very conservative. No one made any appreciable notice to his presence. Everyone had small cloth bags or valises. There was discarded trash on the ground; he saw no trash barrels. George assumed that the men were waiting for the opportunity to sneak into Greece.

George stood a few yards from the gate looking at the surroundings and for someone who might be there to greet him. After a few moments had passed a young man approached George. He was in his mid twenties, with a pleasant olive colored face, of medium build, and a few inches shorter than George. For a moment, George assumed this must be a family member.

Nearing George, he asked in English, "Do you need help? I see you looking for someone."

Realizing that the man was a not a family member, but surprised that he spoke in English, George answered, "I'm waiting for my relative."

The stranger said, "My name is Kocho. Are you of Albanian descent?"

"No, I am of Greek descent. My name is George."

"Are you thirsty?"

"Yes."

Kocho quickly turned around and walked across the gravel lot to the ramshackle makeshift structure on the far side of the open area. The building was crudely made of unpainted used wood with a roof made of rusted tin sheets. George thought it looked as though the structure was used by people who sold drinks or food. Because of all his baggage George didn't move an inch. He was making sure it would remain secure. Kocho returned with two bottles of apple juice and handed one to George.

George asked, "How much do I owe you?"

"Nothing. You are the first American I've ever seen."

"How do you know I am an American?"

"By your clothes and baggage."

George felt at ease and explained that his parents were born in the Greek villages and that his aunt was supposed to meet him. George was getting anxious and unsettled because she had not shown up. He had no idea whether she had gotten his letters telling her of his arrival. Because of the inadequate Albanian postal service mail didn't always get delivered.

George had sent three letters to try to guarantee a delivery. He was explicit on the date and time of day of his arrival. George had researched the travel information with an Albanian group in Boston and an elderly family friend named Arthur. Arthur was born in George's mother's village and had returned to Albania many times. The Albanian government allowed this friend to visit because he was born there.

About an hour had passed since George had entered Albania, and no aunt or relative appeared. In the meantime, the young man asked him many questions about America. This helped pass the time. George did not ask questions about Albania. He was leery because he didn't know who Kocho really was. Seeing that Albania had been ruled previously by a totalitarian communist government, George wasn't about to get into trouble asking the wrong questions.

Kocho relieved the situation by saying, "I'll wait with you until your aunt arrives. This is no place to be stranded."

Kocho did not speak Greek nor have any distant Greek relatives, but he told George some Greek travelers had been robbed on the main highway. He told George that times were bad and that a Greek diplomat had been robbed and left with only his underwear and his car. He wanted to be sure that George was safe. Of course, George appreciated his concern and thanked him. Not knowing if his aunt or anyone would ever arrive, George didn't know what to do. He thought, 'Do I have to go back across the border or do I venture on somehow?'

Kocho informed him there were no taxis or bus service at this Albanian custom border crossing. George hearing a motor vehicle driving across the no-man's land and through the Albanian chain linked fence turned around and thought he recognized the car. It looked like the same one that was parked at the Greek gate, with the man that the Greek custom official said would take George to his destination. Because so much time had passed, and because no one else had come through the gate either way George had forgotten about the car.

George said to Kocho, "He looks like the man I could have hired to take me to my family's village, but I told the custom official I was meeting a family member. Maybe I can hire him now to take me seeing that my aunt or any other relative hasn't arrived, otherwise I'll have to go back to Greece."

George and Kocho waved as the car went through the second gate; the driver approached them slowly and stopped. George's Albanian companion walked to the driver's side. Because it was a warm day the car's front windows were rolled down. George couldn't understand what Kocho said to the driver, but Kocho knew what George wanted.

Kocho returned, "He'll take you for two thousand drachmas."

George said, "Good." Kocho related the message to the driver.

The driver had a young dark haired boy sitting in the passenger's side; George couldn't tell his age, but he was probably twelve to fifteen years old; he looked underweight. The boy jumped out, took George's luggage and grocery bags with little effort, put them in the rear, and then slid into the back seat as George got into the front. George thanked Kocho for his help and company and off George went wondering if this unknown make of a car or George would even make it to the bottom of the hill.

Chapter II

George Stamos and his older sister Eli were the first children from their father's family to be born in America. Their father, Vlassi, arrived alone in 1922 as a sixteen year old. His passport was forged so his age said he was eighteen, and Vlassi, as it turned out, was the only family member to immigrate to America. He had one older brother and two younger brothers and four younger sisters. Vlassi's oldest sister was fifteen when he left.

George's father never talked about his marriage or his Albania family to Eli or George. He was most secretive about his past life for some reason, even about his marriage problem, separation (1931), and a divorce (1936), from George's mother; it was an arranged marriage as were all marriages at that time in the Greek-Albanian villages. The tradition was brought to America, but this marriage didn't last long nor did the tradition. George's grandmother told him that her husband had made the arrangements.

George and Eli were brought up by their father in Boston, Massachusetts. Rather than question their stern father they adjusted and didn't ask any questions about family matters. When George was twenty three (1953), Vlassi secretly moved, and there was no communication with Eli and George until 1964. George had heard that his father had gone west to Ohio or Illinois.

One day there was a knock on the Stamos' front door. George and his wife, June, were both home. He said, "I'll get it." It was May 15, 1964.

George opened the door. There was a well dressed man standing there with a smile on his face. It took George a second before he recognized that it was his father. Vlassi appeared older, his face was thinner and lined, he had lost most of his hair, and he seemed shorter. George was at a loss, and it took a moment before he knew what to do. George finally said, "Come on in." Vlassi extended his hand and entered. Vlassi wanted his son in his life again.

Vlassi visited many times in the course of one year. He got a job in Boston working at a bakery. He had been a baker before the 1930s depression. At times, George and June would drive the hour to Boston to visit him. Vlassi seemed to be in good spirits.

George and June would invite his father for dinner, and sometimes Vlassi would stay a couple of days. George would take him for rides up north to see the White Mountains or some of the local lakes. They were developing a pleasant relationship. They wanted to know more about each other, but Vlassi never said much about the previous eleven years. He was still the secretive man about his past. He only related that he had lived in Chicago, had remarried and divorced. He sold his home and wanted to see Eli and her three daughters, George and his wife, and to be back in Boston. He wanted to help George financially, but George needed no help. He was quite comfortable in his situation.

Vlassi, while working making doughnuts, had a minor stroke in early May, 1965, a year after he returned from Chicago. His right side was affected, but not severely. When he was discharged from the hospital, George brought him to his home to rehabilitate. Two weeks later, George and June were both home when Vlassi had another stroke watching television. He was taken by ambulance to the local hospital. The doctor treating Vlassi told George and June that his father had a massive stroke and would not recover. George telephoned the local Greek Orthodox Church for the priest to give his father his last rites. An hour later the priest arrived, said the proper prayers for Vlassi, and when the priest completed his religious duties, Vlassi died.

One evening, a few days before Vlassi died he talked to George and shared some of his past and about his family in Albania. As it was, June was not at home. Maybe he felt at ease being alone with George. He told his son that his passport was forged and that he was not sixty-one, but only fifty nine. His passport was forged because he could not enter the country alone if he was only sixteen years of age. He mentioned his family in Albania and said that his three younger sisters and one brother were still alive. Two brothers had passed away in 1960, one was fifty-seven, and the other brother was thirty-seven. A sister had died in 1960 when she was fifty-three. Vlassi's father, Vangeli, died in 1958, at seventy-seven, and his mother Krisidio died in 1959. She was sixty-nine.

George was surprised that his father was telling him about his family, but his father, obviously, was aware that life was closing in on him. One never knows how a person will act when facing death. Vlassi never mentioned anything about George's mother. George let his father talk about whatever he wanted. Just the fact that he did was enough for George. George didn't interrupt or ask any questions.

After Vlassi died, George became the executor of his estate. Going through his father's possessions he found an address book with names of his father's relatives in Albania. George was thrilled! How exciting to be thirty-five and discovering, for the first time, his relatives in Europe, and seeing their names and addresses for the first time.

George set the address book aside and told June he should write to his aunts and uncle to let them know of their brother's passing. Not a delightful way to write for the first time. George let a couple of weeks pass before he decided it was time to write that letter. He looked for the address book, but it was nowhere in sight. George and June looked everywhere, but it was not to be found. They had no idea where it was. He was distraught and disappointed in himself, and June felt his despair. How could he ever find their names or addresses without the book? It was a communist country with no diplomatic relations with America, and there was no one to turn to.

George's mother didn't know any of his father's family's first names. Also, although most of his mother's generation probably knew some of his father's family most had died except his grandmother and her older sister. George's grandmother knew the village and had known of the family, but she never met any of them. Her family considered Vlassi's family to be peasants, uneducated, and poor. George's mother's family was wealthy and educated. Also, George's grandmother had left Albania in 1920 when she was twenty-five with George's mother who was ten. With the war of 1912, and the country becoming Albania, life was stressful with a young child, and she had no exchanges with a peasant family living in another village. With that, George sulked and went on with his life.

George was an electronic researcher during this period of his life. He worked on military research programs for large electronic companies. He was tall, with curly dark hair; dark blue eyes, of medium build, and fairly good looks. His wife, June, was a prenatal doctor and she loved to paint oils and watercolors in her spare time. She was of English blood, and her family had been here for many generations. June was very pretty, with long brown wavy hair, large brown eyes with long curled-up lashes, and a model figure. She had modeled clothes during her college years. They were married in 1953, but she bore no children. They both loved the outdoors, and most sporty adventures. They had met at a mountain club organizational camping excursion in New Hampshire and were members of the Appalachian Mountain Club. Hiking and camping were their favorite activities. Marriage was good, and they lived in a modest home outside of Manchester, New Hampshire.

George would bring up the subject of the address book many times with his sister, his wife, relatives, and close friends. When he related the story it always brought tears. June felt empathy for George, because she knew he was angry at himself for losing the address book. How could he ever find out where his relatives lived?

Aware that Albania had isolated itself from the rest of the world there was not much anyone could do. Time passed on, but that image never left him. He thought that maybe some day he would be able to go to Albania and search for family members, but for now Albanian visas for Americans were out of the question. George would have to wait for that to change. George knew the names of his mother's and father's villages, but who was living there was a big question.

Seven years after Vlassi died, June was diagnosed with ovarian cancer. The only treatment during those years was to operate and remove the cancerous cells. June was hospitalized a few times following her diagnose, but there was no improvement. This was all before chemo was the norm for treating most cancers. The two family's visited her at home and while she was hospitalized. It was a difficult situation for all.

A year later June passed away. George, the families, and friends were devastated. The thought of Albania was put on the back burner for George.

With the passing of time, George started to date about three years after June's death. George dated a few ladies, but he didn't want to go steady or get married.

He was a bachelor for four years when he met Lesley. It was love at first sight for both of them, but neither one wanted to marry and she wanted no children. Lesley was a dental hygienist. She was of mixed blood, Irish and English. Lesley had a pretty face, blonde hair down to her shoulders, striking blue eyes with long eyelashes, and a curved figure. They moved in together and became a happy couple. George explained to Lesley all about Albania and his family living there, and how he had lost his father's address book. The only answer Lesley could give was that maybe in time things will change. George accepted that answer and went on with his life.

Chapter III

George was in his three car garage going through some old boxes, sorting out things to save, give away or throw away. The boxes took up one car-space. It was one of those projects that he always wanted to do, but had never gotten around doing it. Well, this one Saturday he decided, today is the day.

After going through two boxes, he was searching through a large box of papers, envelopes, and old magazines when he saw a small, black leather book sitting at the bottom. He picked up the book and opened it. The first thing that caught his eyes was his father's handwriting recognizing it from when he was a young boy. Riffling through the pages seeing names and addresses, George realized that he had just recovered the lost address book; the date today was May 16, 1990.

He went running in the house yelling, "I found it, I found it." Lesley put her oil brush on the easel and said, "What are you talking about?"

"The book, the book. I found it. I can't believe it. I found it."

"Found what book?"

"My father's address book, The Albanian address book. Can you believe it? I found it. I can't believe it. Twenty-five years later, almost to the day my father died and I found it. I always believed that I never threw it away, but who would believe that we had it all that time. When or how it got into that box is a mystery, but who cares now. I have it. We can celebrate tonight, and I will write letters and hope for an answer. WOW! Twenty-five years!"

Tears were falling from Lesley's eyes and George's eyes were watered. George got on the phone and called the best restaurant in Manchester and made reservations for two. They would buy a bottle of champagne and make a toast to their find, and to his relatives. The prospect of going to Albania was a dream that would possibly become a reality.

George said, "First we write a letter. But to whom? That will come later after we get down on earth. Right now I'm floating on a cloud."

Chapter IV

A few days after George found the address book, he and Lesley sat down together on the couch and looked at the black leather address book; it reminded George of a spy novel when the detective discovers the answers to his clues. They were going to discuss whom they would write to regarding Vlassi's death, explain the delay, and that George was Vlassi's only son. It would be nice to introduce George and his sister Eli to the family living in Albania.

Sitting and passing the address book back and forth to each other, George said, "We should obviously write to my father's only living brother."

Lesley replied, "And maybe his youngest sister. He did tell you that one sister had died."

For some reason George remembered his father telling him that his youngest sister wrote more than his other siblings. Of course, George knew that the older brother had died and the remaining three sisters were younger than Vlassi. Checking the addresses, George saw that all the brothers had lived in the same village. Two sisters lived in a different village, and one lived in yet another village. They decided to write to the one brother, Yannis, who lived next to George's mother's village, and the two sisters living in another village. George's mother knew the name of his father's village, the one listing most of the family.

George drafted a letter of four pages. Lesley edited the letter and shortened it to three. It expressed their condolences and an apology for not writing sooner, also why the delay and that George wanted to visit the family. Three letters were mailed the next day; it was May 20, 1990. Now they had to wait for a return letter.

In the meantime, no diplomatic relations between Albania and America were in force. George did some research and found a Free Albanian organization in Boston that sent clothes and other materials to Albania. They gave George the address of an Albanian embassy in Rome and told him to write a letter for permission to visit the country. George wrote, but he never received a return letter.

George and Lesley waited for a letter from Albania. Two months had passed and still no letter. They started to think that the letters were never received or that maybe the relatives didn't live there anymore. Maybe they had better write another letter.

Lesley remarked, "We could write a letter to a different sister."

George responded, "Let's wait. We know nothing of the postal service there, and we know it is a country with a difficult past. Maybe the entire family left the country, as my mother did. "

George and Lesley returned from work a few days later, and going through their daily mail they found a slip from the post office indicating a registered letter. George went to the post office the next day after work and retrieved the letter. He held the letter in his hand and in the upper left corner instead of a return address there was a blue square with lettering, ME AEROPLAN, and underneath, par avion. There were four colorful foreign stamps, and red and blue checkered squares circumventing the envelope. In the lower left corner there was another stamp, and underneath in red letters, R, and GJIROKASTER Nr 153. It was mailed July 5, 1990, and received at his post office July 24th. On the reverse side there was a name; Vassilis Stamos, Glifada, Argirocastro, Albania.

George felt he had found the gold pot at the end of the rainbow. He drove home, went flying into the house and called to Lesley, "It's a letter from Albania. The first name is not familiar, but it is from a family member."

Lesley eyes reddened, and George couldn't wait to open the letter. The returned name on the reverse of the envelope was not the name of his Uncle Yannis Stamos.

The name was Vassilis Stamos, but the address was the same one that they used for his uncle. George got his letter opener and sliced through the top of the envelope. He pulled out two light tan pages colored with light blue lines. The writing was very neat with perfect Greek letters. George translated the following letter for Lesley.

To my cousin George. We just received your letter and are very glad to have gotten it—and especially that we can converse with you, your family and especially our cousin Eli. We were very upset when we heard about the death of your beloved father, just as much as it would have affected you of our beloved father's death-Yannis.

All of this began from 1960 to 1965. If it won't upset you-let me begin to tell you these painful memories.

In the beginning of '60' our Aunt Urania died right before we were to do her forty days our beloved grandmother Krisidio died – and preceded with the death of a young Uncle Kostas, and then an older Uncle, Spiros. After all this pain my father tearfully built the new house. He said, "I am only a small branch."

As I wrote this letter it brought tears to my eyes, and in '65' with all the pain and suffering brought upon the death of my father.

So then, in the new house my father placed a black cloth out-not only for the death of Vlassi, but also for the death of all the other siblings, and within that year, one fall night he closed his eyes and he too never woke up again.

Those are the painful stories of our family.

I Vassilis that is writing this letter am so happy that we can share the affairs of the heart together. I used to send you letters before, but they would return, because the address wasn't right.

Our Aunts, Violetta, Olympia, and Evanthia tried to also. They're all doing very well. They all send you and your cousins their love. Their families come from your father's village.

I, Vassilis am the youngest son of Yannis, and together with my mother, Amalia, wife Violetta, and my two children Nicholas and Alex, live in the village of Glifada. I live in the home that my father built with his hands. My sister, Eleni also lives in the village.

In your letter you said how you would like to get in touch with all of your relatives. It would be our pleasure to do so.

The road to doing this is very easy. You have to write to the Albanian embassy in Athens, Greece, which we did for you and are mailing it to you. You have to sign this, date it, and send it to the embassy. Ending up, we wait with enthusiasm your reply and your visit. We send you many kisses and all our love, Vassilis and all the family to all of your relatives. I'm sending you two pictures from my wedding (June 6, 1987).

My address is: Vassilis Yannis Stamos

Gjirokaster Albania

For a few moments neither George nor Lesley could say anything. Both George and Lesley had tears running down their cheeks.

Finally Lesley said, "Can you believe that letter?"

George swallowed and said, "What a beautiful letter. I'm saddened by the deaths, but it is hard to believe that I got an answer. Who would have ever known after twenty-five years? I wonder how Vassilis knew my father had died. I'll write another letter tonight and fill out the enclosed visa application to the Albanian embassy in Greece. We never did get a reply from Rome. I'll go to Albania as soon as I get that visa. It would be good if you went also, but one thing at a time, let's celebrate."

Nine days later, on August 2, 1990, George received another registered letter. It had been mailed July 27, 1990, but the return address was not from Vassilis, it was from his Aunt Evanthia Anastasi, the youngest sister of Vlassi. She lived in Gjirokaster (Argirocastro). George was thrilled when he signed for the letter. Three letters sent and two received.

George went home excited. "Hey hon, guess what-another letter from Albania." George and Lesley sat down to read the letter. Of course, like the other letter it was written in Greek.

With all my love George, how are you? As I am writing you this letter, we are all doing fine, and I hope the same for you. I had just received your letter, and was glad to hear that everyone is doing well. I am so happy that my nephew is writing me letters and keeping in touch.

The pain that I felt for my brother is the same pain I feel for you.

You and Eli should be proud and happy about Eli's children. I again send you my sympathy about the death of your father.

In your letter you said how you would like to come and visit me in Agyrokastro. You can't understand how much I hope that you want to come and that a visit here comes true. I am waiting patiently for you to come.

My loving nephew, I would like for you to give me your telephone number. George, I am here with my husband Sotir, my son, his wife and their two little girls.

I send you my love from this distance.

Love and kisses to everyone,

Evanthia

George and Lesley were excited that his aunt was still alive. She had written a beautiful letter and wanted to speak to George on the phone, but she never sent her telephone number. George now had to write a letter to this relative. How exciting.

George was wondering if he was going to hear from the Albanian embassies in Athens or Rome. He called the Albanian organization and they told him, "They will probably not return a letter. They've been doing that for years to Americans. Maybe they will write because the government has changed somewhat, but our experience is that they will not write. Do you have the Paris Albanian embassy address?"

"No."

"Do you have a pen?"

"Yes."

"Here is their address."

George wrote down the address. George thought, "Another embassy to write to."

"Well write to them. Give them details about your family living there. Also, that they have been writing to you to tell you to visit. Maybe they might reply. Good luck."

"Thanks for the help. Good-bye."

George felt disillusioned. That would be the third embassy and now even more waiting; Albania had only three embassies in the world. Maybe he'd be lucky and one would answer, but what else could he do? George had received mail from Evanthia and Vassilis, but still no letter from an embassy.

About two months after writing, George received a letter with an application for a visa from the Paris embassy. Of course George immediately answered. During this interim his Aunt Evanthia had gone to the officials and signed a notarized document saying she would sponsor George on his visit. This was submitted to her Albanian officials, and George sent a copy of the letter to the Paris embassy, thinking, "They did send me an application; maybe this will inspire them to answer." He even wrote a three page letter and attached to the application explaining his family's background, and all the relatives he had living in Albania; to no avail. It was never answered. George grew more and more frustrated and disappointed. How could he ever get to Albania?

Over the course of two years, George and his Albanian family members continued writing to each other. Sometimes they would write and say that they had written, but no letters arrived. George would write, but it became obvious that some letters never arrived or were received. Some letters took a long time to arrive to George, or to family members. It was evident that the Albanian postal service was inadequate. George realized that a country that was under a restrictive government wasn't going to change over night. All he could do was wait.

In the meantime, there were no answers from the three Albanian embassies. How frustrating, even though relations with America had improved since 1990. How was George going to get a visa if the embassies wouldn't answer? One day in July, 1992, George decided to call the

Albanian organization that had helped him in the past. Lesley was in the back yard working in her flower gardens.

Talking to a gentleman, George told him about his problems with the embassies. The man replied, "You can go to Albania now. America and Albania have diplomatic relations and you can get a visa. Go to Athens to the Albanian embassy and they will give you a visa. Things have changed over there. Give them a call when you get to Athens. Also bring clothes, patent medicines, and food, or whatever you can carry. Albania is in dire straights."

George replied, "Are you kidding? I can go? Really? Boy, that's good news. I can't believe it. I'm glad I called. I'll do as you suggested about bringing items. I've been trying for a couple of years to go over there. You've been great. Thanks for all your help. I don't know what I would have done without it. I'll make plans today and go as soon as I can. Once again, thanks. Good-bye."

"Good-bye and I wish you safe travel."

George got off the phone and went to the garden to tell Lesley the good news.

"Hey Lesley, guess what?"

Lesley was on her knees weeding around her flowers, "What?"

"We're going to Albania."

"What do you mean we're going to Albania? Did you hear from an embassy?"

"No! Remember that Albanian group in Boston I've talked to?"

"Yes."

"Well, I just phoned them and they said that Americans can go to Albania. The man said I had to go to the Albanian embassy in Athens to get a visa, but there would be no trouble. Isn't that great news?"

Lesley jumped up and put her arms around George and gave him a big kiss and a big hug. "Boy, that's the best news I've heard around here for a long time. Can you imagine-a trip to Albania? How wonderful!"

"We're going to take our vacation days and go in September. It will take some time to plan this out, but we have a month or so to do it. What do you think of that? I'll go first to make sure all is okay and I'll call you and give you all the details. Then you can fly and meet me. How does that sound?

"Wow, that's sounds exciting. We could tour some of Greece too. We've always wanted to travel there."

"Yes, it all sounds too good to be true; Albania and Greece, family and villages, Athens and whatever, a dream of a lifetime. I'm going to call my aunt and tell her we're going to Albania."

George's aunt, Christina, was his mother's younger and only sister. She was born in Boston in 1921. She had three daughters, was widowed, and lived alone in Boston in a senior citizen housing development. She had been sickly as of late, but she seemed to be doing all right now. She always told stories about her mother's past. How her mother, Penelope, lived under Turkish rule, about the war in 1912, and about Penelope moving to America in 1920 with George's mother who was ten, and Penelope's older sister Eleni and her husband Dimitri and their two daughters and a son. Penelope's father was a Greek priest and a doctor. Her husband's father owned a hotel and a candy store in Argirocastro. Christina's father, Nicholas, went to America nine years earlier (1911), and he owned and operated a barber shop in Boston. Nicholas died in 1942 at an early age, fifty-two.

George returned to the garden after talking to his aunt. His aunt had advised him not to go, as she had been reading about all the problems in Albania, Greek travelers getting robbed, no strong government in control, and the lack of infrastructure. She was afraid for his safety. George brushed that all off. He told her he was going no matter what the problems were. He'd been to other problem countries, even ones under states of siege. George told her not to think of the worst, but how exciting it's going to be visiting our parent's villages and homes would be.

During the previous two years Aunt Evanthia had written to George more than any other relative had. Knowing that George wanted to visit, she helped him as much as she could and told him what Greek border to cross to enter into Albania. Also, George had received a detailed travel itinerary from the Albanian organization in Boston many months ago-they had assumed one day he was going to get a visa.

Aunt Evanthia called one time at 5:30a.m.; it was 11:30a.m. in Albania. It was a very brief call. She explained that she never sent her telephone number because she's had never had a telephone. Evanthia said, "I called because I wanted to hear your voice, and I knew you could never call me, and I have only a few minutes to talk." That explained why she never gave George her number.

After the initial introductory letters from relatives, correspondence became infrequent. Vassilis wrote, but infrequently. Of course, the postal service didn't improve as time went on. So who knew how many letters were never delivered? It seemed that Aunt Evanthia was most interested in his coming, so George felt that she would be the one to tell of his arrival. Besides she didn't work, and other relatives probably had jobs, and, of course, there were many relatives he hadn't written to.

Figuring out the logistics of travel to the Albanian border, George booked with Lufthansa for an August 31 flight. He would fly overnight to Frankfurt and then take a morning flight to Athens. He also booked a flight for Lesley to arrive the following week. George figured that when he arrived in Albania he would scope out the situation, call Lesley, and let her know if it would be all right for her to travel to Albania, and how to get a visa. If difficulties developed she would cancel that flight, and George would let her know of his departure from Albania. Then she could reschedule a flight to Athens, and he would meet her there. Their return tickets would be booked on the same flight.

He wrote three letters to Aunt Evanthia explaining his date and time of arrival in Greece and then to Kakavia. He prayed that one of the letters would be delivered.

George and Lesley discussed their live-in situation and the Albanian family's attitude about marriage. Of course, somewhere in George's letters he had told him that his wife, June, has passed away, but he had told them about Lesley.

They decided that when George arrived in Albania he would tell the family that his wife, Lesley, was coming to visit. George assumed that family traditions were still in existence in Albania, so it would ease the situation if George and Lesley were considered married. He wouldn't say that they were married, but just refer to her as his wife. George didn't know how the family would react to Lesley as a live-in partner, and he didn't want to upset the family or cause a difficult situation. Actually, George and Lesley felt like they were married.

Chapter V

George Stamos arrived in Athens, Tuesday, September 1, 1992, at 1:08p.m. Departing the plane, passengers rode a bus to the terminal, passed through a passport check, and then retrieved their luggage. George then had to go through customs where they stamped his passport, but they didn't check his luggage. George asked an official if he knew the location of the Albanian embassy in Athens. First the official said, no, then yes, and finally no. George went to the Olympic Airline's office and inquired if they knew. There was a round-about conversation between the staff, but they admitted they didn't know. George went to a Greek tourist office at the airport and asked if they knew where the Albanian embassy was. They said no, but they would try to see if there was a telephone number. They found a telephone number and called, but no one answered. They said they found no address. George randomly asked a few individuals in the airport, but they had no idea. At least he had a telephone number.

George spent two hours at the international airport and the tourist office trying to locate the Albanian embassy. George was patient but he was wondering how he was going to get to the Albanian embassy. He realized too much time had elapsed and that his business with the Albanian embassy or the U.S. consulate would have to wait.

George had to go to the domestic airport as he arrived at the international airport, and no domestic Greek airlines tickets could be booked there. He went outside and hired a taxi. He was lucky to find a taxi because the Greek driver said the taxis were on strike; George had purchased Greek drachmas at a bank in Boston in preparation to have Greek money on his person.

Arriving at the domestic airport, George tried to purchase a ticket to Ioannina, but all flights were booked that day and also the next day, but they said he could fly to Preveza tomorrow and arrive midday and then take a short bus ride to Ioannina. George had told his aunt that he would be at the border in the afternoon on September 2nd, and he was going to be on time, even if he had to hire a private plane or if he had to walk.

After George purchased his ticket, a generous Greek man of middle age asked if he needed any help to carry his bags. This Greek man, named Constantine, worked at the airport; George guessed he looked haggled.

George said, "Πρέπει να κάνω μια κράτηση σε ξενοδοχείο (I have to make a hotel reservation)."

Constantine replied, "Κάντε κράτηση ξενοδοχείου εδώ. Ελάτε, θα σας δείξω πού. Εάν χρειάζεστε βοήθεια, θα είμαι στο πλευρό σας (Make a hotel reservation here. Come, I'll show you where. If you need help I'll be at your side)."

"Ευχαριστώ (Thank you)."

George paid 12,000 drachmas ($80) for a first class room located a city block from the Mediterranean Sea. Constantine waited at his side and then helped George carry his bags outside to a taxi stand. George had three bags, two weighed fifty-seven pounds total and his handbag weighed fifteen.

At the designated taxi stand there were no taxis in sight. Constantine wished George a safe trip to Albania, said good-bye and left. George offered a tip, but Constantine refused. After fifteen minutes and no taxi, and no Constantine, George didn't know what to do. He knew no one in Athens. While George was pondering the situation a semi-uniformed man approached him.

"Ψάχνετε για ένα ταξί (Are you looking for a taxi)?"

"Ναι, μου είπαν ότι είχαν απεργία όταν ήρθα με ταξί από το διεθνές αεροδρόμιο, αλλά ήλπιζα ότι ένα θα έρθει. Δεν γνωρίζω κανέναν στην Αθήνα και χρειάζομαι να πάω στο ξενοδοχείο μου. Δεν ξέρω τι να κάνω. (Yes, I was told that they were on strike when I came by taxi from the international airport, but I was hoping one would come. I know no one in Athens and I need a ride to my hotel. I don't know what to do)"

"Έχετε τη διεύθυνση του ξενοδοχείου (Do you have the hotel address)?"

"Ναι, έχω την επιβεβαίωση της κράτησης και τη διεύθυνση. (Yes, I have the address and hotel confirmation)."

The man checked the address and said, "Καλά, δείτε το λεωφορείο εκεί πέρα (Well, see that bus over there)?" It was parked across the street.

"Ναι (Yes)."

"Εγώ δουλεύω στο λεωφορείο, και ο οδηγός είναι ήδη στο λεωφορείο. Εργαζόμαστε για τη δημόσια εταιρεία λεωφορείων. Θα σας μεταφέρουμε για 1500 ($10.00) δραχμές (I work on the bus, and the driver is in the bus. We work for the public bus company. We'll take you there for 1500 ($10.00) drachmas)."

George looked at the bus. It was the type of bus you'd see in any large city. George couldn't believe his eyes, or the offer. George replied, "Εντάξει (OK)."

The worker grabbed George's two large bags and they entered the bus. The driver, sitting behind the wheel, said hello. George took out his 1500 drachmas and handed it to the worker, sat down and off they went. There was no one else on the bus. This was amazing.

George said, "Αυτό δεν θα συμβεί ποτέ στην Αμερική (This would never happen in America)."

The bus driver asked, "Ποιο μέρος σκοπεύετε να επισκεφθείτε (Where do you plan to visit)?"

"Τη Βόρεια Ήπειρο. Έχω οικογένεια εκεί. Αυτό είναι το πρώτο μου ταξίδι. Θα πρέπει να πάω αύριο στην αλβανική πρεσβεία να υποβάλω αίτηση για θεώρηση (Northern Epirus. I have family there. This is my first trip. I have to go tomorrow to the Albanian embassy to apply for a visa)."

The driver replied, "Άκουσα ότι δεν χρειάζεστε θεώρηση τώρα πια (I heard you don't need a visa now)."

"Πραγματικά (Really)?"

"Ναι, κάποιοι φίλοι που γνωρίζω δεν χρειάστηκαν μία πρόσφατα. Αυτοί έχουν γεννηθεί εδώ και πήγαν χωρίς θεώρηση." (Yes, some friends I know didn't need any just recently. They were born here and they went without visas)."

"Εγώ θα καλέσω την Αμερικανική πρεσβεία στην Αθήνα και θα ρωτήσω. Θα ήταν υπέροχο αν δεν χρειάζεται πια θεώρηση. Θα τηλεφωνήσω νωρίς αύριο το πρωί. Ευχαριστώ (I'll call the American embassy in Athens and inquire. That would be great if I didn't need one. I'll call early tomorrow morning. Thanks)."

"Παρακαλώ. Πώς θα πάτε στην Αλβανία (You're welcome. How are you getting to Albania)?"

"Αεροπορικώς μέχρι την Πρέβεζα, μετά με λεωφορείο μέχρι τα Ιωάννινα, και στη συνέχεια θα πάρω ένα ταξί μέχρι την Kakavia (I have a flight to Preveza, then a bus ride to Ioannina, and then I'll take a cab to Kakavia)."

"Σας εύχομαι να έχετε ένα ασφαλές ταξίδι. Να προσέχετε τον εαυτό σας στην Αλβανία. Υπήρξαν προβλήματα με ταξιδιώτες από Ελλάδα (Have a safe travel. Watch yourself carefully in Albania. There have been problems with travelers from Greece)."

George thanked him. The bus driver said, "Έχουμε σχεδόν φτάσει στο ξενοδοχείο (We're almost at the hotel)." The drive to the hotel took about fifteen minutes.

The bus turned down a small street. The hotel's entry way was a ramp wide enough for two cars. The driver handled the bus like it was a bicycle, and parked it in front of the main entrance. The worker took George's two bags and carried them inside and dropped them at the front desk. George gave him a tip and said thank you.

George checked in and went to his room which was in front and on the fifth floor. George, after tipping the bellhop, walked to the window and looked down. The bus was still parked there. George took out his camera and photographed the top of the bus. He still couldn't believe what had just transpired.

George called the American embassy to inquire if he still needed a visa for entering Albania; the embassy was closed. After showering and changing clothes, George went down to the front desk and inquired about a restaurant. The clerk told him of a nice restaurant within walking distance-good food, and on the water.

He made the short walk and went inside the restaurant. He was met by a young man; George saw tables inside and out. He asked for an outside table and the man led him to a table with a beautiful sea view. The only other customers were a young couple at a table facing each other kissing softly and quietly laughing and drinking wine on the other side of the room. George was satisfied and he sat down. George couldn't believe he was in Greece facing the Mediterranean Sea as the copper and carnelian red sun was setting over southern Europe. His thoughts went across the water to Lesley, wishing she was there with him, but he knew it wouldn't be long before she would be at his side, and tomorrow, if all goes as he planned he would be in Albania.

Greek bus

Chapter VI

Early the next morning George had his continental breakfast: yogurt, coffee, juice, bread and Swiss cheese. He called the American embassy; a female answered the phone and told him he needed a visa. He asked her where the Albanian embassy was. She gave him the address and George checked out. The hotel told him they would get him a taxi. In fact, it was a private car, but George didn't care.

Fifty minutes later, through narrow streets and heavy traffic, George entered the Albanian embassy. George told the driver to wait for him. Entering the brick three-story single-family-home-like building, and sitting at a front desk, he explained to a pretty young girl, speaking Greek, that he is an American and that he is inquiring about a visa to Albania. Time was running out for George to get to the domestic airport. The girl got up and went into an office behind her desk; the door was wide open. In a matter of seconds she returned and said, "No visa."

George was shocked. He inquired in English, "No visa. Why not?

The girl said again, "No visa."

George politely said, "Can I please talk to the consulate?"

The consulate, from inside his office said loudly in English, "No visa!"

The consulate, obviously hearing George, walked out of the office and facing George said, "No visa."

George asked, "Why not?"

The consulate said, "No visa, you need no visa."

"I can go to Kakavia and enter Albania without a visa? I'm an American."

"I know you're an American. Yes, no visa required."

"Thank you, I'm on my way, thank you."

George turned around and flew out the door and told the driver, "Τρέξε στον εγχώριο αερολιμένα. Hurry! (Go to the domestic airport. Hurry!)."

After a roller coaster ride, that cost 2700 drachmas ($18.00) George arrived at the airport. As he was checking his bags the propellers were turning, and with George running, the plane was ready to go. He was the last person to board the flight. In fact, he was sitting down and buckling up as the plane started to taxi.

It was a small two propeller plane with twenty seats. Leaving Athens, George could see how mountainous Greece was as they headed west toward the Ionian Sea. The mountaintops were mostly denuded of growth. Patches of earth and rock abound, groups of homes edging the blue sea, and the sky was cloudless. The plane ascended over a wide strip of water with land on both sides. Patches of orchards could be seen. With built up emotions George considered the fact that he is heading toward his heritage. The mountains are growing in altitude, and wide arroyos are visible. He prays to God for thanks and for a safe journey. The stewardess was blonde, pretty; blue-eyed, tall, and Greek.

The plane landed at Preveza at 12:10p.m. George had to cross a narrow strip of water on a ferry. This cost him 60 drachmas (40 cents), a ten-minute taxi ride costing 300 drachmas ($2.00) brought him to the bus station. All this took was less than a half hour. The bus leaves at 1:15p.m. for Ioannina, 1300 drachmas ($8.66), an eighty mile drive.

With a few minutes to spare, George entered a coffee shop for a quick cup; there is a group of men sitting at tables playing cards. Smoke is swirling above their heads and one woman is completely dressed in black. Some men were drinking coffee or just talking. George could tell by their way they looked at him that they knew he wasn't a local man. No one nodded. Outside the sky is blue, the temperature is comfortable, and the air smelled pleasant. There are signs on all the buses, even on the bus ticket;

"MACEDONIA IS GREEK!" stating Greece's opposition to Macedonia becoming a country.

George boarded the bus for Ioannina and sat next to a window. The seats are cushioned and comfortable. Many passengers boarded the bus, mostly women with packages, and some with young children.

A young man sat next to George and said, "Γεια σας, το όνομά μου είναι Στράτος (Hello, my name is Stratos)."

George replied, "Γεια σας, το όνομά μου είναι Γιώργος. Χαίρομαι που σας συναντώ (Hello, my name is George. It's nice to meet you)."

Stratos said, "Δεν είστε από την Ελλάδα, από πού είστε (You're not from Greece, where are you from)?"

"Είμαι από την Αμερική, αλλά πώς ξέρετε ότι δεν είμαι από την Ελλάδα (I'm from America, but how did you know I'm not from Greece)?"

"Μιλάτε με προφορά (You speak with an accent)."

In English Stratos said, "We can speak American. I have lived in America, in Chicago. I need to practice my American. By the way, your Greek is good. My American has an accent. So we both have accents."

George said, "Well, that makes us equal. Do you live here now?"

"Well, not really. I'm here visiting my home and my grandparents. My parents live and work in Chicago. Actually I'm going back to Chicago in a few days. My parents own a bakery in Greek Town. That's in Chicago. Have you ever been there?"

"Yes, I have been to Greek Town. I've had dinner in a place called the Parthenon."

"We sell them Greek pastries, what a small world."

George asked, "What do your grandparents do?"

"They are farmers. They grow wheat. My father used to grow wheat, but he wanted to go to America. He opened a bakery, and my mother, my brother and I work there. It is called Mediterranean Pastry Shop. It's on Halsted Street, number 806. We sell to Diane's, the Parthenon, Rothedes, and other restaurants. If you ever go to Greek Town ask for Stratos Taoultsides. That's me. They all know me."

"I'll try to visit the shop whenever I visit Chicago, and of course, I'll ask for you."

Stratos asked George, "Where are you going?"

"I'm going to Albania. My parents were born there. I'll be the first member of my mother's family living in America to return since they left in1920. My father was the only one to immigrate to America from that side of the family; he arrived in 1922. He never returned to Albania."

"Really, that's very interesting. That country has many problems. I hope you will be safe there."

George said, "I have many relatives there. I'll be all right."

Arriving in a small town, as the bus slows down, Stratos says, "I'm getting off to see my aunt. It was good to meet you. I hope your travels are safe. And don't forget Chicago."

They said their good-byes, and George sat looking out the window at the town as the bus drove away. It was a quaint village with stone structured buildings and a few elderly men sitting on benches under shade trees. From there the bus ride was beautiful through the variegated mountains, farmed valleys, and verdant hillside pastures. The Pindus Mountains are extremely high, jagged, saw toothed, and rock-bare. The lower mountainous areas have many evergreens and oak trees. The ride was fast and safe.

Arriving at Ioannina, George hired a taxi for 5000 drachmas ($33.33). Traveling through the mountainous terrain, small villages and farmlands George has the driver make a quick stop for food in a fairly large village. Driving 75-80 MPH they arrived at Kakavia at the approximate time that he had told Aunt Evanthia he'd arrive. He couldn't believe the day, or the timing, or the roller coaster ride as he had to grab the interior strap and hold on more than once. He felt blessed and fortunate!

George paid the driver, collected his luggage and food bags and entered the Greek custom building passing Greek soldiers who were fully armed with automatic weapons and mingling about the complex. Those standing near the entrance smiled and said hello. George was anxious with all the security, but their attitude eased his concern.

Chapter VII

⁓

George tried to get comfortable in this strange make of a car. His thoughts went back to Kocho's remark about robberies to Greek travelers. In back of him was this young boy. Did he have a gun? Were they going to rob him when they got further down this secluded hillside road? How could he protect himself? He was nervous about being in Albania and in this strange car.

When George was traveling to Kakavia by taxi he stopped at a grocery store in a Greek village and bought cheese, coffee, sugar, rice, canned sardines, flour, butter, dry beans, and various processed packages of meat. It cost eight thousand drachmas ($53.33). He couldn't believe the cheap prices. Not like in America. So, in addition to his luggage he had bags of groceries.

They hadn't driven too far when the Albanian-Greek driver started to talk to George. He didn't talk to him in Albanian, but in Greek. He asked, "Where do you want to go?

"Glifada, it is my father's village. He left Albania when he was sixteen to live in America, but my relatives still live here."

"Are you Greek?"

"Yes, Greek-American, but I was born in America. My mother was born here also-in Morista."

"I am Greek also and I come from Kostensa, a village further north of where you want to go. My son in back will help carry your bags for

36

you when we get there. He is a good son. I have two more sons and a daughter. I am happy to meet an American, especially one whose parents were born here in Dropoli. It is dangerous now to travel on this road for Greek Nationalists, but they are only being robbed-no physical harm. If Albanians see Greek license plates they stop them on the road. A Greek diplomat had been robbed further north of here. He was left with only his underwear on. My name is Leonidas. Welcome to Dropoli. It is the district's name for the Greek Villages."

"My name is George, and I'm happy to meet you. My aunt was supposed to meet me, but no one from the family appeared. That young man who talked to you was very nice. He told me he would stay with me until someone arrived. He did mention that there were robberies on this road. I didn't know what to do. I was thinking I might have to go back into Greece, so I'm glad that you stopped."

Leonidas didn't reply, but he had a smile on his face. George turned around and the young boy nodded and smiled. George felt at ease and lucky, so far so good. He didn't feel threatened, and he was on his way to his father's village. Leonidas told George he would point out and name all the Greek villages as they drove by them. The road was in very poor condition, like the car, but the car managed to move along.

If there were any robbers, none came out of their hideaways. They probably knew the man, his car, and the fact that only George's face was visible, and he looked Greek or possibly Albanian. If he was a rich Greek traveler, he wouldn't be in this junk car.

George checked the interior of the auto. The seats were well worn, the headliner was torn, and the front dash was unimaginative. There was no radio or any identifying symbol as to the maker. The body's outside paint was faded, and it had few minor dents. It was not made by a Western European manufacturer, maybe Bulgarian, Romanian or Russian. George thought, "Who cares, as long as we get to my destination safely?"

They finally got down to the main road which was in a wide valley with spectacular views of mountains on both sides going south and north. It looked like a small two lane country road in northern New Hampshire, but in poorer condition. Leonidas told him that this road goes to the capital,

Tirana. George didn't say anything, but he was now seeing how poor the country was. If this is the main road, what are the conditions in the rest of the country? He knew he was back in a third-world country again, and he could expect anything.

They drove by beautiful agriculture fields, but it was past harvest time. In places, George saw large grassy fields with shepherds tending large flocks of sheep, a few goats, and a dog. In other grassy fields he saw a few cattle. George also saw large concrete half shell-like looking objects on the sides of the road. They had narrow slit-like openings facing the south and west. They looked old and not in use. He couldn't figure what they were, but he did not ask. As they drove past villages that seemed to be mostly to the west of the road, Leonidas would give the names. There was very little motor traffic, but there were a few people walking or riding donkeys. Some were women wearing a white cloth on their heads; most of the men had hats.

George blurted out in English, "So this is Albania. What else can I expect?"

Leonidas with a questionable look said, "There is your mother's village. The next village will be your father's."

George looked at his mother's village, sitting on the lower side of this mountain. He looked for her family's home. He had seen a picture of it many times, and he knew he would recognize the house if it came into view. As they passed, George thought that he saw it. George started to well up inside. To him this was all unbelievable.

When they arrived at Glifada, Leonidas said, "This is your father's village."

George didn't know what to say. He looked and saw homes further up the mountain side than his mother's mountain. Flashes of thoughts went through his mind, but George couldn't say anything. The reality of his whereabouts settled in the bottom of his stomach. It was like looking at the Grand Canyon for the first time. It takes what seems like a life time to realize that you're awake and not in a dream, and a pinch wouldn't change the results.

Leonidas went across a small bridge over a dry weedy ditch. George assumed the ditch carried water during the rainy season or when the snows melted. Leonidas started to drive up the unpaved rocky mountain road, but George knew to proceed further they definitely needed a four wheel drive vehicle or a tractor. Even a donkey would do.

The so-called road took a sharp curve to the right onto a steeply slanted large smooth rock, but the car slowed and spun its wheels; finally the car stopped. Leonidas tried again to go forward, but the wheels spun with a high pitch; George sat there amazed. He knew the car wasn't going anywhere.

George said, "Its okay, I'll get out here." Leonidas paid no attention and tried again with the tires burning rubber. George said loudly, "Leonidas, I'll get out here, you'll never make it."

Leonidas took his foot off the accelerator and looked at George and said, "I guess I can't go any further."

"Leonidas, that's okay, I can walk the rest of the way. I'm in good shape, don't worry. I'll get help from my family. My cousin Vassilis Stamos lives here."

They all got out, and the boy took out George's luggage and grocery bags. George looked at the tires and saw that they were bald as a baby's head. George was thankful that they got as far as they did. He handed Leonidas the two thousand drachmas and a tip of five hundred and fifty drachmas ($17.00). The ride would have cost a lot more money in America. George thanked him, and Leonidas returned the gesture. In the meantime two young ladies, about five hundred feet away, one on a donkey and the other at her side were going up the mountain.

Leonidas yelled, "There is an American here to see Vassilis Stamos. Tell him he needs help with his bags."

George wished him well, in his broken down car, and said good-bye to Leonidas and his son. Leonidas backed down to a point where he could turn around. Leonidas waved, and off he went. George was very thankful for his help and for the safe ride. George stood waiting and contemplating about the day and wondering who was going to appear. He was in the family's hands now.

Main highway to Tirana (capitol)

Chapter VIII

⎯⎯⎯

George, standing on the flat smooth rock waiting for someone to appear, viewed the surroundings. There were some small trees and just a few large trees. The mountainside was dotted with small bushes, cactus, various green ground plants, clumps of visible grass mixed with a rocky soil, and a lonely magpie looking bird. He also saw a couple of small stone buildings that looked empty and in need of repair. The open view allowed him to see down the mountain to the road he had arrived on; there was no traffic, and there were no homes anywhere in view He heard the braying of donkeys, the tinkling of bells on goats, the bleating of sheep, and the murmur of the wind, but no human voices.

About ten minutes later he spotted a male's head approaching over the rise on the rocky road. Then the whole body came into view. George and his cousin Vassilis recognized each other from exchanged photographs. Vassilis had a big smile on his face. George returned the smile.

Vassilis was handsome, with lots of dark wavy brown hair, and brown eyes. He was in good physical shape, and had a great smile; he was thirty-six. George could see that Vassilis was very happy to see him. They embraced then kissed each other on the cheeks; they both had tears.

After the hellos Vassilis said, "How did you get here?"

"I came from Kakavia by car. Aunt Evanthia was supposed to meet me, but she never showed."

Vassilis didn't respond verbally, but with a nod his head went upward.

"A Greek man and his son from Kostensa said they would bring me here. He drove me to this spot but couldn't go any further because of the road's poor condition and his bald tires. Anyhow, I didn't know where your house was, so it was best we stopped here. I can't believe I'm here, and I'm glad you are here also."

"You sure have a lot of baggage, Come, I'll help you." Vassilis grabbed the two large suitcases, and George took the food items and his shoulder bag. Up the hill they went.

Vassilis said, "One of the village ladies came to the house and said an American man is down the hill. It caught me by surprise. I thought it must be my cousin George. Who else would come to see me from America? I had no idea you were coming. How come you didn't let me know?"

"Well, you have no telephone, and Aunt Evanthia has been writing to me on a steady basis. She even called me one morning and said she can't wait until I arrive. I wrote to her and gave her the approximate time of day, and the day I would be in Kakavia. This is the day, and I was on time, and here I am. I don't know why she wasn't there. I'll have to tell you the difficulties I had trying to get here. Some are comical and some are trying, but here I am, and I can't believe it. How far do we have to walk, those two suit cases are heavy?"

"Not too far. See that curve in the road up ahead? We go around the curve and then up the hill a short distance. Are you tired and feeling good?"

"Me, I feel great. I'm wondering how many times my father walked this road."

George was taking in the sights. The road led up to the main village built on the side of a mountain. He could see stone walls and stone houses with stone roofs bordering the rocky undeveloped road. Sheep and goat droppings lay everywhere between the rocks.

Vassilis said, "That's my home, there on the right."

George looked at the high solid stone wall with a solid large metal gate. It reminded him of a prison wall. The only visible objects beyond the wall were the over-lying stone slabs that made the roof top. He looked up the steep hill and saw more walls and homes. He couldn't make out where the road or the homes stopped. Vassilis opened the metal gate, stepped aside, and told George to enter. George took a deep breath and passed into the courtyard. This was the home that Vassilis described in his first letter, the one that George's father's youngest brother built with his hands. It was a one-story stone home, and it looked peaceful and charming; it was breathtaking. George knew he was taking a step back in time.

When George learned that it is customary in Albania to take off your shoes and put on sandals or slippers when entering a home, he thought of all the animal droppings on the road. Vassilis supplied George with beautiful leather sandals; Vassilis put on old slippers. About then a pretty young lady appeared. Vassilis introduced his wife, Violetta. She had dark flowing hair, light skin, was of median height, had a slim shapely body and a beautiful white-toothed smile; she was twenty-seven. She greeted George with kisses on both cheeks, and he returned the gesture. George showed her the bags and explained they contained groceries. Violetta took the bags and disappeared.

Vassilis took George and the remaining luggage to a bedroom and asked, "George, do you want to lie down?"

George replied, "No, my adrenalin is in full force."

George followed by Vassilis went to the kitchen in the rear of the building; it had the appearance of the late 1800s. There was no modern equipment visible. The water faucet in the sink was gravity fed. Beside the sink there was a small older lady preparing food. It was Vassilis' mother, Amalia; George's aunt. She was dressed in black down to her shoes, with a white kerchief tied over her head, and had long hair braided down her back. Amalia stood about five feet and had a great smile with dimples. They kissed on the cheeks. George called her thia; Greek for aunt; she giggled.

Violetta offered George a small cup of coffee and sweet-fig preserves. This is a typical offering before a meal or when visiting a Greek home. George sat down, and Vassilis followed. The coffee was the espresso kind, and it was sweetened. Not George's favorite. He liked his espresso straight from the pot; black and no sugar. George drank it and thanked Violetta and Vassilis.

From a doorway a young boy appeared. It was their oldest son Nicholas.

He was four, cute, and with big brown eyes. Vassilis introduced him. The boy looked at George inquisitively and went out of the room. They also had a baby boy a few months old; he was sleeping.

Vassilis asked George about his trip from America. Violetta was busy working in the kitchen with Amalia, but she listened. George explained his itinerary after arriving in Athens, the situation at the Albanian embassy, then leaving Athens, crossing the border, the young Albanian (Kocho) helping him, and the extraordinary ride with Leonidas the Greek-Albanian; Vassilis and Violetta listened intently.

Vassilis remarked, "What incredible situations. I would have had trouble dealing with all that. I have not traveled anywhere. Only to Ioannina, and that has been only recently. Tell me about Evanthia."

George could see that Vassilis was agitated. He explained about writing to her and sending three letters to make sure she received at least one. "Of course, when no one appeared I thought of returning to Greece, but I knew I wanted to go on."

Vassilis didn't respond, but he kept moving his head up and down. In Greece and Albania moving the head up is negative and means no, moving sideways means yes. By these actions George knew that Vassilis was upset.

During the conversation, Violetta had dinner ready. She had prepared lamb, potatoes, tomato and onion salad, feta and olives, bread, and coffee. She set the table and Vassilis and George ate while Violetta served them. Amalia had left the room. George didn't know where the young boy was. Maybe he had eaten already.

After dinner Vassilis was telling George about his father dying the same year as George's father. He also explained about the aunt and grandmother dying within forty days of each other. This all seemed so ironic. There wasn't much one could say about these strange occurrences. The Greek Orthodox religion has a special church service forty days after the death of an individual.

Vassilis told George, "I'm educated and I studied to become a veterinarian. There is a dairy farm nearby and I monitor all the animals, doing artificial insemination, injections, feeding control, and inspection for diseases. My pay is forty two hundred leks ($300) a year, thirty five hundred leks ($25) per month."

George was shocked. He couldn't believe a veterinarian received such a low pay. When George told Vassilis the approximate pay for American veterinarian, Vassilis had a look of disbelief.

Vassilis retorted, "That's incredible. Maybe that will change here, but let me tell you about tonight's activity. The village has many Stamos' families. Some are arriving later to meet you. You are the only Stamos from this village living in America. Even though you weren't born here it doesn't matter, you are a Stamos. Is this all right with you?"

"Yes, of course."

George surmised that the word went out soon after he had arrived. How and when, he had no idea; the house had no phone. George assumed that news traveled quickly in this mountainside village and that Vassilis or Violetta had told someone that an American was here. Then of course those women that Leonidas yelled at when they entered the village.

Vassilis continued, "Some of the family members live in Argirocastro. It isn't far from here. Some live in other parts of Albania and in the nearby villages, and now some are in Greece working. There are not many jobs in this country. The economy has not returned since the fall of communism. The country is very poor as you will see when you go to the city of Argirocastro. The Albanians call it Gjirokaster. We Greeks call it by the Greek name. We do not speak Albanian here in the villages or teach it in our schools. We even raise the Greek flag. We refuse to fly the Albanian flag. There are many problems between the two factions. You will see and hear more as you visit the country. Thank you for coming here. You do not know how it affects us all. I am thirty-six, and besides meeting a new relative and having never met an American… by the way how old are you?"

"I am sixty-two"

"You are? I believe you are the oldest man in the entire family. Maybe Spiros and you are the same age, I don't know for sure. Wait."

Vassilis left the room. He returned after a few moments with a smile on his face.

"My mother says you are older, maybe a year or two. You will meet

Spiros in Argirocastro. He lives there with his son, his daughter in-law, and grandson. That does make you the oldest man in the family. Our aunts are all older than you. Evanthia, I believe, would be five years older than you, and she is the youngest aunt. Are you aware that in our Greek custom you are the patriarch of the family? That is quite an honor."

George didn't know what to say. Did that bring responsibility? How would these families react to that? George didn't have any answers. He would just be himself- a family member visiting family. In America the oldest male member of the family receives respect for the most part, but nobody refers to him as the patriarch. George would take it in stride.

Not long after this discussion visitors began to arrive. George heard Violetta greeting them. Seeing that Vassilis and George were sitting at the kitchen table, Vassilis told George they were going to another room. Once again Vassilis had George leave the room first and directed him to a larger room which had a couch and two beds. George entered, and Vassilis followed, telling George to sit on the couch. Vassilis greeted the men as they entered the room and introduced each one to George. Then George and Vassilis sat on the couch. The men sat on the beds facing George. Before long more men arrived, more introductions, and then the visitors ceased coming. George wondered how he would remember all their names. The room was crowded with men sitting and some having to stand.

There was a soft tone of whispers among them until Vassilis cleared his throat and said, "George, our cousin from America wants to address you all, but before we turn this meeting over to George, I thought you would all like to know that I found out that he is the oldest man in our entire family-older than Spiros."

Heads turned to each other with surprising looks among themselves, and the whispering began again. A moment later the room quieted down; you could hear the wind whistling on the building's eaves. All eyes turned their attention towards George.

George spoke, "Hello, I am the son of Vlassi Stamos. He was born here in 1906, and he was the only one in the family to move to America. I was born in America and have lived there all my life, and I am happy to be able to finally visit here in this village. I have been trying for a long time."

Before George could say another word, a Greek Orthodox priest and another man walked into the room. George got up as did everyone else. The priest greeted Vassilis and then George; both kissed the back of the priest's hand, which is customary.

The priest turned to George, and said in English, "Hello, my name is James Laskaris. I live in Saint Petersburg, Florida, but I was born here in this village. I return as much as I can. It is a pleasure to meet you. This is my cousin Arthur; he is a teacher here in Albania and he speaks some English. I heard you had arrived. You don't know what it means for these relatives to have you visiting here from America. I'm not aware that any one of them has ever met an American; especially one that was born there, and a Stamos. There have been some older villagers who were born here and moved to America when they were very young. They return home to visit their family, but they are not from this family. The Stamos family is the largest family here in the village. Here, let's sit down."

When the priest and George sat every one else followed. With their attention returning to George, he paused to scan their faces. From memories of his father, he saw familiar features that defined the Stamos family: he could see his father's eyes in this one, a chin in that one, and a smile in another. George was astounded by all the facial similarities. Even when some of them spoke the sounds of their voices reminded him of his father's. George was welling up inside.

The men were asking George about America, with the priest also asking a few questions. What did he do for work? Did he own a home and a car? Was he married, and did he have children? Was there plenty of food and clothing? What's America like? What was the government like? How much did things cost? What did jobs pay? During the questioning each man stated his relationship in the family. For George it got confusing as to who was who. All he knew was that they were all his cousins and he was old enough to be to some, a parent. The querying lasted late into the night. It seemed that nobody wanted to go home.

Even though George had had a long day, he was very interested in answering every question. He enjoyed their inquiries, because he understood that they knew nothing about George or his country. They knew George did very well financially. They could tell by his clothes and by the fact that he had traveled to Albania. None of them made enough money to go anywhere or could travel during Hoxha's regime. Now they were in a state of survival, for them and their families. It was a sad state of affairs, and George was overwhelmed as to how to help all of them.

Finally Father Laskaris said, "I have to go home, I have to travel to Tirana tomorrow. It was a pleasure to meet you. Thank you for taking your time to sit here. This is a big day for this village and the families. I'm sure you will see every one again. Have a good and safe time here in Albania, and God bless you."

The men decided it was also a good time to go home. George stood at the doorway and kissed cheeks and shook hands as the men repeated their names as they left. It was a tremendous night for all.

Vassilis said, "It's time to retire. You must be tired. It has been a long day for you."

George acquiesced, and Vassilis led him to a bedroom. Vassilis told George, "The bathroom is outside to the left of the front stairs, close to the road. Take a candle with you. You can wash at the sink in the kitchen. I'll see you in the morning. I have to go to work, but I'll not be gone long. Goodnight."

"Vassilis, I need to call my wife. I told her I would let her know I arrived safely, and if it is alright for her to travel here. It seems okay, so I need to get to a phone. Can you arrange that?" George asked.

"Of course, we'll do that tomorrow."

"Good, goodnight and thank you for everything."

They went their separate ways, and George finally retired. His thoughts of the day went through his head as he dozed off to sleep in his uncle's home.

Aunt Amalia and goat

Nicholas

Chapter IX

George woke up to a sunny day and to the sounds of a donkey, a rooster, and distant barking dogs. He felt afresh, but he needed his coffee. He went into the kitchen and was greeted by Amalia and Violetta.

Violetta said, "Kalimera (good morning), I'll make you some coffee. Did you sleep well?"

"Kalimera, yes, coffee would be good, but please do not use sugar. I like it sketos (black and strong)."

Violetta raised her eyebrows and then smiled. She thought no one else in the family drinks it like that, but I guess that's the way he likes it. "Would you like a double cup?"

George went over to Amalia and kissed her on the cheeks. She giggled and smiled, and said, "Kalimera."

"Kalimera. Yes, a double cup. Thank you."

George sat down and Violetta served him yogurt, honey, bread, and a double cup of strong coffee. He put honey over the yogurt and stirred; that's the way Greeks like to eat yogurt, with bread.

After he ate, George said to Violetta, "Come into the bedroom, I need to give you something."

She followed, and George went to the heaviest valise. He put it on the bed and opened it. It was full of non-prescription medicines and some clothing.

George said, "I brought all this medicine and clothes for the family. I don't know how to distribute it, but you and Vassilis will know what to do. There are aspirins, Tylenol, antibiotic salves, digestive pill remedies, bandages, tooth brushes and paste, and so on and so on. I didn't bring liquids. I was afraid of breakage. As for clothes, there are socks, underwear, shirts, blouses, and sweaters. As for the valise you can keep it. I don't want to take it home."

Violetta's eyes opened wide. She knew everything would go to good use. Albania was in need of many such items.

"Vassilis and I will take care of this. You don't know how much we need these things. In the village, Vassilis is used as a family doctor. He'll find plenty of ways to use them. Plus we can give some items to other family members. Vassilis told me that one of the bags was very heavy. He couldn't figure out what was in it. Thank you. Wait till Vassilis gets home, he won't believe it."

They went back into the kitchen, and Violetta told Amalia about the medicines and clothing. Amalia smiled and said, "That was very thoughtful of you. How did you know to bring this?"

"I talked to an Albanian organization in America, and they've been helping me in many ways. They told me to bring these items. I wish I could have brought more, but I knew I had to carry everything, so I did the best I could. I have to call my wife. She wants to come here. Maybe she can bring a few things. Is there a phone I can use nearby?"

"No, but you and Vassilis are going to Argirocastro and you can call from there"

"When can we do that?"

"When Vassilis comes home. He has probably already made the arrangements. Do you want more coffee or anything else?"

"Another cup will be fine, remember, sketos (no sugar)."

"I will make it the way you like it." She smiled with no raised eyebrows.

George took his coffee and went outside onto a front porch, saw a chair and sat down. He could see all the way down the mountain to the road he had come in on. Across the wide valley he could see a long high mountain range. The mountains were hazy, but looked rugged with sharp multiple peaks. He could see the stone slab roofs of a few houses below and to the right. On the valley floor there was a large flock of sheep and a shepherd with his dog in a large grassy area; the sheep looked tiny. There were many large square and oblong acres of farmed sections, but they were fallow. The sections had bushes circumventing them. George sat and thought about how many times his uncle had sat there, also seeing the same sights. He couldn't believe he was here in the village. A dream comes true.

George didn't know how long he sat there. Every once in a while Violetta would come out and ask if he needed anything. In the meantime, little Nicholas was in the side yard playing. He would come over and look at George but turn away and then play. George would say something, but no response. George figured he was being shy.

The sun got higher and the haze diminished. George walked around the family's courtyard, checking out the grapes on the overhead arbor, the few vegetables still growing, and a few fruit trees in terraced plots below the house. One was a pomegranate, and another was a fig tree. The arbor provided shade from the hot sun in the late summer days. He surmised that the land was well-used. George was about to return to the porch when he heard Vassilis say hello.

George said, "Kalimera (good morning), you're home earlier than I thought. Did you have a busy morning?"

"Kalimera. Not too busy. I've made plans for us to go to Argirocastro so you can call your wife. It will be evening in America. A friend is coming with a car to take us there. Did you have a good-night's rest?"

"Yes, I can't wait to call Lesley. We'll have to make arrangements to pick her up at Kakavia. What time is your friend going to be here?"

"Ten thirty. We have to go down the mountain and meet him at the bridge."

George looked at his watch. They had a half hour. "I'm ready to go whenever you are."

"Let me go into the house, and I'll tell Violetta and say good-bye to Nicholas. Do you need to take anything with you?"

"I want to take my camera. It's in my shoulder bag. Vassilis, I have

American dollars and Greek drachma. Do I need to change it into your money? By the way, what is your money called?"

"Lek. You can use any money that you have or exchange it in Argirocastro. American dollars will go a long way, but you should use drachma or the lek here in Albania." When you return to Greece, the lek will be invalid.

They went into the house, said good-bye and walked down the mountain. Arriving at the bridge, a red car was parked; it wasn't in much better shape than the one George had ridden in from Kakavia. Vassilis introduced the driver to George and off they went. They passed villages and some individuals walking on the road. There was little traffic. George read a sign for Gjirokaster, the Albanian name for Argirocastro, 7 km. The road got busier as they entered the city. The city's buildings were mainly to the left, on the main highway, and appeared to be built upon the mountain side. There were only a few buildings along the edge of the main highway to the right aside the leveled valley. The driver took a left onto a wide main avenue. As it turned out, it was the widest street in the city, and you could see it rise upwards toward the mountain's top. The thoroughfare was busy, with a few more cars and trucks. Many people were walking about.

Vassilis told the driver to stop at a particular building off the main road. Exiting the car, Vassilis said something to the driver in Albanian. He turned to George and said, "This is where you can make your call. When we get inside, write the telephone number on a piece of paper and hand it to the lady behind the front desk. When she makes the connection, she will direct you to a closed booth to enter. She will speak Albanian. I will be with you and I will talk to her. It might take some time. I'll explain later the complications we still have."

George followed his instructions. There were a dozen or so people doing the same procedure. A few people were going in and out of old wooden phone booths used in America in the 30s and 40s. After fifteen minutes the lady called George and said, "Go to booth number four." Vassilis translated, and George entered the booth and closed the door.

He picked up the receiver that was attached to the wall; it was at least fifty years old. George said hello expecting to hear Lesley's voice. A man's voice in accented perfect English said, "Who are you?"

George said, "I'm trying to call my wife, there must be some mistake."

The man replied, "Yes," and hung up.

George went to Vassilis, "I got the wrong connection, what do we do?"

"We have to do it all over again."

George and Vassilis waited another twenty minutes. George couldn't understand the problem, but he realized he was not in America. Just about the time that George was going to say something to Vassilis, the lady looked at George and said in Albanian, "Go to booth number one." George assumed what she said, but Vassilis translated.

George said hello, and the same man answered, only this time he swore at George. George tried to explain where he was and that he didn't dial. The man said, "I'm on the other side of the world in Australia, and you have woken me up twice, I'm in no mood for excuses." George heard a loud slam.

Vassilis saw George come out too soon for a phone call. He knew something was wrong. When George approached he said, "I got the same wrong number."

"We'll return later and try again. Maybe you'll have better luck. Let's go and exchange money for leks. I'm sure you will find this interesting."

Vassilis and George walked out and returned to the main avenue. They walked slowly up the hill, and before long they approached a large crowd of men milling around and busily talking almost in the middle of the street. A few uniformed policemen were standing off to the side watching the activity.

Vassilis entered the closely crowded men and spotted a man he knew. The two men talked briefly and Vassilis beckoned George, who was on the crowd's edge.

Vassilis said, "How much money do you want to exchange?"

"Thirty thousand drachmas ($200)."

The man (the money exchangers are called Kambists) said something and Vassilis said, "He will give you a better exchange if you give him American dollars. Besides, you will need drachmas when you return to

Greece, but remember, any remaining leks in your pocket are not useful in Greece. Greece will not accept them."

George got nervous because of the policemen watching. George thought, what was taking place was illegal in all the countries he had traveled in. He certainly didn't want to get arrested in Albania. Vassilis noticed George's agitation.

Vassilis said, "Don't be nervous, the government doesn't care, even if it is against the law. The police are here to keep everything peaceful."

George made the exchange of two hundred American dollars and received ten percent more leks than the local bank would have given; two thousand and eight hundred, and the ten percent; two hundred and eighty, (a total of 3080 leks), plus there was no fee for the exchange. It seemed like a lot of money in Albania. The actual buying power of one lek was equal to ten dollars in America. You could buy a loaf of bread for the Albanian price of twenty-five cents. Clothes and housing were much cheaper also. One lek went a long way. When George was a young boy during the depression, he remembered that a loaf of bread sold for a nickel. He also thought that he would give them any remaining leks to the family. If he needed more leks they could return here and exchange more money.

They then walked back to the telephone office. Twenty-five minutes later and the results were the same, except that the call was to Germany. George decided to try his Aunt Christina in Boston (she is nine years older than George). This took even longer, but he entered the booth and his aunt answered. She was happy that all was well. Of course, she asked many questions.

George told her what had transpired in the village, and gave a brief history of how he got there. He explained that he wasn't able to reach home. He asked her to call Lesley and say all is okay, and for her to arrive on the date they had scheduled.

"Tell Lesley to schedule a flight to Ioannina, Greece, from Athens with Olympic Airways before she leaves home. She'll arrive at the international airport, but she'll have to take a taxi or a bus to the domestic airport. She can ask about getting to the other airport; maybe there's a shuttle. Tell her to ask about the taxi strike also. She then has to hire a taxi from Ioannina to Kakavia on the Greek border. They are not on strike in Ioannina. I left her instructions, but I want to reiterate the plan. Do you want me to go over it again?"

"No, I wrote it all down."

George knew the approximate time she would arrive in Ioannina and how long it would take to get to the border. He continued, "I'll be there at the border gate, and if I'm not there for some reason, tell her not to enter Albania, just leave and have a good time in Greece. There is no way she can call me or anyone. And by the way, tell her to bring lots of toilet paper, they have none here. She can buy some in Greece during her taxi ride to the border. The driver will know where to stop for some. Before she hires a taxi, have her ask the taxi driver if he speaks English. She knows how to say that in Greek. Oh, tell her to expect a fast and furious drive in the taxi, and tell her I love her."

Christina laughed, "I'll call her now or early in the morning (Albania is six hours ahead of America) and give her the message. Are you sure she can do this alone?"

"Are you kidding? She can do anything she wants, she is not meek. I'm sure nothing will go wrong for her or for me. Tell her I'll be there to meet her. Okay? Thanks for everything, I'll have lots to tell you when I return. I've seen my mother's village from the road. Take care and don't worry about me, I'm in good hands. Love you, thanks and goodnight."

"Goodnight sweetie. Hello, and my love to the family there from me"

George exited the booth with a smile on his face. "I talked to my aunt, and she will call my wife that all is okay."

Vassilis said, "I'll get us a ride back to the village unless you want to see more of the city. Are you hungry?"

"No, I would like to see more here, but right now I want to see my mother's village. I know what the house looks like from photographs. Can we do that?"

"Whatever you want to do is fine." I'll get a taxi. We can return here, no problem."

Although there were few vehicles on the avenue, Vassilis hailed a car; it had no markings. How Vassilis knew it was a taxi was beyond George.

They got in and headed back to the villages. Once again, the car was a wreck!

As they passed villages and those rounded cement structures on both side of the highway. George asked Vassilis, "What are those structures?"

"They're military bunkers for soldiers with guns to hide in. The government told us that the imperialists were coming, mainly the Americans from the west and the Greeks from the south. That's why the gun holes face the south and the west. The larger bunkers are for people to hide in; every village has at least one. We waited fifty years and they never came. Why would America invade Albania? What a waste of money. What a stupid government we had."

They drove past Glifada. Arriving at Morista the driver pulled off the highway and stopped. There was a large building at the base of the mountain and near the highway. The village was much lower on the mountain, not like Glifada, but it had many more homes. Vassilis paid the driver and George started up the hill walking on stony gravel and sheep and goat droppings.

George excitedly said, "I can see the home from here. It is the largest home in the village. My great grandfather had it built, and my mother was born in it. I can't believe it; I'm here."

There were a few people walking about as George and Vassilis headed up the hill. They greeted an elderly couple going down hill. George, being in front of Vassilis, stopped in front of his mother's home. It had two floors, many large windows, and a large walled-in courtyard. Passing through the large metal gate, they followed a cement walkway to a veranda with ten steps. George knocked on the front door and a petite elderly lady wearing a colorful dress and an apron answered.

"Hello, I'm George Stamos, and my mother, Areti Doulas, was born in this house. I'm visiting from America, and I came to visit my father's village, Glifada, and especially this home. This is Doctor Vassilis Stamos, my cousin from Glifada."

The woman had a surprise look, "Come in, I am Areti's second cousin. I can't believe it. From America! I have heard of Doctor Vassilis Stamos. How do you know this house? Did you ask someone?"

"No, I recognized it from old photographs."

"Photographs? Please come in, come in."

"Yes, my grandmother had a photograph of this village, and another picture of this house hanging on her wall since I was a little boy."

George and Vassilis entered into a large marble-floored foyer which had a stairway aside the rear wall above an elegantly tiled walled fountain. There were three blue wooden exquisitely hand-carved doors on each side of the foyer and one in each rear wall corner. Upstairs, there was a blue wooden-railed balcony circumventing the foyer, there were six rooms with blue doors, and a large wooden hand carved double door with glass, which opened to the outside. George couldn't believe his eyes. He knew his great grandparents had been rich, but he never expected this. George and Vassilis started to remove their shoes.

"My name is Sophia Papajanis, and my husband is in that room; she pointed. Please go in. You do not have to remove your shoes."

George replied, "I don't mind taking my shoes off."

George entered the room and Vassilis followed. They saw an elderly gentleman sitting and reading. He got up with his arm extended and said hello. He was thin, dressed in worn clothes, and he wasn't much taller than Sophia, but he had a strong grip.

Sophia continued, "This is my husband, Kostas. This is George Stamos from America and his cousin Doctor Vassilis Stamos from Glifada. He is Areti Doulas' son. Her grandfather and my grandfather were brothers. My mother and Areti are cousins. Areti left here when she was very young. I wasn't born yet. I can't believe you're here. Here, sit down."

Sophia had short grayish hair, large brown eyes, a pleasant smile, a dainty posture, and like everyone George met, she was thin. She excused herself and left the room. During her absence Kostas asked George about his travels to Albania. In the middle of a sentence Sophia returned with watermelon, grapes and coffee, all on a beautiful tray. She served George first, then Vassilis and her husband.

She sat and asked, "Will you stay for something to eat?"

"No thank you. We can't stay long. I arrived in Albania yesterday, but I really wanted to see this home, I've heard so much about it. I wanted to know who lived in it. I thought maybe a stranger. My family didn't know. My mother will be surprised that you live here with your husband. I have heard about you and your father and mother, but my mother didn't know if your mother, Sevasti, was alive or not. She said it had been a while since she received any letter from your mother. We also knew that the government had taken possession of the house."

"Yes, it was occupied by the Italian army from 1939 to 1944 and used as officers' living quarters. Then the Albanians took control from them until 1969. They used it as a school, had animals living on the second floor, and they removed all but a few hand carved wooden ceilings and cornices. We are poor, so we have not been able to replace the damages. When can you return? I have room for you, and you can stay as long as you like."

"I can't stay right now. It is getting late and we have to return to Glifada, but my wife is coming from America soon, and we'll make arrangements to come and visit. It would be a pleasure to sleep in the home of my mother, grand and great grandparents. Also, we can spend more time talking, and you can show me the rest of the house."

"Would you like more coffee?"

"No thank you. We'll finish our drink and then we have to go, but I'll be back."

George got up and everyone rose. They kissed each other on the cheeks and said their good-byes. George and Vassilis walked down the steep path and saw some vehicles sitting at the bottom; one looked new. The same driver was there. George was surprised, but Vassilis knew he'd be there. Unknowingly to George, he had told him to wait. They got in and drove back to the bottom of Vassilis' mountain home.

George asked Vassilis, "How much did you have to pay for the driver to wait? I'm glad I didn't stay too long."

"Two hundred and eighty leks ($2.00). He would have waited until we returned. I told him we wouldn't be too long because it would be approaching dusk."

"Boy! That would have cost a lot more money back home. I knew it was getting late, and Violetta would wonder when we would return for dinner.

Besides I haven't eaten since this morning, but I'm so excited I don't care if I eat. What about you?"

"I left early this morning and had a snack at work before I returned."

The return trip was quick, and the hike up the mountain was refreshing. George entered the house and was met by Aunt Amalia. They kissed on the cheeks and she said, "Did you talk to your wife and enjoy Argirocastro?"

"Yes I did, and Argirocastro looked interesting, but I talked to my aunt. She'll call my wife, but we left and went to Morista to see my mother's home. We just returned from there. My wife will arrive in Albania on September 6. I can't wait."

Violetta came into the room, having heard the conversation. She had a large smile on her face. "I'm happy for you. It will be nice to have your wife here. I want to meet her. Is she Greek?"

"No, she is of English and Irish origin, with blonde hair and blue eyes. She knows very little Greek. I'll have to go to Kakavia to pick her up."

"Don't worry, the family will help you. You have many relatives living in Argirocastro to visit. Some in Tirana and many other places. Are you hungry? Dinner will be ready very soon."

"I'm excited about meeting as many relatives as I can; my wife is very anxious to meet my relatives, and yes, I am hungry."

After refreshing himself, George was told that dinner was ready. It consisted of the same fare as the first dinner: lamb, potatoes, tomato and onion salad, feta and olives, bread and coffee. The family excused themselves for having the same meal. They were very apologetic, but after the meal they served yogurt with honey. George knew they were embarrassed, but times were tough. It is traditional for Greeks to be very generous when feeding guests.

After eating, Vassilis and George retreated to the front porch. Darkness had settled in, and many stars were visible; the village had very few streetlights (bare bulbs). Soon after they sat, Violetta served them coffee in small cups and saucers on a tray. Across the wide valley they could see the concentration of two small mountainside village lights, and way off in the distance a larger village's sky reflection; George was told it was Libihovo.

Vassilis was explaining his family. He had two older sisters and one older brother. The oldest sister and the brother lived in Argirocastro; the youngest sister lived in the village.

"You will meet the sisters, but my brother is in Greece working. He returns occasionally with money and goods. The youngest sister is a recent widow. The Stamos family is very large and now somewhat spread out, but many still live in this village."

"How many years has our family lived in this village?"

"About eight hundred to one thousand years."

George replied, "Really? Oh my!"

George didn't know how true that was, but he suspected that the family history went as far back as anyone knew. George's thoughts wandered while thinking about his heritage. He was amazed. A thousand years is a long time. He couldn't wait to tell Lesley and his family back home.

Vassilis told George, "The Stamos family is the largest family in the village. Just wait until you meet them all. You have met only a few."

As they were talking and drinking their coffee they could see a few cars traveling on the highway below. George was looking north when he saw many vehicle lights stacked one right after the other come into view heading south. As the lights were approaching more lights came into view. George counted the vehicles. There were twenty-eight tractor trailers in a column, and the sound of motors and rolling tires rose up the mountain side. It was an incredible sight.

George turned to Vassilis and asked, "Where are they going?"

"Returning to Greece. The Greeks are sending food and supplies."

"You will see many more trucks as you stay here longer. When communism fell, our whole infrastructure collapsed. There were no seeds for farmers, factories closed, transportation fell apart, and food, medicine, and clothing were in short supply or nonexistent. The older generation wants to return to communism, because it wasn't as bad as it is now. The younger generation wants democracy and freedom. They know it will take time to recover. In the meantime things are bad."

"I saw in your garden you have a few vegetables."

"Yes, I had saved some seeds, but now that fall is approaching we can't plant. We have to go to Argirocastro or Greece to get food. I don't have a car, so I've gone only once to Greece with a friend or we ask friends to get us something. The Greek custom officials let us go freely because we are Greeks. Albanians cannot cross without difficulty, if at all. They sneak in at night. The soldiers catch them and return them, but they try again and again. It is a very difficult situation. That is why you saw many Greek soldiers. They are patrolling the border."

During the conversation, Violetta returned and asked if they wanted anything. The young son came out and kissed his father goodnight. He just looked at George with a smile, and then Violetta said goodnight. Amalia was somewhere. George had not seen her since they returned.

As the night passed, Vassilis talked about the family. George learned that their grandfather was a shepherd who would take his and other family's sheep into the mountain grasses for days. He was well-respected and a spokesman to the communist party for the village. He mediated many problems between villagers and communist officials.

Vassilis said, "There are seventeen first cousins including you and your sister. Tomorrow we will go back to Argirocastro. You'll meet our two aunts, my sister, and some of their children. It will be a very busy day. They know you are here, and they want to meet you. Are you up for all that? I don't want to over-exert you."

"Don't worry about me. I'm in good health, and it all sounds great."

George couldn't figure out how everybody knew he was there, but he didn't ask. All he knew was that the grapevine was working. They watched a few more trucks pass and village lights turn off. It was time to go inside and say good-night and retire.

George, lying in his bed, thought of tomorrow and the days ahead. He was anxious for Lesley to arrive. He hoped that her travels would go well. She was a strong woman, and he trusted her judgments. She had traveled to Europe in her college years with girlfriends and saw the usual British and French tourist spots. Traveling to Greece and Albania would be somewhat different, but she knew not to enter Albania if George wasn't there to meet her. The thick stone walls silenced the building except for the dogs barking in the village as he drifted off to sleep.

Telephone Office

Chapter X

The next morning George awoke to a bright sunny day. Vassilis told him after a breakfast of coffee, bread, and yogurt that everybody but Amalia and the two boys were meeting a car and would be going to Argirocastro to visit their three aunts. The aunt from Kassanda would be there. George thought the wonders of how words travel when phones were almost nonexistent. George got his camera, and Vassilis, Violetta, and George walked down the mountain and waited for the car to arrive.

After about ten minutes a red car arrived. This car was in better shape than the others George had ridden in, although the make was still foreign to George. They all piled in; George sat in front. Vassilis introduced George to the driver.

"This is Aleko; his father is Spiros, our cousin, the one near your age; Aleko works in the telephone office. We are going to Aunt Penelope's home. Aunts Stavroula, Evanthia, and Evanthia's granddaughter will be there, and then we'll walk to my oldest sister's home for dinner. She is a great cook. You will like her husband, Kristos."

Aleko and George greeted each other and talked briefly as they drove toward Argirocastro. The car entered the city and went up the main thoroughfare and then made a few sharp turns onto rough narrow gravel roads. They stopped high on the mountainside. Everyone got out except Aleko; he had to return to his job.

Walking up a few concrete steps they faced a more modern home.

Removing their shoes, Vassilis opened and held the front door open to allow George to enter first. George peered in quickly and noticed that the home was furnished above the standards he had seen in other homes. Sitting at a table were the three aunts.

Vassilis introduced George to his aunts. Penelope, the oldest, was wearing black clothing down to her shoes and a black cloth kerchief-like headdress. She was wearing a skirt down to her ankles, and black stockings and a long-sleeved white blouse with a buttoned down black light jacket (George had seen a picture-1900-of his great grandmother wearing the same style clothing). Stavroula, the second oldest, was similarly dressed, but her headdress was a white cloth. Evanthia, the youngest, was also dressed in all black, but her dress reached just below her knees, showing her black stockings, and also a black headdress. George went over and kissed and hugged them one at a time. His thoughts went to his father. He knew they were looking at him as if he was their brother. The two oldest aunts started to cry. Violetta decided to join them, and George and Vassilis had tears. Aunt Evanthia had a big smile.

Aunt Evanthia introduced her granddaughter, Sophia. She was tall with long black hair reaching below her shoulders, big bright brown eyes, a pretty face, and a shapely but slim body. She was wearing a red and black colorful cotton dress. She was eighteen, spoke English, and wanted to practice her English. George knew that Evanthia was only five years older than himself. She was thin, had perfect teeth. Her face resembled his father's. She had stern eyes, and was spry. The other two aunts were in their seventies. Penelope and Stavroula were slightly heavier than Evanthia, their facial structures had family resemblances, and they were both somewhat sickly. When the emotions somewhat settled Sophia served fig preserves with coffee. George expressed his thanks for a perfect cup of coffee (he had overheard Violetta telling Sophia how George liked his coffee).

The aunts asked many questions about George's father, George's and Eli's family, and about America. George spoke in Greek and in English so Sophia could translate into Greek. She did an excellent job. Once in while she had trouble with a word, and George would help her. In return George asked about their family, how many children they had, and where the other two aunts lived. Stavroula lived in a village next to Morista with her husband and children. Evanthia lived not too far from Penelope with her husband. Her son lived upstairs with his wife, and another daughter lived up north with her two daughters. She was Sophia's mother.

While everyone was talking, an older man and a very pretty young lady entered the room unnoticed. Vassilis saw them and introduced them immediately. The gentleman was Penelope's husband, Taki, and the lady was their daughter, Margarita. She was in her late thirties, and her facial features resembled George's sister. Margarita had strikingly pretty face and sky-blue eyes, long wavy brown hair, and a Hollywood figure; she was wearing a bright yellow dress, which accented her hair. She was married with two children. The children were attending private schools, and her husband was away on business. Taki was elderly, stocky and short. He had straight shoulders, thinning hair, and a strong handshake. After introductions, Margarita brought out ouzo for the men. Vassilis refused; he said he didn't drink alcohol, and the women weren't served, except for Evanthia; she asked for a glass.

Aunt Penelope told George she remembered very little of his father; she was just a five year old girl when he left, Aunt Evanthia wasn't born when he left, and Aunt Stavroula was a baby. They were anxious to see George. As George had thought, they told him that looking at him was like looking at their brother. A chill went up his spine. He was the long-lost brother-a daunting experience for George.

As time was passing, everyone, except for Aunt Evanthia drank more ouzo. They had coffee and watermelon and listened to each others' questions and answers. They were all curious about George and Eli and America, and George was learning more about the family and Albania.

George asked if he could take pictures. Everyone agreed. He reached into his small bag and retrieved his camera. Taki asked if he was a professional seeing the Nikon F-2 with a 105 mm portrait lens attached. George told him he had been taken pictures for many years. It was a hobby. The family murmured among themselves. George took many photographs, and Sophia took some for George after he gave her some quick instructions; he wanted to be in some of the photos. No one else owned a camera, so this pleased them very much, and they asked for copies. George told them he would send copies after he returned to America.

When things settled somewhat and as time passed Vassilis informed everyone that it was time to leave as they were walking to his sister's home so George could meet more of the family and for dinner. He would bring George back to Argirocastro after George's wife arrived. All the aunts commented about Olympia, Vassilis' sister's great cooking. George was excited about the upcoming meal and meeting more family. The three aunts invited him and his wife to visit and stay overnight. Evanthia couldn't make the same offer, for an overnight stay, as she only had one bedroom.

George replied, "I will visit all of you with my wife. She'll be here in two days and I'll make arrangements to visit after she gets settled in. I want very much to meet your husbands and children. I've been to two villages and here. Now I can visit another village. Besides, I want to see more of Argirocastro. Vassilis has told me how beautiful the tiled streets are. It was beautiful to meet you all. We are all blood, and it's too bad it took me so long to get here, but I know you understand why, and living so far apart it's not easy. Until next time, I love you all."

George got up from his chair and all but the aunts rose. George did the cheek kissing and said his good-byes. Once again, George was let out the door first. Vassilis and Violetta were happy that all went well, and walking down the road there was much conversation.

Vassilis asked, "George, do you mind walking to my sister's home? It's down the mountain."

"No, it will give me time to contemplate what just transpired. Besides, I like to walk. Meeting my aunts for the first time was quite an experience. Just think, I'm sixty-two, and I just now met them. Unbelievable after years of trying."

Vassilis said, "Good, I understand."

George said, "I didn't say anything to Evanthia about not meeting me, and she never inquired how I got to your house. I don't understand."

Vassilis replied, "I'm glad you didn't. Everyone is upset with her that she didn't tell the family you were coming, and more upset that she didn't meet you or make other arrangements. She received your letters. Sophia read the letters to her. Some members of the family have had trouble with her. You're here now so don't think about it."

Violetta grabbed George's arm, "You don't know how happy the family is that you are here, and that is very important."

Continuing down the road George thought as he walked behind Vassilis and Violetta. They walked holding hands and talking. George was happy to have met his aunts, and now he was going to meet another relative. His thoughts traveled to America and to his Lesley. George knew Lesley was preparing to travel, and he missed her; just two more days. He thought of how Albania was so different, even being a European country.

George was quietly daydreaming when Vassilis said, "We're going right, and then a left. We'll be there soon."

Vassilis and Violetta stopped in front of a home on a narrow partially paved rutted street. The home had a long porch on the second floor facing the bottom of the mountain, and the home overlooked homes below.

Vassilis knocked and a pretty round faced lady opened the door and he said, "Hello, this is George. This is my sister, Olympia."

Olympia said, "It is so nice to meet you, come in please."

Of course, George entered first, shoes came off, slippers came on, and kisses were exchanged; the routine was always the same. George liked it, but he would have to tell Lesley the routine. The house was fairly large and well furnished. Olympia introduced her husband, Kristos who was as tall as George, and in good shape. He had a handsome face with dark features and a thick head of salt-and-pepper hair. Olympia was not thin, and George could see the Stamos resemblance. She had thin streaks of grey hair, but no wrinkles, except for crow's feet next to her hazel colored-eyes. She had a beautiful smile. George immediately felt warmth towards her.

With everyone settled, Olympia and Violetta left the room and Olympia returned with tsipouro (an alcoholic drink made from grape skins) for George and Kristos; this aperitif, or ouzo, is always served to men in Albania with a small glass of water. She then brought in fig and plum preserves in small decorative china bowls, small china plates with silver spoons, and also loukoumi (Greek jellied candy covered in powdered sugar). She had made the candy and preserves. She asked who wanted coffee. The men replied yes.

With the women out of the room Kristos made a toast to George; a swig and then a sip of water, and maybe a small serving of preserve or candy. This procedure was duplicated in every home, if available in those hard times, before a meal or when guests arrive even for short visits. The typical procedure is you are given small spoons, saucers, two water glasses, a preserve, coffee, and a liqueur. You put your spoon in the preserve and take a portion and then put it into your mouth to clean everything off the spoon, put the spoon in one glass of water, drink a little water from that glass then drink a little of the liqueur (tsipouro or ouzo), then maybe drink from the other glass of water and then finish with a cup of Greek coffee. It is expected to make a noisily sip as a sign of appreciation. George knew the custom from when he was a small boy. It was going out of favor with younger Americanized Greeks.

The men talked and drank tsipouro (there was a decanter) and coffee. To George's surprise the coffee was made to his liking. He was aware that it didn't take long for word to get around. The woman returned and the questions came. George described where he lived and about America, his profession, his salary, his car, his house, and about democracy and capitalism. They couldn't believe how much money he made. They wanted to know why America hadn't sent money, food or medicine. Of course, George had no definitive answers. To them George was rich, especially because he could afford to fly and travel.

George asked Olympia and Kristos about their living conditions. He assumed because of their nice home and furnishings they were somewhat well off.

Kristos said, "I was a shoe maker, and Olympia worked in a utensil factory, making spoons, forks, knives, and other items. We live on twenty eight hundred leks ($20.00) per month. We were actors and toured the country in our spare time for extra money. We have lived in this house since we got married thirty-two years ago. We have a daughter, thirty years old, and two grandchildren, a boy seven and a girl eight. You will meet my family and son-in-law, George. He has the same name as you."

As Kristos was talking there was a knock on the front door. Olympia opened the door and a woman and two children walked in. Vassilis went over and greeted the guests with Olympia. They came over and George got up and Kristos followed.

Vassilis said, "This is my oldest brother's wife, and their two children. He is in Greece working and his two older daughters have jobs there also. You will not meet them, as they can't leave right now. His name is Vangeli; this is Margarita, and their son Dimitri (14 years), and daughter Anthoula (16 years). They live not too far from here. Anthoula is learning English. I see she has brought her English book with her. They are going to have dinner with us."

George said, "It is so nice to meet you. I'm sorry I can't meet your husband and daughters, but please give them my regards. What are the names and ages of your daughters?"

Margarita replied, "Madeline is twenty-three and blonde and Amalia is twenty with dark brown hair."

Dimitri had brown eyes and hair, broad shoulders and bulging muscles, and a shy, awakening smile. Anthoula had blonde hair, blue eyes, a young girl's figure, and a pretty face. The mother was attractive, with dark hair, dark eyes, and a laugh that was charming. George thought to himself, his relatives are quite handsome.

By then the meal was announced. No one moved until George got up, and then everyone followed. He was showed the way to the dining room and then where to sit. George entered the dining room first, and sat down first and at the head of the table. He started to pay attention to this his being first. He assumed that because he was a guest they were honoring him.

Olympia served a fantastic meal of baked lamb, okra with tomato, pilaf, pickle eggplant, green and red pepper salad with garlic and peppercorn, tomato and onion salad, cut squares of corn meal cooked with feta and wild greens, yogurt, hand made philo dough baklava, Amstel beer, and Fanta for the youngsters. Everyone told pleasant and funny stories, making each other laugh.

After the table was cleared, coffee and tsipouro were served as was milk for the youngsters. Once again the conversation turned to America. They were very curious about the lifestyle, and its politics. They had been taught that America was their enemy, and everything in America is bad. Of course, they were waiting for America to invade. Eventually they realized that Enver Hoxha had lied and ruined their country. Now they wanted to catch up with the rest of the world, as Albania was very antiquated, and few modern conveniences were available. Albanians are very proud and not lazy, but they don't have enough money to travel, buy cars or buy modern equipment. There are few jobs and less available food. Those who can grow food are fortunate. George thought, what can you buy on fifteen or twenty dollars a month? You can't buy expensive products from other countries making twenty dollars a month.

George decided to change the conversation and take photos. He told them that he had his camera and wanted to take pictures of everyone. He took out his F-2 again. This brought some low vocal tones and whispers. George took individual portraits, family shots, different group pictures and then the entire group. He then had to show everyone the camera and they all looked through the viewfinder. Someone asked George how much the camera cost. When George told them, they knew they would never have that much money, at least the way things are. Everyone settled down, and George returned to his chair.

George turned to Anthoula and asked in English, "Can I see your English book?"

She got up and retrieved the book and handed it to George. He perused the contents slowly; it had been printed in 1988. Everyone was quiet, waiting for George to say something. After a few minutes he told Anthoula in English, "I have found many errors. I want to look some more."

Anthoula asked, "No understand, is book bad?"

George replying in Greek said, "Bad? I found many errors, especially in spelling and grammar. This is not a well-written book. When I get home or in Greece I'll send you a better book for you to learn English. I'll send a Greek-English dictionary, also an English-Greek dictionary. Speak in English. Is this a school book?"

"No, I go private school. Book only one."

Replying in English "You're doing okay. Of course, you'll have to use this book for now. Do you understand?"

With a gleam in her eyes and a big smile, "Yes, thank you."

George inquired if Dimitri was learning English also. The mother told George he loved wrestling and boxing. He wanted to be a boxer. George could see the physical results. The boy had a big smile on his reddening face.

The day was passing and nighttime was approaching. Vassilis' brother's family lived close by and Vassilis had to secure a ride back to the village before darkness closed in. Good-byes were said, and Olympia told George to return with his wife and stay over, and Margarita invited them for lunch or dinner. Anthoula said she couldn't wait to try her English again.

George was quite pleased with everything. Many invitations to visit relatives. He hoped that Lesley and he could get it all in. Although they had the remainder of the month, there was Greece to visit also, especially Athens. Vassilis left and returned, saying he had found a ride home. George was amazed at his competence in executing his ability to obtain rides so quickly. George also thought anyone with an auto was for hire.

During the ride home George asked Vassilis, "Why am I always first to enter a room, to sit down, and to exit?"

Vassilis replied, "George, not only are you a guest and from America, but you are the oldest male in the family. Remember? The Patriarch!"

This was a little too much for George to accept, but customs are what they are. To some degree he liked the attention.

Another day was passing, but George was satisfied with all the day's events. Although life in Albania was difficult, the family tried their best not to show signs of their difficulties. They shared their love and their happiness in meeting their only relative from America.

George thought of his travels in Bolivia and Peru to areas that were primitive and underdeveloped. He felt safe and protected here, but the food was not abundant and varied. This reminded him of a meal of a roots prepared by an indigenous lady (Jivaro tribe) in the upper Amazon. It was simple, but tasty. Of course, Albanian meals are a little more elaborate and also tasty.

Military bunkers

The Aunts-Penelope, Stravoula, and Evanthia

Chapter XI

The next morning after breakfast, when Vassilis was at work and Amalia was with the boys, Violetta took George to the home of his grandfather where Vlassi and his brothers and sisters were born. It wasn't a large house, considering the size of the family. George could see that it was old and in need of repairs, but it was higher up the mountain village road, and it had a grand view.

Violetta knocked on the door, and a woman's voice was heard to say loudly, "Enter." The entryway was dark as they walked into the living room. A short lady dressed in black with a white headdress and a white apron entered from another room with a surprise look on her face.

"Please excuse me, I thought it was a neighbor, I'm busy making feta and my hands are messy. Please sit down. You must be George. Wait, I'll get my son, and I'll return in a few moments. I'm so sorry."

George heard her call for her son who was out back somewhere. "Theodore!"

Violetta said, "That was your Aunt Ollga. She was married to your Uncle Kostas."

With so many relatives, George knew it would be somewhat difficult to remember all their names and how they were related. While George was thinking about this, in walked a tall strapping-built man with slight streaks of grey in his hair. George remembered his face from the first night when the group of men visited.

In a deep bass voice he said, "Hello, I am Theodore your cousin, it is good to meet you again. My mother will be here shortly. How is your visit going?"

"Very good, it is good to meet you again also. I wanted to see the home where my father was born and where my grandmother and grandfather lived. Do you live here?"

"Yes, I live here with my mother and my wife Mariana and my two year old son, Panajotis. Mariana is in another village visiting her mother for a couple of days. Panajotis is with her. You'll have to return for dinner and meet them."

"Yes, I would love to arrange that. My wife will be here soon. We will do that then."

Violetta excused herself and left the room. There were conversations about Theodore's work and George's. Theodore was asking questions about America when Violetta and Ollga returned with a tray of coffee and plum preserves; George and Ollga made their formal greetings. The coffee was made to George's satisfaction.

George asked, "You're making feta? Do a lot of the families make it?"

"Yes, in the villages most families make their own. My mother taught me when I was a little girl."

"Would you tell me how it is done?"

"Yes, it is quite simple. You take fifteen liters of sheep's milk, heat it to 85 C (187 F), cool it to 35 C (97 F), add one teaspoon of rennet and mix gently, cover for one hour, and then filter it through a cheese cloth for eight to twelve hours, then add salt and form cakes. It formulates in thirty-five to forty days. Then refrigerate at 5 C (41 F) to 10 C (50 F). If you make a larger amount, make the added adjustments."

George thought it sounded like a lot of work and obviously would be time consuming. He knew he would never make it or ask Lesley to do it. It was easier to go to Greek or Middle Eastern markets and buy imported feta. He knew that the feta he had eaten in Albania was delicious, but he hadn't given it much thought as to whether or not if it was hand made. George thanked his aunt.

She smiled, "Are you going back to America and make some?"

"No, I don't think so, but I'll enjoy it while I'm visiting, and also realize how it is made, thank you."

"When you return for dinner you must stay over and eat feta."

Everyone laughed. George was having a good time.

George asked, "Do you have your own sheep?

Theodore replied, "We have a small flock and a couple of goats. One of the men in the village takes them to pasture with other villager's sheep. The families pay him for this work."

George said, "Fresh milk, fresh cheese, fresh meat, how wonderful. We have to go to stores and get everything, unless we drive out to the countryside to a farmers' market."

Ollga replied, "It was much better when we had communism. Now there is nothing to buy. Food is in short supply, and the men and women can't find jobs."

George said little. He knew times were tough and he didn't want to add to the conversation about communism. He just listened and nodded his head in the affirmative (sideways). The conversation was similar to conversations during other family visits; questions about George, his family, and America. He in turn asked about Aunt Ollga, Uncle Kostas and his grandparents. Aunt Ollga said that George's grandmother had been a beautiful lady-one of the prettiest ladies in the village and that she had a pleasant personality. Everyone had loved her. When she died it was a great loss to the family and the village. George's mind drifted, and he was saddened that he had never seen her face, held her hand, or talked to her. After two hours or so, George wanted to leave and spend more time seeing the village, knowing he would return and spend the night there with Lesley.

George got up and said politely, "I'm afraid it is time for me to leave. I want to tell you it was a good to meet you Aunt Ollga, and I had a nice visit."

Aunt Ollga and Theodore also thanked him for visiting. They told him to return with his wife for dinner and to stay over.

He said, "It would be a pleasure. I'll let you know after my wife arrives."

They kissed good-bye, and George and Violetta started for home. They met many villagers who were outside their homes and some exiting their homes as they walked down the road. There were babies and toddlers, but no school-age children. The villagers waved and smiled. Some came forward and said hello asking his name and where he was from. When George said Stamos, smiles came over their faces. He also saw some of his men relatives who had visited that first night. They came over and talked briefly. Of course they kissed on the cheeks and shook hands.

There were even goats and sheep traveling on the road, but they paid no attention to the people. Some animals stopped and lingered in front of homes, and the owners gathered them to be put in their pens. George, passing a building, noticed it had red painted letters depicting it as the communist party meeting building. The front door was hanging on one hinge.

"Well, now you have seen the village and your father's birthplace. Most of the villagers know you are visiting, and the word must have gone out that you were at Kostas' house. They were waiting to see you when you walked down the mountain. They are not routinely out like that. What a nice greeting for them and you. So what do you think?"

"Personally, I loved it. What a beautiful village, but I didn't see many children."

"In the villages the children are in school."

Arriving home they met Vassilis walking up the graveled road. They greeted each other and Vassilis said, "We have to go to Argirocastro to see Aleko and his father. I want to ask Aleko if he can take us to Kakavia to meet your wife. I asked him already and he said he would see if he can get off work. You can also meet his wife and father. His father is almost your age, remember? Where were you coming from?"

"My father's and our grandparent's home; I met a lot of villagers."

Violetta said, "The villagers came out of their homes to see George. It was exciting."

Vassilis asked, "How nice, George how soon can you be ready to go? Are you hungry?"

"No, I'm ready to go now. I need to get my camera."

"Good, a car is waiting for us."

The driver seemed to fly in another different style foreign car. He was quiet only his hello was heard. George inquired about speeding tickets.

Vassilis laughed and told George, "There are not many police who have cars, and right now many don't care, but that will change as more people get cars."

Entering the city the driver drove to a high rise apartment complex and let them out. The buildings were five stories high with no elevators. George was told that the buildings were fairly new. They were in poor condition and looked one hundred years old. They walked up four flights of stairs, and Vassilis knocked on one of four doors.

A pretty pregnant lady answered. George insisted that Vassilis enter first. Inside Vassilis introduced George to cousin Spiros, and Rezarta, the pretty pregnant lady; Aleko's wife. Spiros had broad shoulders, was taller than George, with a handsome round face and a bald top. Rezarta was the same height as Lesley, with long, light-brown wavy hair with dark blondish streaks, a small tilted nose, and a gracious smile, and she was very pregnant.

She said in perfect English, "Welcome to my home."

George was surprised, "Hello. You speak English. You are the third person I've met who speaks English. Do you mind me asking where you learned to speak English without a heavy accent?"

"In college. I am a school teacher. Aleko told me about you. I wanted to meet you to practice my English. A few friends of mine speak it also, so we practice together, but it will be nice to speak to an American relative. Do you mind?"

"No, I need to use my English so I won't forget it."

Rezarta and George laughed, and Spiros and Vassilis wondered why they were laughing. She spoke Greek and related the English, and they laughed also. Just then a young toddler appeared. He was cute as a button.

Rezarta said, "This is my boy, Artioli. He is three."

George approached the boy and held out his arms. Artioli allowed him to pick him up. George spoke softly, and mumbled nothings in his ear, and the boy chuckled; they became friends.

Vassilis asked, "When will Aleko be home?"

Spiros answered, "He will be home soon to get something to eat. Aleko said you want him to go to Kakavia with you and George to get his wife."

Rezarta inquired, "I want to meet her. Maybe I can go too. Do you all want coffee?"

The men said yes, and George told her how he liked his. She looked at him but said nothing. The men sat down at a round kitchen table in a small room next to the kitchen. George looked into a very small so-called kitchen; there were no cabinets. Rezarta was using an electric hot plate to boil water.

Vassilis answered Spiros, "Yes, I did ask Aleko if he could help."

George asked to use the bathroom. He walked into a small room with no shower stall, but a rubber hose with a shower head on one end. No porcelain toilet, but a hole and concrete cutouts to place your feet (the villages had outhouses), and as in the villages, communist books were being used for toilet paper. That is why he told Lesley to bring toilet paper. There was a fifty-five gallon wooden water barrel with a large ladle for flushing, and a very small electric water heater to heat the water. The water pipes and electric wiring were as antiquated as in the village homes. It brought back memories of the wiring he saw in animal barns in the forties. The more George saw of European- Albania the more amazed he became. He thought to himself, this is Europe and the twentieth century! While these thoughts were mulling in his head Aleko returned home briefly and affirmed that he could take George to get his wife in between his job. He would be at the bottom of their hill tomorrow at 2:30 p.m.; it was a Sunday. George and Vassilis thanked him.

George asked Aleko, "Do you always work on Sunday?"

"No, but I usually go in every day or part of the day. I have maintenance duties."

Aleko had a gentle demeanor, similar facial resemblances to George's father, broad muscular shoulders, a sound body, was slightly shorter than George, and had a receding hairline.

Because Vassilis had to return to work to check on a sick animal and take George back to Glifada they said their good-byes, walked to the main avenue, and Vassilis managed to hail a car, and off they went. It was another warm sunny day, and the traffic was minimal. Arriving at Glifada Vassilis walked George to the house and left to go to work. George realized that the family would accompany him everywhere.

George greeted Violetta and Amalia and sat on the porch with a cup of coffee. His thoughts went to America and to Lesley's travels. He was so occupied, time had passed and Vassilis returned from work almost unnoticed. George immediately excused himself.

George felt apologetic, "My mind was across Europe and the Atlantic."

Vassilis said, "Yes, I understand. Dinner is almost ready."

Aleko returned with a surprise visit to Vassilis' home after they just finished dinner and asked George if he would spend the night with his family. They wanted to spend more time with George, and then go to Kakavia, stopping to get Vassilis on the way. Rezarta was also going to Kakavia. She was very excited to meet an American woman, especially a family relative. George quickly packed his necessities and returned to Argirocastro.

Sleeping was difficult for George. He was anxious for the arrival of Lesley. His thoughts went to her traveling alone in a taxi from Ioannina to Kakavia. Yet he knew she would be safe. He wished that she spoke Greek fluently. She only knew some of the most common phrases: *kahleemehrah* (good morning), *kahleeneektah* (goodnight), *ehfkhahreesto* (thank you) *me agapi* (my love), and a few more.

Chapter XII

George woke up to the sounds of dogs barking, donkeys braying, roosters crowing, and car horns honking; the same noises as in the village except for the car horns. The household woke up excited. Even Artioli sensed the excitement. George wished that Lesley's travels would go well and that her entry into Albania would not be too complicated. He also thought about the small car carrying five passengers and luggage.

George spent the morning playing with Artioli and talking to Spiros and Rezarta. When it was almost time to leave Aleko returned home. A woman who lived upstairs arrived to take care of Artioli; Spiros had errands to do. Artioli fussed some, but they had to leave. Rezarta and George walked down the four flights of stairs and met Aleko at the front door. They drove to the bottom of the mountain at Glifada; Vassilis was anxiously waiting at the roadside. The ride to Kakavia was exciting, but the passengers remained solemn.

Arriving at the Albanian border, George and Vassilis got out; they were the only ones to cross over to Greece. Rezarta and Aleko remained with the car. There were no other cars in the Albanian lot, but the lot was full of men either trying to cross the border, or waiting for someone coming from Greece. It had the same appearance as when George had first arrived.

Vassilis and George had to show their passports to the Albanian soldiers at both gates. Vassilis spoke in Albanian and told the soldiers that they were there to meet an American lady at the Greek border, and they would be returning. The soldiers waived them through with no discussion.

They met three cars driving slowly in the no mans land. The cars were returning to Albania packed with goods inside and tied down on their roofs. One vehicle had a small refrigerator on the roof. Vassilis told George they were Greek-Albanians bringing goods to their village homes after working for Greeks. Only a few Albanians are given Greek work visas.

Vassilis had to show his Greek visa, which he had procured before George arrived, and also his Albanian passport so he could enter through the Greek gate. He told the official that they were there to meet George's wife. George had his passport in his hand. The Greek official, remembering George, looked at it briefly and just waived him through.

It was a warm day, and they didn't see Lesley outside the compound. They entered the main building and looked around, but did not see her. George knew they were early. He had planned it that way just in case she arrived earlier than planned. They were about to sit when all of a sudden Lesley appeared. She had two suitcases and her hand bag. Under her left arm she had a large cache of toilet paper. Vassilis made a comment about the paper to George and smiled. After kissing and embracing George, she told him she had been there an hour and was getting bored, but she knew she was somewhat early.

George said, "I'm sorry we weren't here earlier."

Lesley replied, "There was a change in one flight, so I got here earlier than expected, but I knew you'd be here. Still I was getting somewhat anxious."

George introduced Vassilis. Vassilis greeted her and kissed her on the cheeks. In Greek she said hello. Vassilis had a big smile. Vassilis grabbed her luggage, and Lesley held onto the toilet paper. She had already completed the official paperwork.

Passing through Greek Customs, Vassilis had to show his visa and passport again, Lesley had to show her stamped passport, and the same official waived George through without looking at his passport. At the Albanian gates and office, Vassilis said something and was waived through. Lesley had to get stamped and show her passports to the soldiers; George was waived through. Once again the Albanian immigration official was not friendly even with Lesley, but it was not the same official as when George first had arrived.

Lesley made comments to George about the difference between the Greek and Albanian officials, and the condition of the Albanian side compared to the Greek side. George had a lot to explain to her about Albania. He hugged her to his side as they walked toward the car. Aleko and Rezarta got out of the car to meet Lesley. They hugged and kissed, and Rezarta spoke in English, which surprised Lesley. Everyone piled into the car, luggage and all. It was a tight situation, like the circus with thirty people coming out of a Beetle, but no one complained, as the excitement overwhelmed them all. Aleko had parked on a slight grade; George never noticed that every time he had got into the car it was running. Aleko rolled the car, jump-started the motor, and off they went; some chuckles could be heard.

George said, "If the car stalls there are enough of us to push it all the way to Glifada."

That brought many laughs. The ride to Glifada seemed to pass quickly. Aleko crossed the entrance bridge and parked on the hill. Everyone got out; Aleko and Vassilis carried the luggage and the toilet paper. Rezarta climbed the hill with a strong gait even though she was eight months pregnant. Following the group, George told Lesley that they won't let him carry anything, as he was the oldest male in the family. She in return called him an old man. They both laughed.

Aleko said, "We can visit shortly. It won't be safe to leave the car too long."

Violetta was standing at the front door to meet them. She had an inviting smile and her eyes were glowing. She kissed Lesley and gave her a big hug. Lesley returned the gesture. Aunt Amalia met them in the foyer and spoke to Lesley in Greek, welcoming and inviting her to the house. Nicholas grabbed Lesley's hand and told her to pick him up. George translated, and Nicholas and Lesley kissed, and Nicholas perkily went outside. George now knew the boy liked women.

After settling in, Lesley and George went into the kitchen. Violetta had made coffee, and put out fig and plum preserves; Lesley's coffee was sweet. With George now having to translate, Lesley discussed her trip to Albania. She had been able to get a taxi to the domestic airport, and everything had gone smoothly. She loved the ride through the Greek villages and mountains, although the driver drove fast. The family listened intently as George translated.

Vassilis said laughingly, "There she appeared with a large package of toilet paper under her arms. George, did you tell her to bring some?"

"Yes."

"It's been awhile since we've had any. Thank you."

"You're welcome; we'll leave some in a few homes."

Young Nicholas came into the kitchen and stood next to Lesley. George said, "I think Lesley has a new friend. He hasn't been that friendly with me."

Violetta said, "Yes, my son likes the ladies."

Everyone laughed, and then laughed again when she translated it for Lesley. George had to catch up on things back home, so the two of them briefly discussed things in a quiet tone. George explained the situation, and the family understood.

Vassilis and George discussed their itinerary for tomorrow and for the rest of their days in Albania. George said he wanted to visit his mother's village, the three aunts, cousin Spiros and his brother and their mother, his father's home again, Vassilis' older brother's wife and children, and Vassilis' two sisters. He also wanted to tour Argirocastro and its ancient fort. There was much to do and many places to go. The time would be well-spent.

Vassilis said, "I'll make arrangements for a ride to your mother's village and to Argirocastro. Of course the visits here are no problem, and I'm sure Aleko will be very accommodating. What do you want to do tomorrow?"

Aleko spoke up, "I can take time off. We want you and Lesley to stay over."

George said happily, "Sounds good to me." After translation he asked, "What about you Lesley?"

"Whatever you decide is all right with me."

George, "Let's see if we can see someone here in Glifada tomorrow. It would give Lesley a chance to rest and adjust to the jet lag. Theodore wanted us to stay over. You said your sister Eleni wanted us to visit her home, and Spiros said to visit his mother and his brother. There is much to see here."

Vassilis, "I'll talk to my sister, and what is jet lag?"

"When you fly long distances and the hours of time between countries are many, it takes time for the body to adjust to the hour changes. It is six hours difference between our home and yours. They call it jet lag. Someday you will fly and you'll find out."

George asked Lesley, "Do you want to rest some?"

"No, I'm fine. I can't believe I'm here."

Rezarta said, "Aleko, it is getting late, we had better leave. We'll see you later at our home."

Aleko, "Yes, we left the car too long."

Good-byes were said and a lot of kissing was done. After they left George said, "Vassilis, I want to take Lesley outside to show her your courtyard and sit on the porch."

Vassilis, "Good, I'll get more chairs. We can have more coffee."

"I'm all right with what I have. Lesley, do you want more coffee?"

"No thank you, I feel okay."

George got up from the table, excusing himself and Lesley, and took Lesley outside to see the courtyard, the gardens, the fruit trees, and the beautiful view; young Nicholas followed. After viewing everything they went to the porch to sit; Nicholas quietly sat on Lesley's lap. Vassilis came out and joined them. After a while Nicholas got up and played in the yard, and Violetta brought out the young baby for them to see. He was wide-awake and smiled joyously. His skin was cream-white, and he made cooing noises. Amalia was in the kitchen preparing dinner.

Lesley and George enjoyed the view while relaxing on the porch. Vassilis excused himself and returned in twenty minutes, saying that they were to see his sister Eleni for lunch at her home tomorrow. Violetta served dinner at 7:00 p.m. and joined the family to eat. Amalia and Nicholas had eaten earlier. Violetta had made spanakopita (spinach pie with feta); from the last of the spinach growing in the yard; Vassilis served red wine. It was the first time Violetta sat to eat with George. Not too long after dinner Lesley, feeling tired, wanted to retire. Bedtime was 9:45 p.m.; early for George. They fell asleep after making love.

Chapter XIII

L esley and George woke up early to a bright morning sun and the usual village noises. Amalia was outside gathering vegetables, and Violetta was washing the baby. Nicholas was drinking milk until he spotted Lesley. Then he got up and stood by her side looking up at her. Violetta apologized and said she would be finished soon, and then she would make breakfast. There was water boiling on the electric coiled stove.

George said, "We'll go out and get some morning sun." Nicholas followed.

Before long breakfast, consisting of coffee, yogurt, and bread, was served. Violetta told George that Eleni would come for them for lunch and that Theodore invited them to dinner and to stay overnight. George said that Lesley would unpack and get settled. She wanted to rest some more from the long flight, but she wanted to spend time with Violetta and Amalia. Of course George would have to translate. Violetta told them that an older man from the village who spoke some English was coming to visit. He was a retired science teacher and he wanted to meet them both. Besides, he wanted to check on his English. Nicholas sat next to Lesley.

About an hour later the science teacher appeared. He was older than George but was in good shape and had a friendly smile and a firm handshake. He kissed Lesley on the cheeks and said hello in English. His name was Ziko Goritsas. Nicholas left to play.

Ziko, while having his coffee, inquired about America and about Lesley and George. Lesley talked about her job. Ziko liked that because of being a science teacher. It must have been a while since he had used English, as he struggled, but overall he got his message across. He told them about his family, the difficulties of Albania's past and its present situation, and briefly he talked about Albania's geological history. One of the subjects he taught was earth science. Lesley was receiving a good education about Albania as was George. It seemed that time passed quickly, and then Eleni appeared.

Ziko dismissed himself and said, "I will try to return to visit again, and I am very pleased to speak English to Americans and a Stamos family member. I taught all the Stamos children here. I will bring my dictionary the next time. Welcome to our village."

After meeting Eleni, George and Lesley walked with her to her home on the far side of the village. She had a large home with the most-decorated metal gate with metal filigrees of leaves, flowers, and vines George had seen in the village. It was beautiful, as was her home. The courtyard had many flowers, fruit trees, and of course, grapes.

Eleni was dressed in black except for her white headdress. Her husband, George died in 1988 when he was fifty-two. She had a daughter and two grandchildren. Eleni was very beautiful, with smooth olive skin, no facial wrinkles, and a nice figure. She was fifty-two, but looked to be in her thirties. Eleni lived alone in this large home.

"I live alone here and it is very lonely. I want to be with my daughter and grandchildren. They live in Tirana with her husband. It seems so far away."

After the translation, Lesley asked, "Do you get to see her often?"

"The bus ride is very long. I go when I can. I miss my husband, and I am very lonely. I am thinking of moving, but everything is so bad now. I don't know what to do. Let's go into the kitchen, I have prepared something to eat."

The kitchen was roomy, but to Lesley it seemed antiquated. George thought, wait until she sees the kitchens in Argirocastro. At least Eleni had cabinets.

Eleni served fig preserves, spanakopita, stuffed eggplant, yogurt and honey, bread, and coffee. She served the coffee the way George liked; Lesley's was sweetened. Lesley and Eleni shared stories about themselves. Of course, Eleni wanted to know all about America.

She asked, "Do Americans like Greek-Albanians?"

Lesley replied, "Most Americans know nothing about Albania or even where it is, and I'm sure they don't even know there are Greeks living in southern Albania."

When George translated, Eleni had a surprise look on her face. "We were told that America was going to invade and kill us. Why don't Americans know where we are?"

"It's because your country was isolated for many years from the rest of the world. There was little news about Albania, and people probably paid no attention if they saw it." George continued, "It will take some time before they do. Albania will have to do something to get in the news, and America never had intentions to invade you. That was Hoxha's propaganda. It was all a lie."

Eleni listened and made no reply. George recognized that Eleni was learning about the outside world. For her it was like being in school again.

The three of them spent a good part of the afternoon together. It was very interesting for all of them, and George felt sorry for this cousin's family situation. Eleni was bright but knew little of the outside world, only what the government or people told her, and what she learned from the Greek stations she was now able to pick up on her sixteen-inch black-and-white TV with rabbit-ear antennas. All outside stations were previously blocked by the Albanian government.

When it was time to leave, George told Eleni that they were going to Theodore's home and spending the night, and they had to make some preparations. They hoped to see her again soon and thanked her for sharing her home and food.

George said, "Eleni, you don't have to take us to Vassilis' home. We can find our way home."

They said their good-byes and left, leaving two rolls of toilet paper in a paper bag. They didn't tell her what was in the bag. Walking through the village, Lesley and George talked about Eleni and her situation and tried to figure out what they could do for her. They both decided that money would surely help. Also, they tried to imagine, someone in her fifties, living in Europe, knowing very little except only about Albania. They enjoyed walking and being alone together; especially George. He'd had no time by himself since he had arrived except when he was in bed.

When George and Lesley arrived home Amalia was sitting on the porch. She greeted them and told them that Vassilis was home. She asked about Eleni and if they were going to Theodore's. Before George could answer, Nicholas came running out and hung onto Lesley's legs.

George said, "Yes, we planned on it. Hello Nicholas."

He looked up and smiled and held on to Lesley's leg. They moved inside after Nicholas let go of her. They greeted Violetta and Vassilis.

George said, "We're going to get ready to go to Theodore's for the night."

Vassilis responded, "They are poor, and there are many living in the house. They will do the best they can, as you will see."

Lesley and George walked up the hill carrying a small paper bag and a night bag. On the way they met a few family members and some residents, but not like before. George introduced Lesley, and she was met enthusiastically.

As they approached the small stone house they were met by four youngsters and a toddler, two young attractive ladies, and Theodore and his mother, Aunt Ollga. One lady was Theodore's wife, Mariana and their toddler son, Panajotis (two years). The other lady was Theodore's youngest brother's wife, Anthi, and her two young children. Kostas was ten, and Elena was eight. Anthi's husband was in Greece working. The fourth child was the daughter of Theodore's oldest brother, who was also working in Greece. Her name was Irini. She was twelve.

It was a busy household and all the children were chattering while everyone was introduced. The children all smiled and stared. Lesley was the only blonde in the room. The children all talked to her even though they were told she did not speak Greek, but that didn't stop them. Lesley smiled, as they jabbered constantly, taking turns. They held her hands and got as close as possible whenever they said something to her. It was a delightful meeting. George translated whenever he could get a word in for Lesley.

Watermelon was served; the women, except Aunt Ollga drank coffee. George and Theodore drank ouzo. Aunt Ollga and Mariana served dinner and the children sat wherever they could, as the table was not large enough to accommodate everyone. Lesley and George sat down and then the others followed. George was placed at the head of the table.

The meal consisted of potatoes; bread, yogurt, and feta, and one piece of lamb for everyone, except for George and Lesley, who got two. George ate his meat reluctantly. He couldn't refuse and insult his aunt and cousin, but George knew they had sacrificed and had done the best they could. How could he ever pay them back? Lesley and George thanked them for the generous meal. With a glass of ouzo in his hand George made a toast to the family; "Ygeia Sou (Good health to you);" even the children joined in.

George told Lesley the story about Aunt Ollga making feta. He then had to translate what he said. Everyone laughed.

The evening went well, and the children asked Lesley and George many questions about America and about them. Finally all the children said goodnight and disappeared quietly even though no one had told them to go to bed. The night passed away, and it was time to retire. George and Lesley were led into a bedroom. They realized that someone had given them their room, but they didn't ask. Where everyone slept was a mystery, because the house had but a few rooms. It was an enjoyable evening, but it was sad, especially for George. He fell into a disturbed sleep thinking about their living conditions. No one in his family in America lived this poorly.

Ex Communist Party meeting building

First graders

Village scene

Village with tractor

Village woman and boy on donkey

Chapter XIV

The next morning they had coffee, bread, and yogurt. The coffee was made to George's liking. Aunt Ollga and Theodore told George that everything in Albania was bad. They apologized for the dinner and breakfast. George said he understood about the food situation, but he and his wife had enough food and were having a great time, and meeting the family was most important. George thanked them for doing the best they could. He was saddened that they had so many mouths to feed, and life in Albania was in dire straights. He could not say enough to thank them.

Lesley and George left, leaving the paper bag which contained toilet paper and fifty American dollars, knowing it would buy more food. They walked down the road, greeting those they passed and entered through Vassilis' gate. They were met by Nicholas, who was playing with a stick. George entered the house and heard someone in the kitchen. He saw Aunt Amalia and Violetta sitting at the table. Of course they got up to greet him. They asked if all went well.

George said, "We had a good time meeting all the children and everyone. I'm saddened by their lack of food. They fed us as best they could, but it wasn't much. I really didn't want to eat anything. You know that food I brought; do you think we could give them some of it? I'm sure they could use it today."

"Of course, I'll send all I have. I'm sure they could use it. This way I don't have to give some here and some there. Theodore and the family need it the most. How many were there?"

George responded, "Nine, five were children. They had little to share, but you know how Greek families are about guests. They gave Lesley and me two pieces of meat and everyone else got one. I wanted to refuse, but ---. I felt silly leaving toilet paper. Yes, giving them the food will be much better. Thanks." George never said he left money.

Aunt Amalia said, "The two husbands are in Greece working. They left recently, so who knows when they will come home with food and money. Meat and bread are rationed, so there isn't much to share. The villagers help each other as much as they can. This is the first time since the Italians and Germans were here that we have been in trouble-especially about the lack of food items and ways to earn money."

Violetta told George, "Aleko is taking you to Argirocastro tomorrow to Spiros' home for a few days. That way you can stay and visit other relatives and not have to return here. Is that alright with you?"

"Sounds good to me. Lesley will like that, but we'll miss being here. You have been very generous, and I love this village, and you."

Violetta smiled and George could see her modesty. "When will we leave?"

"Tomorrow. Aleko will pick you up about 10 a.m."

"I'll go and tell Lesley." She was outside with Nicholas.

George passed the day having a light lunch, talking to Aunt Amalia, Violetta, Vassilis, and occasionally to Nicholas. Violetta cooked a dinner similar to all the others. Of course, they apologized to their guests for the sameness.

George had a peaceful night, viewing distant lights, the nighttime stars, and going to sleep listening to distant village noises. He kept thinking of his family's plight here in Albania, and of what he could do besides give them money. It was a large family: three aunts and fifteen first cousins, all with spouses, children, and grandchildren. The other concern was the lack of items to buy even with money. But not having enough money to feed your family is a sad state of affairs. So many people in the world struggle with this matter every day. Seeing it first-hand among family members was not easy for George and Lesley. They discussed the idea of giving their money when they leave, leaving themselves some to pay for travel; they could get money when they returned to Greece.

Chapter XV

Lesley, George, Violetta and Nicholas walked down the hill to meet Aleko. Violetta walked down with them, because Vassilis was at work and he wanted to make sure that Aleko met them. George told her it wasn't necessary, but Vassilis also told Violetta not to leave them alone. The family was very concerned about their safety. Vassilis had told George that the villages weren't as safe as they used to be because of all the strangers on the road trying to go to Greece. George accepted his concern.

Aleko arrived on time. Lesley and George said their good-byes and got into the car. Aleko told them he had repaired the starter, and the car was now running well. George silently questioned that opinion. Aleko told them he had to go to work, but he would drop them off. Rezarta and his father would be home.

The ride was quick. Many people were walking or riding donkeys or horses along the road approaching the city. There were a few automobiles and trucks. A couple of Mercedes tractor trailers were heading south, one behind the other. Seeing their license plates Aleko said they were Greek. George made comments about the tractor trailers, and Lesley admired some of the large shade trees lining the edge of the road. She thought the mountains in the distance were majestic looking.

Arriving at the apartment complex Aleko walked up to his apartment with his guests, and Rezarta greeted them at the door; Aleko left, saying he would be home about five. Spiros was sitting at the kitchen table playing solitaire. He got up and received his guests with wet kisses.

Rezarta said in English, "He's been drinking tsipouro; I told him no more, you are arriving."

Artioli came running into the room with a big smile and yelling, "Kalimera (good morning)."

George sat at the kitchen table, and the ladies went to another room; Artioli stayed in the kitchen next to George. Spiros started talking, and George was distracted by some loud music outside, below the kitchen window. It was coming from a one-story home surrounded by a wooden fence on a large tract of land to the rear of the apartment building, but it was not part of the apartment complex; it abutted it.

George inquired, "Why the loud music?

Spiros said, "It is a wedding. They are Turks."

George said, "Interesting music."

"The wedding is tomorrow and they will be singing all day, tomorrow, and the day after."

"I would like to go down and see it. Would that be possible?"

"No, no, they are Turks."

Just then Rezarta walked in and asked George, "What are you talking about, the Turks?

"Yes, Spiros said it was a Turkish wedding. The music sounds very interesting, and I like Middle Eastern music. I was asking if maybe I could go down and visit. I have never seen a Turkish wedding. I wonder if I could get permission to take some pictures."

Rezarta said, "I'll go down and ask. I don't think they would mind. They are a very nice family. I have spoken to them so they know me. I'll go now."

George said, "No, don't go now."

Rezarta said, "Lesley, will you go down with me? They probably don't know any Americans. It will be very interesting."

Spiros and George looked out the window and saw Lesley and Rezarta enter the yard and disappear into the home. Spiros made some low guttural sounds. About ten minutes later they came out and returned with big smiles.

Rezarta said, "I told them there is a Greek-American, and this is his wife from America, visiting his mother's and father's villages. He wants to know if he could see your wedding and take some photographs with your permission. He has a professional camera."

The father of the bride said, "Please join them tomorrow at 2 p.m., or now if he wants. I have never met an American. It will be interesting for me and the family and for him too. And yes, he can take photographs. We have no one taking pictures. The father also asked if you spoke Albanian. Of course, I told him no."

George was pleased about the invitation. Rezarta had spoken in English, so she had to tell Spiros what had transpired; Spiros didn't say anything. The rest of the afternoon was spent having coffee, yogurt and bread, sharing personal stories about themselves, and listening to music drifting through the kitchen window.

George played with Artioli and was teaching him some English words, with Spiros also trying to repeat in English. Artioli was in a playful mood. He said many 'gezuars' (cheers in Albanian). He repeated everything George said: coca cola, baby baby bush baby, I love you, wow, and many more words. He commented that he loved Lesley; Artioli was two and a half.

The ladies spent time together, and Lesley watched as Rezarta prepared dinner in her small kitchen using the electric plate for cooking. Lesley was amazed at the lack of cabinets, space, countertops, and the slow-running water from the faucet. Rezarta loved speaking English, and she did most of the translations for Spiros and for Aleko after he returned from work.

After dinner of lamb, string beans, potatoes, yogurt, bread, and coffee, proceeded with watermelon, Rezarta told the family that the schools would not open until October 1st in Gjirokaster (Albanian spelling for Argirocastro) because of the lack of books and materials, and maybe not even then.

"I have to walk one hour up the hill to work. After my baby is born I will have six months off and receive eighty percent of my pay; my pay is $15.87 a month (the lek converted to the dollar). Maybe we can take you there to show you where I work."

Aleko said, "I have to be at work so I can't take her there. I work in the telephone office taking care of the batteries. I make seven hundred leks

($5.00) a week. Our rent, water, and electricity are $32.00-$35.00 (the lek converted into dollars) a month. We buy three liters of milk for twenty-two cents, and a loaf of bread costs twenty-five cents."

Spiros, "I receive a pension of fourteen hundred leks ($10.00) a month."

Rezarta said, "An Oxford dictionary cost twelve cents. I work with a girl called Eli. Her husband is a military officer and makes $40.00 (the lek converted into dollars) per month. They are related to the owner of a fancy castle-looking restaurant in, wait let me think. Oh! Leicester, Massachusetts. I saw her recently, and she wanted me to ask you if you know the place."

Lesley said, "We have gone by it but have never stopped there. How did you remember the name of the town?"

"She showed me a picture of the restaurant the other day."

Lesley said, "We'll have to stop there some day."

Aleko said, "I'll take you to visit the telephone office and show you the upstairs. I'm sure you will find it interesting."

George said, "I'm sure I will. I went there to call Lesley. I had to try a few times before I got through to America, but not to Lesley."

Aleko said, "Yes, the telephone service is old and very bad. We have lots of problems. I'll drive you up the mountain and show you a new system built by the French."

Lesley asked Rezarta if they have picked out a name for the baby. She replied, "Ana for a girl, but we haven't picked a name for a boy."

George said, "Vangeli."

Spiros said, "Too many Vangelis." Everyone laughed.

Rezarta asked, "George. Would you like the name to be George?"

George said, "Yes."

Aleko said, "I don't care."

It was left at that. The conversations were interesting alternating from Greek to English for Lesley and English to Greek for Spiros and Aleko; Rezarta and George translating. Everyone was having a good laugh at the language exchanges. Once or twice Rezarta would err, but she did very well. Finally it was time for bed.

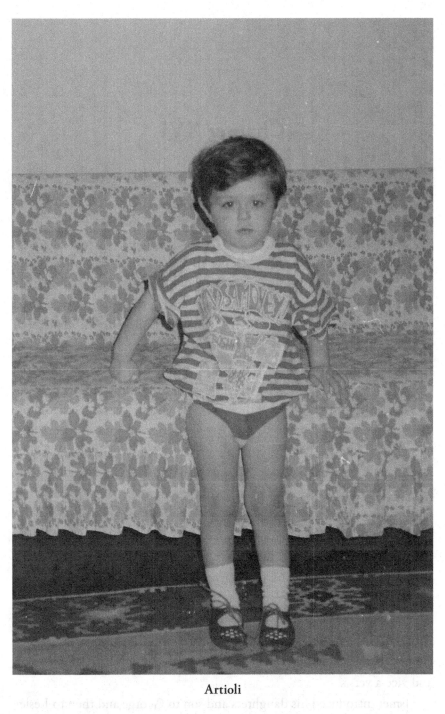

Artioli

Chapter XVI

The next morning after eggs, bread, and coffee, Lesley and George took separate water-hose showers. Not like at home sometimes; they liked showering together. George cleaned his camera lens in preparation of photographing. Lesley and Artioli played. Spiros drank coffee and watched. Rezarta cleaned the dishes and got ready to take her guests to the wedding and Aleko was at work. The music down below was going strong and loud.

Around 2 p.m. the three of them went downstairs and walked into the yard. Spiros stayed home to babysit Artioli. Someone noticed them enter, and a group of men sitting around a long table stopped singing. A middle aged man (father of the bride) approached, and Rezarta introduced her guests. The father's name was Ismet, and the mother's was Haxho. They had five daughters: Vasilika (bride), Vajsaria and Jatjana (bridesmaids), Lilyama, Kozata (the youngest) and one son, Lulzim. Lulzim looked to be in age between Jatjana and Lilyama.

There were younger and older people conversing in groups, standing or sitting at tables, and everyone was dressed in their finest. They stopped whatever they were doing and looked at the visitors. After kissing and hand-shaking, the father brought the three visitors into his home. The men continued their singing, and Rezarta translated English from Albanian and vice-a versa.

Ismet introduced his daughters and son to George and then to Lesley and Rezarta. The bride kissed George on the cheeks and thanked him for coming, and then she turned to Lesley and Rezarta. She was young and stunningly beautiful, with olive skin and long flowing wavy black hair and dark-brown almond eyes.

George was invited to sit on the couch; the bride sat next to him. Lesley sat on the other side. The bride's mother brought in tsipouro, plum preserves, loukoumi (candy coated with powdered sugar), and soft drinks for the ladies. After many gestures of 'gezuars' (a toast), and well-wishes for all, and a welcome to the wedding, George asked if he could take some pictures. He said he would mail copies to the family. The father said something to his daughter and four of her sisters; they all went to another room. Of course, when he took out his Nikon everyone stared.

Before long, the bride came out in her beautiful white gown. George took many photographs of her, with her family and with her friends. She went back inside and returned with her two sister bridesmaids, who were dressed in beautifully different colorful satin shiny long gowns. The two younger sisters returned wearing fancy colorful cotton dresses. George knew that they had spent the morning decorating their over-the-shoulder length hair-dos. George was quite busy with repeated photos, individual photos, and then the entire wedding party and the immediate family. Rezarta, Lesley, and George remarked about the beautiful women and handsome father and son.

There was an elderly slim lady sitting quietly by herself in one corner of the yard next to the house. She was dressed in black from head to toe; she was less than five feet tall. George thought she would be a good subject to photograph. She had an interesting facial structure.

George asked the father of the bride, "Can I photograph that elderly lady sitting over there?"

The father said, "She is my grandmother, and she is deaf. Because she can't hear, she isolates herself, and she does not want to have her picture taken."

The other guests were very cooperative about having their photos taken, and George was having fun. Lesley and Rezarta watched while they sat at a table. The men never stopped singing except when they had their photos taken; there were no musical instruments.

When George finished and everyone returned to what they were doing he was invited by one of the men singers to sit with them. The men greeted him while the ladies went to a women's table. George was told (finger pointed) to sit at the head of the table, a complimentary position.

There were appetizers and bottles of tsipouro for the men spread on the table. George took a clean glass, and a man filled it. One of the men said something to George. George looked for Rezarta; he waved and she came over to the table.

George extended his arm, "That gentleman said something to me."

The man repeated what he said. Rezarta translated (they were speaking the Albanian language); "He wants to know if you want to hear folkloric music?"

George, "That would be wonderful."

The men returned to singing a cap-pel-la. After a few more sips of tsipouro, and with George listening intently, he started to sing the notes (George had a classical music background, learning the violin when he was ten), not the words of course, just the notes; they were singing in Turkish. George followed the music closely and sung with them.

After a few songs one of the men spoke to him. George had to call Rezarta over and inquire what he said. "He asked, how do you know the songs if you don't know the words or the Turkish language?"

"Tell him I can closely follow the music from my past musical studies. Of course, I'm not perfect. I sound okay because of the tsipouro."

When she translated, the men all laughed. She left, and they resumed singing. Again they stopped, and another man said something to George. Rezarta was called over again; the man repeated what he said.

Rezarta said, "Tell him that we dedicated the last song to him."

When she walked away the singing men raised their glasses toward George with a loud, "Gezuar (cheers)!" George welled up inside and thanked them in Greek. The men acknowledged and smiled and raised their glasses again. George knew it had been a successful visit. Rezarta had also told the group of men that George would return tomorrow to take some more photographs.

Food was served-soft drinks, beer, wine, and tsipouro (the wine and tsipouro were locally made; probably in someone's courtyard). The food consisted of roasted lamb, shish kabobs, potatoes, eggplant, feta, yogurt, bread, and tomato, onion and green pepper salad. Rezarta went over to George and told him she was feeling tired, so they decided to leave. They said their good-byes, and Rezarta told the family that George would return tomorrow for the final day and do some more photography.

Rezarta climbed the four flights of stairs, saying she was not feeling good. She went into her bedroom to lie down. Lesley checked in on her and said she was all right, and just felt tired. Spiros did not ask any questions about the wedding other than whether George took pictures. Lesley said she'd had a good time and that it had been very interesting. Artioli went into the bedroom to join his mother, and George sat down to talk with Spiros.

About an hour later Aleko returned home. Rezarta had taken a short nap and was in the kitchen preparing dinner. She said she was feeling better. Aleko told them that his Aunt Rita from Tirana was coming today by bus; Rita was Spiros' younger sister, but only by two years. Spiros was looking forward to seeing his sister; he didn't get to see her often.

Lesley asked Rezarta, "Does she speak English?"

"No, but she is quite a lady. You'll enjoy her company. She always makes us laugh."

Aleko asked George, "Did you go to the Turkish wedding?

"Yes, it was wonderful. I took lots of photographs, and we ate and drank, and I sang."

Aleko asked, "What do you mean you sang? American songs?"

"I sang Turkish songs with a group of men sitting at a long table. Tell him, Rezarta."

Rezarta replied, "That's right; he even got up on the table and danced."

Aleko said, "No he didn't. You can't sing Turkish songs. So how come you sang?"

George answered, "Because they were singing. Well, I only sang the notes. I had taken many photos, and one of the singers invited me to sit with them, plus I wanted to be close to the singing as it was. I was really enjoying the music. Before I knew it I started to sing, and I was having a good time. Maybe it was because of the tsipouro."

Aleko laughing said, "Oh, you were drinking tsipouro, well that will make anyone want to sing. What did the men do?"

George said, "They liked it, and they sang a song dedicated to me."

Aleko with a smirk said, "Good, now you're not only Greek and American, but now a Turk."

Spiros proclaimed loudly, "Not a Turk!"

Briefly George translated the conversation to Lesley. Quietly Lesley asked George, "Why is Spiros so blunt about the Turks?"

George told her, "I'll tell you later."

Rezarta thought she would change the subject. "Aleko, what time do you think that Rita will arrive?"

"I think she'll be here by six or no later than seven."

Rezarta said, "Good, she'll eat with us. I'll peel enough potatoes. Let me see if we have enough bread and lamb. If not you can go and try to buy some."

Lesley went to the kitchen and said she would peel potatoes. Rezarta said she needed more meat and bread. Aleko was out the door saying he'd be back soon. Spiros lit a hand-rolled cigarette and played solitaire, and George talked to Artioli, teaching him more English words. It was warm outside, and the windows were open, and the music drifted loudly up from below.

George thought about Spiros' attitude towards the Turks. Spiros' parents and grandparents had lived under the Ottoman (Turk) Empire, as had many generations before. The Ottoman Empire throughout Greece lasted from 1453 to 1829, but not in Northern Epirus (Albania). The last Turkish rule ended in northern Epirus in 1912. This area was considered part of Greece until then, but it was not under Greece's control. Being under a foreign country's authority is not acceptable especially for the Greeks. Spiros had probably listened to stories about conditions from his parents and grandparents.

Rita arrived about 6:30 p.m. and was warmly greeted by everyone. She was tall and slightly overweight, and she resembled her brother in facial features, except she had a full head of hair. She had a great laugh and displayed a full set of white teeth. Rezarta brought out the tsipouro and Rita joined the men. Spiros rolled two cigarettes; one for himself and for Rita. It was the first time that George had seen an Albanian woman smoke.

Rita told about her ride from Tirana (it is 88 miles and it took five hours), telling funny stories about the passengers and the scenes on the way. She had everyone laughing. George thought that here is an aunt who is a marvelous raconteur. Rita had a refreshing and wonderful personality.

Rita went into the bathroom and came out asking Rezarta," Where did you buy the toilet paper?"

Rezarta told her, and Rita replied, "Who travels from one country to another with a large package of toilet paper? Only in Albania!"

She then went into stories about the book pages she was using for replacements. She said, "I read a page (quoting a communist passage) and then use it."

She even quoted a few more passages. She had everyone laughing. Later in the night, another glass of tsipouro, and another cigarette for Rita. Aleko finally told everyone that tomorrow would be a busy day; more of the wedding at midday and then a visit into the city.

There is always time to laugh even when times are tough. Sometimes you hear laughter at a funeral. It keeps the spiritual atmosphere alive.

Turkish bride and groom

Turkish wedding family

Chapter XVII

Aleko had gone to work the next morning, and Rita stayed with her brother as the others went to the wedding two hours after breakfast. They walked into the yard and were received warmly again, and the men were sitting at the table singing. The bride and bridesmaids were in their formal gowns talking, hugging and kissing their immediate family and all the other attendees.

As George was doing some photographing, the groom arrived, walking into the courtyard dressed in a dark blue suit, white shirt and tie. He was handsome, sporting a thick black moustache and groomed straight black hair and was tall and slim. He slowly approached the mother and father, kissed, and shook hands, and words were exchanged, and when they finished their obligations George photographed the wedding couple and more of the family, and then the groom went out of the yard beyond the fence and stood by his car.

The young bride started to cry and hug her parents, and many others were crying. Lulzim, the mid-teenage brother, was dressed in a white shirt and black pants. With a bottle of wine in his hands he started to walk towards the groom's auto. Everyone stood and watched the boy sprinkling wine in front of the bride's path. She followed slowly, emotionally sobbing, as were most of the invitees. The parents wanted to follow, but they reluctantly remained close to where she had started her departure. This was the final act of leaving her family's home. George photographed the ceremonious exit.

When the bride entered the car and drove away the gate was closed and the singing and partying continued. George thought how beautiful-all this formality mixed with joyousness and sadness. It made an unforgettable impression, and he had the photographs for posterity.

George learned that another celebration was to take place that day at the home of the groom's family. The wedding was to be that morning. They would sleep together in the afternoon, and then they would celebrate again at night. George thought about all the partying before and after the wedding.

Once again, George was invited with a wave to sit with the singers and join in; he was given the same seat he had sat in the previous day. The same group was there as were a young man, maybe thirty, and an older man, both of whom had beautiful singing voices. George thought the music was mesmerizing.

Rezarta and Lesley mixed with the family relatives and friends. During the singing and drinking, the men stopped, and one of the older singers said something to George. George called for Rezarta to translate. At the same time, the thirty year old man wanted to know why George didn't know the words, but he knew the music.

Rezarta addressed the older man's translation, "The men want to tell you that the last song was dedicated to you. They sang that you are now part of their family and history." To the young man Rezarta said, "He forgot all the words." All the men laughed except the young man. He had a stunned look!

George raised his glass with a joyous, "Gezuar (good health), tell them thank you, I feel honored."

Not long after, Rezarta said to George, "It is time to leave, but if you two want to stay you can."

Lesley and George knew it had been arranged to do something else in the day with the family, and there were enough daylight hours left in the day. George got up, and the men stopped singing. There were many good-byes, kisses and many thanks.

When they got upstairs they saw that Aleko had returned home. He said he wanted to show them something up the mountain and his workplace. Tomorrow they were going to visit Olympia and the ancient citadel.

Spiros was going to stay home to take care of Artioli; everyone else piled into the car and Aleko told them he was going to the telephone office. George related the story of trying to call Lesley and the man in Australia they woke up twice, and the call to Germany, and of course, how long it took to be able to phone America.

George and Lesley followed Aleko into the building. Rita and Rezarta remained with the car. George showed Lesley the booths he had to go into and the procedure of getting a phone call. She shook her head amazed. There were a dozen individuals standing about the room waiting to be called; because of Lesley's American clothes the women checked her attire and some smiled.

Aleko took them up a flight of stairs to a long room directly above the entrance and telephone booths. There were some small offices to the side, but what took George and Lesley by surprise were four long tables with many telephones sitting there in front of as many wooden chairs. Aleko said these are the monitoring telephones. Every telephone conversation was listened in on during the communist regime, even if you were an official in the communist party; they trusted no one.

There was a telephone book lying on one of the tables. George picked it up; it was thin without many pages. The book had been printed in 1991, and it was the only book for the city of Gjirokaster (Argirocastro). The city's population was about twenty-five to thirty thousand. George quickly counted the names, there were 388 names listed; it was hard to believe.

They left the building, and Aleko drove up the main thoroughfare and finally onto graveled twisting roads to an area high up the mountainside. There was a new metal tower and a small building where he stopped. He explained that it was the new telephone system built by the French government, and more telephones were to be added to the system, but he didn't know when.

From this vantage point the view was spectacular. The entire city sat below, and the ancient stone fort was to the right and below, sitting on a level area to the south. Aleko pointed out all the government buildings, schools, and a soccer field, and Rezarta showed them her school building. You could see all the way down the city's long straight main thoroughfare to its ending at the north and south highway. It was a crystal clear day for photographing; many pictures were taken of the city and the family. They returned home to spend another day in this ancient tiled city.

Lesley and George had received many invitations from relatives in Argirocastro. These included an invitation to Aunt Evanthia's for a lunch, to Aunt Penelope's home for dinner and to sleep over, to Vassilis' sister Olympia's for a dinner and a night's stay, to his older brother's wife's apartment for a dinner or a lunch, and they had to have a major tour of the city and its famous citadel. Then back to the villages, Aunt Stavroula's home, George's mother's village for a sleep-over, village home visits, and who knows what else. Their flight to America was scheduled for September 29th. They would have seventeen full days in Europe, of which they had to include time to tour parts of Greece. They had to leave Albania Wednesday, September 23rd, leaving eleven and a half days with the family.

Lesley and George were invited to spend midday at Aunt Evanthia's home the next day to meet her husband and their son and his family. For the evening they were invited along with Spiros and his family to Aunt Penelope's home. It was going to be a busy day. Aleko would drive George and Lesley to visit Aunt Evanthia and return to drive them to Aunt Penelope's, where the others would meet.

After another dinner with Rezarta and company Aleko drove George and Lesley back to Vassilis' home before dark and quickly walked them up the mountain. They had not prepared to stay another night in Argirocastro; Aleko would be back the next morning for a return trip to Argirocastro. Besides, for George and Lesley Glifada would contribute a quieter night than the city, even if a donkey brayed.

Argirocastro and road to the fort

Argirocastro scene from mountain

Argirocastro showing brick work

The main avenue in Argirocastro

Chapter XVIII

Lesley packed a few items for a return stay in Argirocastro. Lesley and George said good-bye to Nicholas and Aunt Amalia after breakfast, and with Violetta as their companion, they trudged down the mountain. Aleko met them on the main highway to Argirocastro and dropped them off at the unimproved road to Aunt Evanthia's. The thoroughfare was somewhat busy with people strolling. George noticed the money exchangers and a few cars and trucks. It was a Saturday, but not like a busy Saturday back home.

They arrived at Aunt Evanthia's home, which was on a level area a few feet above the road just out of view. There was a large metal fence and gate in front. They were met by the aunt and her husband, Sotir. He was very tall and thin with a pleasant narrow face, thinning hair, and intelligent cunning eyes. You could see that he was once a handsome young man. Their home had an upstairs apartment where their son and wife lived with two children. George and Lesley were shown the front room for sitting; Aunt Evanthia left the room to get coffee and preserves. While George talked about America Sotir listened intently.

Then George asked Sotir what it was like with the Italians and the Germans invading and occupying their country. Just about then Sophia came into the room. She had been helping her grandmother in the kitchen.

Sophia said, in Greek, "My grandfather was in the mountains fighting. He was a Partisan. This is what we called our citizens that had fought against the Italians and Germans. They didn't come home for days or weeks at a time. He is a hero, and very respected." She ended by kissing her grandfather on the cheeks; he smiled. George translated for Lesley.

Sotir remained quiet; he only nodded to accept the compliment. He had a quiet and gentle manner about him, and he was a soft spoken man. No one, when seeing him, would suspect that Sotir was a war hero.

While Aunt Evanthia was still in the kitchen there was a knock on the front door. Sophia opened the door and an older couple, Turkish neighbors walked in. They were invited to meet George and Lesley. After introductions and coffee, George found out that the woman worked in construction and that the man was a carpenter. They worked at whatever jobs the socialist government gave them. They had no choice in their vocation, and they now lived on 3500 leks a month ($25.00) (two pensions combined).

Soon after the couple's arrival, Aunt Evanthia walked in and said that lunch was ready. She led them to the rear of the house, to the kitchen. George asked about their son.

Evanthia said with displeasure, "He is drunk upstairs, and he and his wife are not coming."

It was soon apparent from the noise emanating from above that something was going on. Music started blaring and someone stomped on the floor. The noise would stop and then start up again. Luckily the kitchen, where they sat, was in the back, and the noises were emanating from the front of the building. Sophia left and went upstairs; she returned crying.

George asked her what happened. She only shook her head. Lunch was served. It consisted of small portions of meat, string beans, yogurt, feta, salad, and bread. George and Sotir drank tsipouro, and the ladies had milk.

After dining, Evanthia invited everyone to sit outside. Not long after they settled the son threw a bucket of water out of a window where everyone was sitting and yelled out the window. "I don't want that man visiting! I don't want to meet him! Send him back to America!"

Luckily for everyone no water struck anyone. George wanted to go upstairs to ask the son what was his problem. Lesley told him, "Forget it, he's drunk."

George was angry about Sophia's crying and the disrupting behavior, and the way the son was insulting his parents in front of guests, but Lesley was right; he was drunk. Then the son, from an open window, yelled incoherent sentences at his mother. Aunt Evanthia argued with her son to close the window and go to bed, and after all the man's yelling he shut the window and stopped the harassment. With the peace and quiet, George took photographs, and the group sat outside in the warm sun, enjoying the camaraderie and the distant noises of barking dogs and sometimes passing conversations. They were glad there were no vehicles noises to distract them.

Aleko arrived later in the afternoon to drive George and Lesley to Aunt Penelope's home. George and Lesley said their thanks and good-byes to Sotir, the Turkish couple, Aunt Evanthia and Sophia, and gave Aunt Evanthia her gift-bag (toilet paper) from Greece. Entering the car, George inquired about the rest of his family.

Aleko said, "I had dropped them off earlier. The family is waiting for you two," Aleko left them at Penelope's home and drove off saying good-bye.

When George and Lesley arrived Aunt Penelope and Uncle Taki's home was full of family members. George introduced Lesley to Penelope's daughter, Margarita, who in turn introduced her husband, Emir, and their two children, Suela (15 years) and Emir (12 years). The other guests were Spiros, his sister Rita, and Rezarta. Artioli was home with a babysitter. After introductions Margarita, Suela, and Sophia went to the kitchen.

The two young girls returned with tsipouro, beer, Fanta, watermelon, and preserves. The conversation turned to Lesley's stay in Albania, and about her meeting George's family. Speaking in English, Lesley was complimentary and was happy to meet everyone. Of course, this took time with translations and others asking questions. Sophia joined in translating and George let her do most of the translating. It was a joyous time.

Two tables were set, and dinner was served: meatballs, lamb, potatoes, eggplant, half an egg, string beans, tomato and green pepper salad, feta, olives, yogurt, bread, mineral water, beer, and wine-the same as was served in most homes George visited, except there was more meat here. George had been told that meat was rationed. Lamb was more obtainable in the Greek villages because of having their own sheep. He was surprised at the amount of food served tonight. During the meal there were many thanks given and good measures made to the guests, especially to Lesley and George. More coffee, tsipouro, soft drinks, and brandy were served after the meal.

George inquired as to what Margarita and Emir do for work. Margarita and Emir are economists. She was the president of a factory where artisans made hand-weaved rugs, tapestries, ceramics, and rosettes (ceiling carvings). The factory was trying to initiate trade with European countries and if the company didn't make money the government would close the factory or sell it. She said it would sell for 8,400,000 leks ($60,000), but the factory needed another 8,400,000 leks to upgrade it. She showed pictures of some rugs, ceramics, and ceiling rosettes they had manufactured.

George said, "You should sell to America. People would pay good money for hand-made items, and Albanian goods would be new items on the shelves."

Emir explained, "We don't have the infrastructure to ship it there. I'm trying now to transport it to Italy and there are many problems trying to do that. I just sent some ceramics to Yugoslavia using their own trucks, and about America, we don't speak English."

Emir's job was to develop distribution and transportation. Margarita spoke Greek, Albanian and Italian, Emir spoke Albanian, Italian, and some Greek; the son spoke Albanian and was learning Italian. Suela spoke Albanian, Greek, and some Italian

George said, "If you ever upgrade your transportation system, maybe I could help you from America. It would be helpful if you learned English."

Suela interjected, "I'm going to take English classes soon." Her parents were obviously training her early.

Time had passed, and guests had to leave. Aunt Evanthia and Sophia were going to walk home; Aleko was coming to take Rezarta, Rita, and

Spiros home. Sophia said she would come and get Lesley and George tomorrow. They were going to an Orthodox Church with Aunt Evanthia. They could walk to the church or hire a taxi. George and Lesley said they didn't want a taxi; they wanted to walk and see more of the city. It wasn't far and it would be a nice walk downhill. Aleko had to work.

When everyone had left, George and Lesley were shown to a large bedroom and shown the bathroom; it had a regular shower, but no flush toilet (there were imprints for your feet) or toilet paper. George and Lesley would leave their paper bag of toilet paper.

Uncle Sotir the Partisan

Chapter XIX

T he next morning, the household was quiet, with only Aunt Penelope and Uncle Taki there. The rest of the family had gone to Emir's brother's home. George was pleased that he could spend more time with his oldest aunt and uncle. Sophia arrived about an hour later, and after thanks and kisses the three departed from Aunt Penelope's home on foot to walk and get Aunt Evanthia. They were going to attend Sunday Liturgy at the Orthodox Cathedral. George didn't inquire whether it was a Greek or Albanian Orthodox Church. Aunt Evanthia showed her spryness by walking fast and leading the way.

Sophia said to George and Lesley, "The church is in poor condition. Enver Hoxha closed all the churches in 1967. They reopened in 1991. Albania was declared officially as an atheist state in 1961, and no private or public expression of religion was allowed. Hundreds of priests and imams were killed or imprisoned. Only twenty-two were alive at the end of communism. The churches were used as storage rooms, animal housing, or they were completely destroyed. I believe more than two hundred and fifty churches have been restored or built."

George and Lesley listened intently but made no comments. What could they say? It was all unbelievable. Neither China, Russia, nor Cuba declared themselves officially as atheist states.

As they approached the church they noticed that some of the stones and cement had been damaged. It was an old Byzantine style church, but without a large cupola in the center. The roof had overlaying stones-the same as many buildings in the villages had. There was a large bell tower on one side that had four separate openings for bells, one atop the other, and a roof covering the tower. The workmanship by the masons using grey bricks was extraordinary but it had many damaged areas. The main entrance had a stone arch with a door made of large wide pieces of wood, with large blackened iron hinges; the door opened in the middle; you could have ridden a horse through it. Even though some outside stones were damaged the structure was beautiful. The family entered under the large arched entrance.

One of George's interests was churches, especially Orthodox churches. He had visited many churches throughout the western hemisphere; he liked the architecture and their ornateness. George was shocked after entering the cathedral. The narthex was vacant of any fixtures, and the nave looked like a vacant warehouse. What struck George were the walls. Instead of beautiful hand-painted icons on the walls, which are typical, there were only three or four small patches of faded remnants. The walls had been stripped almost completely of major wall and ceiling decorations common to Greek churches. To reestablish the building once again as a church the members had hung a few small framed painted icons on the walls. As for the altar, there were no signs of the original one or of the altar wall either. In its place were two bright brass posts, waist high, spaced apart from each other where the altar opening should be, and hanging curtains duplicating the altar wall, with small icons hanging on the curtain on either side of the opening. Cloth curtains separated the altar from the chancel and nave. The apse was indistinguishable. The same size brass posts, connected by rope, made a passage way up to the altar. The bema, with its altar looked naked of any Christian decorations or relics. The church did have a sand container of which to place lit prayer candles. The candles were thin eight-inch bees-wax colored. There was no pulpit or usual place for a bishop or other church official to sit.

The attending congregation stood in small groups waiting for the priest to appear (there are no pews in Europe's Orthodox churches). In fact, there were not many people attending; maybe thirty.

The priest appeared from behind the curtain and performed a brief liturgy; the entire service lasted only fifteen minutes. Having attended services all his life George was amazed. During the service the attendees seemed confused as to what to do; it was sad. George thought about all the years without any religion. Aunt Evanthia told George that the priest was twenty-seven years old and he had become a priest in ninety days.

Surprised at the brief service, and the attendees leaving, George was about to leave also when Aunt Evanthia told George that she wanted him to meet the priest. As she was saying this to George the priest recognized his aunt, Sophia, and saw the two new faces. The priest came forward. Evanthia introduced Lesley and George to Father Dimitri; they spoke in Greek.

"You come from America, welcome to our church."

George said, "Thank you. I see there is a lot of restoration necessary."

"Yes, it will take much money and time. There is a problem between the Greek and Albanian Diocese. The Albanian government does not want the Greeks to be in control of the churches. The members, mostly Greeks want the Greek Diocese to be in control. It is a major problem, and until that is solved I'm afraid little will be done for restoration. The Greek Diocese has money, and our Diocese and government are struggling right now. I'm hoping they can settle this matter soon. How long are you visiting?"

George answered, "Not too long, another week or so. We have many places to visit in Albania."

Father Dimitri said, "Too bad, I would like to see you again. Can I have your address?"

"Sure. Lesley do you have a pen and a piece of paper? My wife always carries a pen and piece of paper." Everyone laughed and George wrote his address and gave it to the priest.

The priest reverently said, "Thank you, I hope you have a safe trip and that you come back and visit. God be with you."

With Lesley holding George's hand and George translating, they all went out into the warm sun. George thought out loud, "Well that was very interesting."

Aunt Evanthia hurriedly said good-bye and left to go home to be with her husband, Sotir. Sophia stayed with George and Lesley.

Walking the main avenue, they saw a few street vendors selling clothes, many young and older men lingering and smoking on sidewalks, a few families strolling or sitting on benches, and many closed and shuttered stores. The joblessness and depressed business situation were very apparent. George thought, "No wonder the men want to go to Greece for work." The men watched them walk by. Some nodded, some said hello, and some smiled at Lesley. Lesley felt at ease even though so many people were staring at her. Lesley made a remark to George about the staring.

George told her, "Remember, you don't look Albanian, and you're beautiful."

When they arrived at Spiro's apartment building there were a lot of women gathering at a single water faucet next to the front cement stairs collecting water into buckets and jars. Lesley saw that Rezarta and Rita had their own buckets and jars near the faucet.

George, working his way through the women, approached Rezarta and in English asked, "What's going on?"

The ladies waiting to collect water were chattering amongst themselves until they heard George speaking English in his baritone voice; they stopped talking with surprised looks.

She replied, "There's no water upstairs. I'm getting water, and no one knows when the water will be turned back on. It happens a lot."

The women surprisingly moved aside and allowed Rezarta to get her water. Rezarta, George, Lesley, and Sophia continued talking in English as Rezarta filled her containers. Sophia, Lesley, and George carried the water upstairs. George wondered how Rezarta and Rita were going to get two buckets and four glass gallon-size jars up the stairs. Water service was restored the next morning.

Aleko arrived home soon after and greeted them, telling them that they were all going to a restaurant bordering a beautiful reservoir. Many in the family are going also. Aleko said, "It is a surprise gathering for George and Lesley. Aunt Evanthia did not want to tell George at the church. That is why she left in a hurry to get Sotir. I will have to make more than one trip to get the family there."

After some coffee and refreshing themselves, Aleko told them it was time to go. During coffee, Aunt Evanthia and Uncle Sotir arrived. Lesley, George, Evanthia, and Sotir, were the first to go; Aleko headed north. It was about a fifteen-minute ride going north on the main highway to the restaurant. Of course, there were no red lights, little traffic, and the car was crowded and the ride bumpy.

When they arrived at the restaurant Evanthia led them to a large outside deck that was furnished with tables and chairs and faced a large blue reservoir. The reservoir was situated between forested mountains on three sides; the peaks were bare rocks. It made for a natural setting to collect water; the water supplied Argirocastro.

They were met by Olympia and Kristos, Violetta and Vassilis, Vassilis' brother's family; Margarita, Anthoula and Dimitri, and Spiros' brother Thomas and his wife Bereta. Lesley and George were quite surprised. They had no idea that the family had arranged this get-together, and there would be six more people attending including little Artioli, Sophia, Spiros, Rita, Rezarta, and Aleko; what a nice surprise; Aunt Penelope and her household had other engagements.

During Aleko's return trip everyone ordered drinks and sat in the warm sun to talk and enjoy the spectacular view of a large lake and the mountains. Lesley, and especially George, was the center of attention. George was getting to like this but, whispering, Lesley reminded him that they were going home and he still would have to take out the garbage. He smiled and laughed silently.

Almost an hour later Spiros and the others arrived. They joined the family outside while Vassilis went inside to finalize the dinner arrangements for the group of nineteen. The restaurant staff set a long table to accommodate everyone, and with drinks in every ones hands they sat with George and Lesley in the middle facing one another, and the married couples sitting opposite one another; Artioli sat on a high chair at the end next to Rezarta and Aleko; Sophia sat opposite her cousin Dimitri, Spiros opposite his sister Rita, and Anthoula opposite her mother, Margarita. The table setting was beautiful, with white linen, Albanian-motif-designed dishes, and fancy Albanian utensils; maybe made by Olympia.

The waiter came over and announced the menu; they had lamb, two choices of vegetables, eggplant or string beans, fried potatoes, salad, feta, olives, and bread, also beer and wine. George assumed that maybe the restaurant would have more choices and a larger menu. He realized that with the food shortages why would there be any difference in the food offered? After choices of vegetables were settled more drinks were served, many toasts and well-wishes for all, and especially for the main guests; Lesley and George.

They drank and shared stories about Albania and its new beginnings, and about George and Lesley's arrival and now their up-and-coming departure. Laughs exploded, when Vassilis told the story of Lesley arriving with her large cache of toilet paper, and tears flowed when Rezarta expressed her sorrow that George and Lesley were leaving. The meal was served. The food was tasty, and many drinks were consumed. For dessert they had watermelon and yogurt with honey.

George said to the diners, "We're all aware of the rationing of meat, the few varieties of vegetables, but what would we do if watermelon wasn't in season?" This brought cheers and thanks for the Albanian watermelon growers.

When time approached to leave, the tone saddened, but Lesley told them what a beautiful family they were, and that she was happy and excited to be a part of it. When translated this brought tears, cheers, and a welcome to the family.

Aleko finally said, "I don't like to interrupt this beautiful gathering, but I have to arrange trips to get everyone home. Who wants to ride first?"

Vassilis said, "I have two taxis waiting for us, so you have to make only three trips, unless there is another taxi available; I'll go out and see."

George thought, "Leave the taxis to Vassilis." Vassilis returned and said to Aleko, "There are four taxis outside. Two are mine and I just hired one more. That leaves you with making two trips."

Aleko asked George, "Do you and Lesley want to go to Argirocastro first?"

They replied, "We'll wait."

With that overheard, everyone else said they would stay. More drinks were ordered while Aleko left with his entire household.

By the time Aleko returned for George and Lesley the sun was getting low in the sky and sunset was forming various red, orange, and purple hues. The drive home on the lonely road seemed unreal after a special day for all. With the beautiful sunset on their right it made for a perfect ending for a perfect day. The other three family taxis followed all the way to Argirocastro's main thoroughfare. Then the family members all went their separate ways home. Spiros' family and guests set in for a quiet and restful evening.

George considered the family gathering. Whoever would have thought the day would come, visiting a country once closed off to the world, and freedom of speech censured, that George would ever see himself sitting four thousand miles from his home and attending a family gathering for dinner, and everyone feeling at ease to express what they wanted. Thanks for freedom and democracy.

Family dinner guests at restaurant

Varosh Eastern Orthodox Church in Argirocastro

Chapter XX

After Lesley and George had their cup of coffee and said good morning, Aleko arrived with Sophia to take everybody except Rita and Spiros to the ancient fort. Artioli could sit on someone's lap in the car. Driving to the fort Aleko had to manage through narrow and curvy roads. Aleko parked the car next to an extremely long stone wall that bordered the steep road near a cave-like entrance beneath a natural cliff wall. Aleko paid for the entrance tickets. George wanted to pay, but Aleko refused. George wanted to carry Artioli, so he hiked him onto his shoulders. Aleko and Rezarta were worried that George would get tired, but George assured them he would be fine.

The fort's inside corridors and walls were of solid stone and were poorly lit with bare clear incandescent bulbs. There were rooms with armament: ancient swords and guns, World War I & II rifles, cannons, machine guns, hand grenades, and airplane sections. Much of the equipment was German and Italian; George never found out if they had been captured or abandoned.

All the fort's inside doors were thick iron with key-hole locks. There was a room displaying old costumes of men and women from the 1800s and early 1900s and the period right after World War II. George recognized some clothing styles from pictures that his grand and great grandparents wore.

In one large room on display was a hangman's rope noose, and next to it a portion of a woman Partisan's dress. She had been hanged along side another Partisan man. George thought about Sotir and other Partisans, and how they risked their lives to protect their country as best they could.

There was also a prison deep inside that had been used by the Germans. Some rooms had barred doors and some were completely enclosed that were used for isolation. The inside of the fort had very wide circular stone stairs and wide hallways for the movement of many soldiers, if necessary, and openings to the outside for guns and cannon placements throughout inside the walls. Outside there was a large open area surrounded by walls, benches, and pole lights (some had been destroyed). Trash was scattered about. The tour was very impressive. George took many photographs including some of Artioli sitting on a cannon overlooking a steep long drop-off bordering an exterior wall.

Deep in the interior, in one of the large subterranean rooms, there was a snack bar to sit at and have refreshments. The air was cool and no outside noises reached the snack bar. They sat and had cold drinks. Rezarta told a story about the area where Artioli sat on the cannon to have his picture taken.

"Long ago there was a Turkish Sultan who wanted to seduce the wife of a Turkish commandant who had been killed in battle. She was young and very beautiful, and she had a baby boy. One day she went to the same area that George took the picture of Artioli on the cannon. Holding her child, she put a fig in the baby's mouth to satisfy his urge to suckle, and then she leaped out of a tower window. The city is named after her; Argiro.

Lesley said, "That's a beautiful sad story."

Sophia added, "It is believed that the citadel stems from the fourth century. I was also told around the year 568 A.D. It has been used in every war, especially since the thirteenth century. That was when what you see was mostly built. It has a lot of history. Looking towards the south from the fort you can see all the way down the Drinos River valley to the Greek border. We hope that some day the fort will be updated somewhat. They used to have parades, music, and various performances in the open yard, even in the night; it had lights. There hasn't been anything like that for a long time, but as you saw, some things have been destroyed or removed.

Only those items under lock and key inside have been spared. It's a shame, but even so, everyone is proud of the fort. Do you have anything like that back home?"

George said, "Well, we do have old places and forts, but our history is much younger, except for Native American culture. The Spanish didn't arrive until the 1500s, and the English until the 1600s. Thank you for showing us, and sharing its history. It sure is impressive, and it gives me something to think about, and about my family coming from this part of Albania."

Walking back to the automobile Rezarta was having trouble. The thought of seeing some of the city tiled streets was cancelled. Aleko decided to drive home; he went to a neighbor's apartment upstairs to call a doctor. The neighbor had a phone; he had once held a high position in the local police department.

Rezarta went to the bedroom to lie down, and Lesley went in to check on her. Artioli accompanied them but briefly returned to play. When Lesley returned she told everyone Rezarta seemed to be okay.

"I don't have a stethoscope, but I checked what I could."

The household was nervous and sat waiting for the doctor to make a house call. Surprisingly it wasn't too long before there was a knock on the door. Aleko, who had been sitting, jumped up and answered. In walked a fairly young doctor carrying his black medical bag. This was the way it used to be in America.

The doctor, asking for Rezarta, noticed Lesley and George. He inquired in Albanian, "Who are you?"

Aleko replied, "They are visiting from America, they are my cousins."

Sophia interrupted to translate for George and Lesley. Instead of seeing Rezarta he went immediately to George and said in English, "I am a gynecologist, I work alone, but I assist on surgical operations but we have no equipment. Do you think you could help me out? I need many surgical supplies and pharmaceuticals."

George was taken by surprise and answered, "I am a retired science teacher and my wife is a dental hygienist. I don't know what we can do for you, but when we get home we'll try. That is all I can say or do, but you had better see about Rezarta, she's in the bedroom."

The doctor thanked George and Lesley and went into the bedroom. He came out and told Aleko that she was all right, she just needed to rest. The doctor went out, thanking George and Lesley again, and assuring the family that she and the baby were okay.

George and Lesley thought that was a surprising visit-a house call and the fact that one of the doctor's prime concerns was asking for help. It substantiated their opinion regarding the poor condition of Albania. They both made mental notes as to what they could do when they returned home: send food, clothing, and some medical instruments and medicine. Lesley knew she could get some of those items for the doctor, and everyone was glad to know that Rezarta was all right.

After all the excitement the day was passing. Rita made coffee for everyone. The coffee grinder was the only noise, as everyone pondered about Rezarta's condition. While they were drinking their coffee and quietly discussing the day, Rezarta came out of the bedroom and said she felt all right. The women kissed her on the cheeks; Aleko kissed her also. Sophia said she had to go home. Aleko told Sophia he would take her. Rita told Rezarta she would make a light dinner, and Artioli went to play with George. Rita cooked with some help from Lesley. The evening went well, and everyone decided to retire early. Next day they would tour more of the city and maybe see relatives in the city.

George and Lesley retired to their bedroom and discussed their remaining itinerary. The next day was settled, and Wednesday they would return to Glifada, and replenish their supply of clothes, visit with Spiros' mother, and Thursday they would visit Aunt Stavroula and stay overnight in Kassandra. On Friday a visit to George's mother's home and a night's stay-over. Saturday they would return to Vassilis' home and return to Argirocastro to visit relatives and then return to Glifada on Tuesday to prepare leaving on Wednesday; they could leave late in the afternoon.

George and Lesley realized that leaving would be difficult, especially realizing the conditions that his family had to live with. They both agreed that they would leave money and wished they had more toilet paper but knew that a return trip would be promised.

Ancient Castle Fort

Scene from ancient castle's cannon opening

Chapter XXI

During breakfast the next morning George announced his and Lesley's plans for their last few days in Albania. They would leave Albania late in the day on the twenty-third. George explained that they wanted to spend five days seeing parts of Greece. The flight to America was scheduled for the twenty-ninth. They needed to say good-bye to Aunt Penelope and Aunt Evanthia, cousins Olympia and Kristos, and Vassilis brother's wife, Margarita, return to Glifada, and then go to Aunt Stavroula's village, and George's mother's village, Morista.

Spiros said, "It will be a sad day for all when you leave."

Rezarta said, "You had better drink a lot of water for all the tears."

Rita said, "Or tsipouro."

Everyone laughed. Rita's and Rezarta's eyes were turning red. Aleko jumped in and said, "I'll take you to the border and to Aunt Penelope's tomorrow. Vassilis will make arrangements to take you to the other villages. He knows many people who own cars. I'll phone him today from my work and tell him you're coming. There is a telephone where he works. Today we'll go to the center of Argirocastro. Bring your camera."

Everyone except Spiros and Artioli was going to go. Aleko told them he had gotten permission to take the day off. It seemed he had flexible hours. When asked he just shrugged it off. Rezarta told them his job gave him much time off anyhow.

Arriving in Argirocastro they rode on cobblestone-like streets. It

139

reminded George somewhat of the many Boston streets he grew up on, except these stones were smoother and lay closer together. Aleko drove to a spot which he described as the city's main center. There were many people walking about, and many walked in the middle of the streets. The women wore dresses or blouses and skirts, and the men wore dark pants and white collared shirts. They saw no one in dungarees.

It was warm, the air was clear and crisp, and the traffic was minimal. George had Aleko stop a few times so he could take pictures of the different patterns of the tiles. The block stone tiles were arranged in fancy and beautiful intricate patterns. Of course, they were blackened with age but in excellent condition. There were no ruts or potholes. The city, known as the 'Tile City,' had been designated as a UNESCO World Heritage site.

Aleko discharged them in the city's center and told them he would park the car and then find them. George wished he knew where his mother's grandfather's candy shop and hotel had been. Walking about George spotted a dentist's office. He walked in. After he explained where he came from George asked the dentist if he could look around. It seemed that some professionals and shopkeepers spoke Greek. The dental chair was from the 1930s and Chinese. His dental cabinet was almost bare of tools. The dentist explained that he wanted new equipment, but right now it was impossible. George took a photo of the dental chair, the tool and supply cabinet. He thanked the dentist and walked out; he was astonished!

George was scanning the shops when a photography store that had a portrait studio caught his eye. Having delved in photography since his teenage years he became curious and stepped into the shop. Immediately he knew that he had stepped back into the 1920s-1930s. A petite middle-aged woman was the photographer and owner. She told George that her grandfather and father had owned the store, and that she had inherited it from her father. George explained his interest in photography and he handed his camera for her to peruse. She commented that she had never seen such a camera. She in return gave George permission to look around all he wanted, and that he could photograph the shop and her.

Her camera was a beautiful old 8" by 10" format model, in perfect condition, and sitting on a fixed wooden tripod that had shiny brass fixtures. She told George that film was difficult to get, and patrons were not spending money for portraits. George took a picture of her and her camera. He thanked her and wished her well.

Lesley and the ladies looked into craft shops and other shops. Lesley purchased a small hand-knotted Albanian rug. She told George she had room for it in her suitcase. It was colorful and beautiful; she paid thirty-five dollars in American money.

Aleko found the group and asked if they wanted a coffee or ice cream. George wanted to pay, but Aleko refused asking George, "How are you going to ask for ice cream? You don't speak the language." Everyone had ice cream and stood outside, and people watched.

A tall blondish young man approached George and said, in perfect English, "You're American."

"Yes, how do you know?"

"Your shoes for one and the camera for number two. I'm American also, I'm from Indiana. I'm one of twenty-one Peace Corps members here in Albania. I've been here for four months. I'm the only Corps member here in Gjirokaster (Albanian for Argirocastro). I live with a woman doctor and her husband. How long have you been here? There are almost no American visitors, especially tourists, except for those who were born here and have moved to America"

"I've been here since the beginning of September. I'm visiting my parent's villages and relatives here in Argirocastro. My wife and I are leaving on the twenty-third."

"Oh, I see that you are Greek. You said Argirocastro. Only the Greeks call it that. I live here in the city and I need to say it in the Albanian language."

"Excuse me. My name is George Stamos and this is my wife, Lesley, my cousins, Rita, Rezarta, and Aleko. We live in New Hampshire, and my wife is a dental, hygienist"

"My name is John Brand. It is a pleasure to meet you. Too bad you are leaving; it would be great to spend more time with you both. Your wife could meet the woman doctor. Maybe we'll run into each other again. We could have coffee or a beer, I'm usually around town. I have a scheduled meeting to go to now. Anyhow, have a good day. Good-bye."

"You too. Good-bye."

George said, "Well that was an interesting encounter. You never know who or where you will meet someone of interest anywhere in the world. I'm glad he stopped me."

Walking further, Lesley and George spotted a grocery store. Peering inside they could see that it wasn't too large, but they wanted to see what the store was selling. Entering the store, they noticed right away that the shelves were practically bare. In wooden bins in front of the counter there were string beans, eggplants, tomatoes, onions, green peppers, watermelons, and potatoes. Placed on the shelves in groups of three or four were a few different preserves, six bottles of cherry syrup, seven wine bottles, a few bars of soap, and four displays of crackers and cookies with three packages in each display. The front main counter was bare except for an old-style gold-colored cash register. It looked like the cash registers George had seen when he was a young boy. It had a rotating handle on the side to open the cash drawer. The rear and the inside side walls had five continuous connecting shelves. The entire display was neat, and the individual groups of items were spread far apart, giving it an appearance of a not-empty store. George thought it would make a nice oil painting; he was embarrassed to ask for permission to take a photo. If Albanians could only see the supermarkets back home. Those who had gone to Greece had seen what most of the world had for food marts. George thought about the few vegetables for sale. They were the same vegetables served with every dinner he'd been invited to.

Aleko, George, and Lesley left Rita and Rezarta at a bench so Rezarta could rest, and then they continued walking and photographing more tiled streets. The tile patterns changed on different streets, but some were duplicated. George wanted to capture all the streets and their pattern changes on film; the workmanship was extraordinary beautiful.

Lesley said, "Can you imagine the work that went into laying this material? It was all done by hand. And think about collecting, shipping, cutting and laying all these small blocks. Look at the tops, they're not exactly flat. I wonder what it would be like in the winter to drive on it when it is covered with ice."

George said, "Yeah, and the streets are mostly hilly. You can't use studded tires, even if they have them here. It would ruin the bricks. From what I understand they don't have a long deep cold winter anyhow, and how many cars do you see on these roads? My compliments go to all the workers."

Aleko said, "We're all proud of our city. Too bad the economy is so bad, I'm lucky I have a job. I think we ought to head back to Rezarta and Rita. I don't like leaving her too long. She's having the baby next month, and she tends to overdo things. Do you remember how to get back to them?"

Lesley said, "Sure, no problem."

George said, "My wife has better sense of direction than I."

"Good, I'll get the car and meet you there."

Lesley and George took longer than they had planned to find their way back. When they finally located the bench it was empty. They looked around and found everyone sitting in the car on the other side of the street, with smiles on their faces.

Aleko joked and told them, "I called the police to find you. I told them to look for two lost Americans."

Everyone laughed as they headed down the hill for home. Rezarta was tired, but she felt good. Rita was returning to Tirana in the morning. Lesley and George were spending another night in Argirocastro.

Photographer and her camera

Argirocastro city's center

Boys with rationed bread

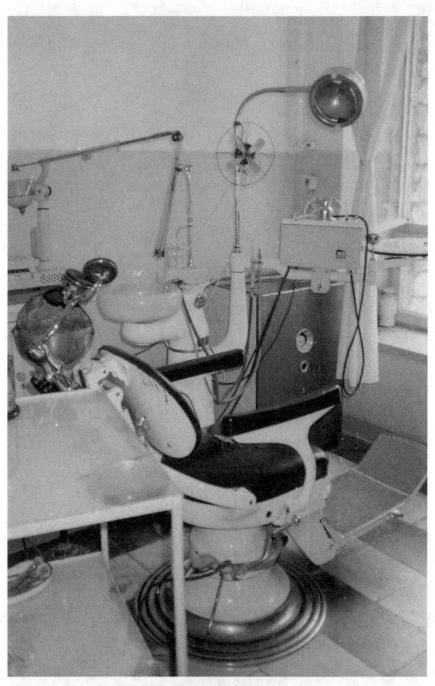

Dentist's chair

School director and faculty

School room interior

Street scene with three children

Street scene with Fort

Street scene with men and fort in background

Street scene with woman holding baby

Chapter XXII

⸻

Another day, another relative, and then another village to visit; Aleko was going to drive Lesley, George, and Spiros to Glifada. Kassandra was in walking distance from Glifada, but George knew the family would not let them walk there by themselves. To have them walk would be inconsiderate to a visiting family member, especially the oldest man in the family walking to Kassandra with his wife.

George mentioned the idea of walking while on their way. He told them he wanted to experience and follow the worn path aside the mountains. After all, Lesley and Georg loved walking. Of course, they knew the family didn't understand their motives. They didn't push the idea, as the family laughed softly when they said they would like to walk.

The remainder of the ride to Glifada was quiet. Spiros went with them, because they were going to meet and visit his mother, Ana. The mother was married to Vlassi's oldest brother, Spiros. George would address her as thia (aunt).

They stopped to see Violetta and Aunt Amalia to tell them they were visiting Aunt Ana that day and then the next day they were going to Kassandra and then Morista, spending a night in each village. After seeing Ana they would return to pack a few items.

Spiros, talking to Violetta said, "Aunt Stavroula will provide a ride from there to Morista. Her son has a car that will take them. Aleko will return to pick them up here midday on Sunday and take them back to

Argirocastro so they can tell everyone good-bye. George, are you ready to see my mother?"

"Yes. Lesley, are you ready?"

"Yes."

Spiros led the way up the mountain and across a rocky path above a ravine. There was a beautiful view looking down the mountain. A lonely donkey was browsing on grass on one side of the ravine not too far away. With his head down he paid no attention to the few people walking above him. The sky was blue and crisp, and some small birds were chirping from a bush. There were only a few homes on that side of the mountain. Behind the travelers the entire village could be seen. George thought about how much quieter it would be on that side. Spiros led them alongside his mother's house and entered through an opening in a stone wall into a large courtyard. Under a large grape arbor there were chairs and a large wooden table shaded from the hot sun; his mother was sitting and crocheting.

Spiros introduced George and Lesley to his mother. "This is George and his wife Lesley. My mother, Ana."

She stood up to hug and kiss George. She was a tall woman; her acute eyes met his. Her hair was almost all black with just a few strands of grey, and her movements appeared strong in stature, her skin was olive, and her face had few wrinkles; she was eighty-eight. She gave George a strong hug and many kisses. She in turn said hello to Lesley and kissed her lightly on the cheeks.

"So this is my nephew from America. Welcome to your uncle's and my home. He would have been proud to have met you. I've been hearing a lot about you."

"I'm happy to finally meet my aunt. I must say you look terrific."

"I do feel healthy for my age. Are you enjoying your stay in Glifada? Your wife is very pretty. She does not look Greek."

"Glifada and my wife are both beautiful. Lesley is English and Irish, and she does not speak Greek. I will have to translate our conversations."

"How nice, I'll get to hear American. This will be the first time for me and in my home."

Just about then Thomas and his wife, Bereta entered the courtyard.

After all the greetings, Spiros came out with plum preserves, tsipouro, water, and Fanta for the ladies. With everyone sitting under the arbor sharing conversations, and with the sun high in the sky, and cumulus clouds floating softly by, the afternoon seemed to pass slowly.

Aunt Ana said, "Thomas and Bereta's son will be here soon. I have made us something to eat. As you know, food is in short supply, but we will sit and eat and enjoy the family."

She had just about finished the conversation when Alex, the son, walked into the courtyard. He had a big wide grin as he walked over to his grandmother and gave her a big hug.

Thomas got up and said to Alex, "This is George and Lesley. You can practice some of your English. He started a class recently."

Alex said in English, "Hello, how are you?" Then in Greek he explained that he is still in the beginning classes.

You could see that Bereta was proud of him. He went around the table and greeted everyone. He's twenty years old and not so tall as his father, but he had a strong build, curly black hair, large sparkling blue eyes, and good looks. He sat down next to his mother.

Thomas asked, "Are you enjoying your car?"

"Yes, very much."

Thomas said, "He bought it recently. It is bright red. It is the first car in this family in this village. He is able to drive it close to the house on this side of the mountain. No one would leave a car at the bottom of the village. He will take George and Lesley to Kassandra. No need for Aleko to drive here to do that."

Spiros said, "Aleko will be here later to pick me up. I'll tell him then."

Alex asked, "What time do you want to go to Aunt Stavroula's?"

George asked Lesley, "Does ten or eleven in the morning sound okay?"

"Maybe ten."

"Alex, we would like to go about ten tomorrow. Is that all right with you?"

"I'll be at the bottom of the hill at ten. Then I can go to work after that. I already told my boss I have relatives from America here and that I would like to drive them to Kassandra. He said, 'That is no problem and bring them by if you have a chance. I would like to meet an American."

With that settled, Aunt Ana said, "It is time to eat. We should eat outside."

Bereta said, "Yes, let's do that. It is beautiful outside."

Aunt Ana and Bereta got up to go inside, Lesley wanted to help also, but Bereta said politely in Greek that they don't need any help. Besides, Alex always helps her. He got up with a smile. George translated.

Someone spread a white tablecloth and then placed dinnerware. Food came out of the kitchen, and Aunt Ana said a prayer. The food was consistent with other meals, but that was understood by everyone; still it was a joyous occasion.

One of the conversations after the meal led to George's father. Aunt Ana talked about Vlassi, "I remember your father. I was a couple of years older, and when he was leaving for America he came to visit to say good-bye. He was excited about leaving, but he didn't want to leave the family, especially his mother. I also remember another time, when we were younger. I combed his hair, and it was very wavy. We never saw him again, but now you are here in his place."

Everyone was quietly listening, and then a pause set in. With the sun getting lower in the horizon Spiros broke the spell.

"It's time to go, as Aleko is to meet me soon, and our guests have to return to Vassilis' home before it gets dark. We have to say good-bye."

George thanked his aunt for everything and for telling him about his father. He wished her well and that he hoped to see her again. Everyone kissed good-bye.

Chapter XXIII

Thomas arrived at Vassilis' home in the morning. He was going to ride with Lesley and George to Kassandra. He told them that Alex was down below waiting. After saying good-bye to the family they walked down the mountain and found Alex wiping his shiny red car.

With a wide smile on his face he greeted them and said, "Good morning. This is my car. Do you like it?"

George said, "Very much. It sure is bright and clean. It's not new, but it's in good shape. How does it drive?"

"It seems to be good. I don't know much about cars, but Uncle Spiros taught me how to drive when I was younger. He was a truck driver."

They all got in and off they went. It was another nice day, and with little traffic the ride to Kassandra went quickly. The entrance road off the main road to the village was partially paved, so they were able to drive part of the way up the mountain. Alex took a couple of turns onto gravel roads and parked beside a building close to the road. Thomas led the way down a narrow path to the home of Aunt Stavroula where a man was building a small structure out of stones. He was chipping away at a large stone to make it square.

Thomas stopped and said, "That is Vangeli, Stavroula's oldest son. Two sons are in Greece working, and the youngest one is joining his brothers soon."

Vangeli looked up and greeted them and said, "Yassas (hello) please excuse me. I'll be inside in a couple of minutes. I need to finish this stone."

Then the group continued on to the main entrance. They had to go through a large patio under a grape arbor; the vines were abundant and contained deep-colored red grapes; Stravoula's home bordered the arbor. The opposite side of the arbor gradually graded downward and provided a spectacular view of the valley and mountains. There was a wide passageway also on that side with another home in view to the rear.

Thomas knocked on the door, and a pretty young girl answered. With a large smile and a twinkle in her eyes she said, "Please come in. My grandmother is in the other room. My name is Fevronia. You are George and Lesley. It's so nice to meet you. She's in the other room sitting. She is waiting for your arrival. My grandmother told me all about you, and this is your wife. You don't have to take off your shoes. I was told that your wife knows no Greek, but I can speak some English."

George said, "I'll take my shoes off. I like that idea. Generally we don't do that in America." Everyone followed George's example.

After they all kissed each other and Aunt Stavroula, with tears in her eyes, she met Lesley. Fevronia left the room. Vangeli entered the house and greeted his guests, excusing himself for being delayed.

Aunt Stavroula's home was spacious and had four bedrooms. She had four married sons. The oldest son, Vangeli and his wife and two daughters lived in the home. The other sons and their families had their own homes. Two of the homes were located on the same property and the other was within walking distance.

With everyone sitting down, Fevronia returned with a large tray of preserves and drinks: tsipouro, water, and Fanta. Her mother and another daughter followed with silverware and glasses. They introduced themselves. Dorothea was the mother and Konstandina was the younger daughter.

Dorothea had a pleasant smile and face, but she was overweight, and George was told that she was sickly. Fevronia had a few freckles under her dark blue eyes, wavy dark hair, and nineteen years old. Konstandina was a bit shy and had unblemished olive skin, dark brown eyes, and straight dark hair; they were both attractive and had young-girl figures. Everyone sat down to chat and get acquainted.

George asked Vangeli, "What are you building?"

"A new outdoor bathroom."

After a few laughs the conversation turned to George and Lesley; Fevronia speaking in English, translated to her family. She struggled some with her English, but Lesley and George helped her when needed. She said that she taught English in the elementary school. Lesley complimented her and made a comment that nineteen was a young age to be teaching.

She replied, "Thank you; I learned English in college. With our new government, they want everyone to learn your language."

Thomas interrupted politely, "Excuse me. Alex and I have to dismiss ourselves. I'm sorry, but Alex has to return to work, and I have to return to Glifada. It was nice seeing you all. We don't get to see each other very often. Our lives are so busy. We should have more cousins from America visiting. Enjoy your visit with our eldest cousin and his beautiful American wife."

George replied, "Thank you, and we will see you again before we leave."

The families said their good-byes, and Vangeli invited them to return and visit sometime. Promises were made, and out the door they went. Then the attention returned to the invited guests.

George and Lesley were getting used to the questions about themselves and about America whenever they met new relatives, for they knew the family was badly informed about America. Plus they wanted to learn about their newly-arrived relative; George and Lesley also felt that they were ambassadors for their country.

Johan, the youngest son, walked in and introduced himself. He was taller than Vangeli and had broad shoulders, blue eyes, and blonde hair; he was thirty-eight. He greeted George with a firm handshake and generous facial kisses.

He said, "George, I know you are staying tonight. When you leave tomorrow stop by my home and meet my wife and children."

"Yes, I will make sure we do that. Thank you."

Eventually a comparable dinner was served, except there were larger portions of meat; George was told that a lamb was killed in the guests' honor. Of course, George and Lesley were grateful. Coffee (sketos, the way George liked it), tsipouro, grapes and watermelon were served when the family retired to a sitting room; Vangeli had made the tsipouro.

The conversations were interesting, and everyone contributed something. They were interested in the amount of money that was paid in America, even for jobs with little skills. They talked about all they could do with higher-paying jobs; they could even travel. Only the two sons had traveled. Of course, nobody was allowed to travel during communist years. How sad to be a prisoner in your own country.

Kalinikta (goodnight) was finally said among the group, and the family retired when it got late. The guests were given a large bedroom that someone had given up for their use. It was beautifully decorated with blue and white Greek motifs and black and white family photographs. George and Lesley drifted off to sleep feeling satisfied that the last aunt's home was visited. Time was running out for them in Albania.

Aunt Stravoula and Fevronia

Chapter XXIV

With the crowing of roosters and the morning light the household became busy with family and guests. Two cars drove on the road next to the home, George thought, not like in Glifada where cars didn't drive on the road next to Vassilis' home. Lesley and George entered the kitchen, and three grandchildren (8, 10, and 12 years old) and Konstandia (14 years) were eating eggs and bread with their milk, preparing for school. With two fathers gone to Greece, their children ate breakfast with the yiayia (grandmother).

Dorothea said, "Kalimera (good morning), I'll have coffee in a few minutes, after I finish with the children."

George said, "Kalimera. Lesley and I will go outside and look around. Take care of the children."

In a few minutes an eight-year-old grandson arrived; he had a large crop of red hair, freckles, and a big smile. The other children came out in an orderly manner, with Konstandia bringing up the rear. As they passed Lesley and George, they looked, smiled, and went on their courteous way with the red-headed grandson, touching George's shoulder, joining the others.

After coffee, eggs, yogurt and bread, Aunt Stavroula, Dorothea, Lesley, George, Fevronia, and another visiting granddaughter, Anthula- who was seventeen with olive skin and striking good looks went out to sit under the arbor and the warming sun. Vangeli went to work on his new project.

Anthula had brought a portable radio with cassettes; her father had bought it for her in Greece. She was playing Greek folkloric music. After a few songs and mutual conversations among the group she changed the cassette and got up to dance. Before long, Fevronia joined her. They clasped hands and danced once around the table where everyone was sitting and then with both of them clutching the corner of a white handkerchief, they took turns spinning around and at the same time circling the table. They invited Lesley and George to join them; they got up and danced under the grapes. After a couple of songs Lesley and George sat down, and the young ladies continued. They danced beautifully as their bodies moved with the sounds of bouzoukis, violin, clarinet, and a drum beat. The situation was beautiful and mesmerizing. They all thanked them when they sat and they told them how beautiful it had been; the music continued softly.

Aunt Stavroula was very communicative, as was Dorothea about George's sister Eli and her children, and about George and Lesley. As the morning was slipping away, the aunt felt tired and excused herself to lie down. She kissed George many times and thanked him for coming to visit; she also kissed Lesley.

Aunt Stavroula said, "I will not see you again while you are here. I don't feel strong. You don't know how happy I am to meet my brother's son and his wife. If you ever return I hope I feel better. Give your sister and her children my love. Good-bye, I love you."

George said, "I love you too. We plan on returning some day. I pray that you feel better soon." With that she went inside.

With the sun at its zenith Fevronia with tears in her eyes, asked George, "When do you want to leave for Morista?"

"I would like to arrive around mid-afternoon. Not that I'm in a hurry to leave here, but our time and days in Albania are very busy. So many people to see, and places to go."

"I understand, I'll make a small lunch. Morista isn't far from here."

"I noticed that it is really close. Lesley and I would like to walk there. Is that possible? We wanted to walk from Glifada to here, but everyone said no."

"Anthula and I will take you there. With all of us, and the two of us returning it will be safe. Besides, the path is not too close to the main road. I'll ask my father if it is all right. He should be here soon for a break."

George thought of the National Geographic Magazine about Albania in an issue dated February, 1931. George had read the article before leaving for Albania. It told about the mountain clans, the thievery, the protection of clan areas, and about traveling with an Albanian woman. If you were robbed or assaulted, or if you had any trouble traveling with a group, as a tourist, or with other clan members, and an Albanian woman was with you it was considered a cowardly act and the male or male's instigators would be considered cowards and put into a disgraced position forever. So it was safer to travel with an Albanian woman in the group, but Vangeli would be considering the safety of his family with the change of times.

Anthula and Fevronia went inside when Dorothea noticed Vangeli. He came over and said hello and went into the house to wash up and get something to drink. It wasn't long before the young ladies came out with a tray of feta, tomato salad, olives, bread, and soft drinks. Their father followed.

During lunch Fevronia asked her father, "Would it be all right if Anthula and I walk to Morista with George and Lesley?"

Vangeli said, "That would be all right. When are you going?"

"Sometime after we eat."

Vangeli said, "Make sure you get home before it starts to get dark."

George said, "We have to stop at Johan's house."

Vangeli said, "That's not a problem; you'll pass by his home on the way."

After clearing the table, the young girls went inside. Lesley excused herself to prepare to leave. She came out with their overnight belongings telling, George that she had left the bag of surprise (the supply of toilet paper was almost gone).

Vangeli and Dorothea thanked George and Lesley for coming and told them they hoped they would return someday. Also, that maybe the other two brothers would be here to meet them. They hoped to return with money and start a business.

The girls returned ready to take a walk. Good-byes were said and off they went heading toward Morista with Lesley and George following. It didn't take long before they reached Johan's home. He was outside repairing a broken rung in a chair. With open arms he greeted them with a smile.

"Hello, I'm glad you stopped by. Unfortunately my wife is visiting with her mother. The boy is in school, and she has the baby girl."

George said, "That's too bad. I was looking forward to meeting them. We are on our way to visit a relative of my mother and the home where my mother was born. Maybe you know the family; Papajanis."

"I know two sons and the home. It is very large."

"Yes."

"Your son has red hair. We saw him this morning. Does your wife have red hair?"

"Yes. Do any of you want something to drink?"

Everyone said they were fine. Johan excused himself saying he wanted to show George something. He returned briefly with a rifle. Everyone except Johan looked surprised. He had this big smile.

Johan said, "I just got this rifle. The family never had a gun before, except maybe during the wars. It is Russian and it works really well. I can use it to hunt or just have it here, I'll put a bullet in it so you can fire it. Have you ever fired a rifle before?"

"Many times, I was in the army for four years."

"Oh, here shoot at that wooden stump."

A little surprised and somewhat reluctant, George took aim and shot. The women plugged their ears and closed their eyes. The bullet hit the stump, and you could see some wood splinter. George handed back the rifle and thanked him. Johan had a grin from one corner of his face to the other.

"You are the only one in the family, besides me, to shoot it. I got it two days ago."

"It seems accurate. Your brothers will like it. I'm sorry we can't stay, but we have to go. I don't want the girls getting home too late. I hope to see you again. When you go to Greece make some money, and say hello to your wife. Tell her we're sorry we didn't get to meet her and the baby. I hope we will next time."

"I understand. Good-bye."

Turning to the right over her shoulder while walking away, Anthula said to Johan, "Bring the baby when you visit next."

They continued walking one behind the other and in places two abreast. The path gave views in all directions. It was a warm sunny day with a slight breeze coming up from the valley. There were a few patches of trees, many ground plants, and there were small birds to keep them company. The young girls talked and danced a few steps as they sang. Lesley and George followed, listening, laughing softly, and watching. It was their first long nature walk in Albania, and they were being entertained.

They reached the outskirts of Morista. It was a larger village than Kassandra or Glifada and had many homes. They could see many graveled roads and people walking about. Those they met they greeted. Some of the people they met had surprised looks on their faces. The girls met a few people, mainly younger people, they knew. Everyone nodded and said Kalispera (good afternoon). Some asked the girls what their family name was. They would reply, "I know your father or mother or grandparents." George mentioned his mother's name a few times. Of course, they knew that name and welcomed him to the village. Some stopped and talked longer. Everyone was polite and understood when they explained they had to move on. Meeting these villagers, George felt the way he felt when he first arrived.

They reached the family home and entered the gateway which was beside the building's front. Once inside the wall, it gave them a new prospective. The girls stopped and looked at this large home with amazement. They knew of no home in Glifada or Kassandra that was this large.

They both asked George, "This is where your mother was born? Your family had to be very rich. It is very beautiful. Look at all the land inside the walls. We always saw this house from the road, but to see it this close and inside the walls, well it sure is beautiful."

When they knocked on the door a tall man opened the door. "Hello, you must be George. My mother told me you and your wife would be arriving today. Please come in, I am Sophia's son, Christopher. She is very excited. Who are these young girls with you?"

"Hello. These are my cousin's daughters from Kassandra. We walked from there, and they showed us the way. This is Fevronia and Anthula Louvaris. Their fathers are brothers, and this is my wife Lesley. She doesn't speak Greek so I will have to translate for her"

"It is nice to meet you. I understand some English, but I can't speak many words, and I know the four brothers. My father is in the sitting room, and I'll tell my mother you are here. Can you girls stay for drinks?"

Anthula answered, "We can stay a short while."

Fevronia replied, "Something to drink would be fine. It is warm outside. My father didn't want us to stay too long. He'll get nervous and run along the trail to see if we're all right."

That brought a few laughs. They entered the sitting room and Christopher's father, Kostas was reading a Greek newspaper. He got up and everyone was introduced and kissed and shook hands. Christopher left the room to tell his mother. He was gone just a few moments when Sophia appeared carrying a tray of preserves, water, tsipouro, and cold Fanta.

Greeting everyone, she said, "Does anyone want coffee?"

There were no replies so she sat and with George translating Sophia said to Lesley, "How do you like Albania?"

"I find it very beautiful and interesting. Everyone is very friendly, and George's family is all handsome. I'm having a good time meeting all his relatives. There are many, so I'm having trouble remembering all the names. A few of the names are new to me, but I'm enjoying everything."

Sophia said, "I understand. I can't imagine what it would be like to go to America. I know it is a very big country and very different than here. We are not modern- very poor, and a new government. Many problems, but it will take time to solve everything."

Christopher said, "I can see a little progress already."

After the young ladies had preserves and Fanta they got up to go home. It was not close to dark, but they felt it would be safer to go then. They told Lesley and George how much they had enjoyed their company and to write them. Christopher got paper and pen, and they swapped addresses. Fevronia had a big smile and tears, and Anthula had a dimpled smile. They kissed George and Lesley good-bye, and out the door they went, commenting on the size of the sitting room, the blue hand carved doors, and the foyer with the indoor water fountain.

George and Lesley stood on the front porch and waved as the girls went through the gate. When George and Lesley reentered the house Christopher met them in the foyer and asked if they would like to take a tour of the house plus put their belongings in the bedroom.

George replied, "We'd love to."

"Let's start where you'll sleep."

Entering the bedroom on the first floor, located on the front corner opposite the main sitting corner room, Lesley sighed as she entered the room seeing the beautiful carved wood and cornices on the ceiling.

It was a very large bedroom with many large windows. It was sparingly furnished with two bureaus with mirrors and a standard-sized bed with a soft hand-sewn colorful comforter. There were some old black-and-white photos on the walls. The windows had beautiful light-blue hand-made drapes. The marbled floor had two large hand-woven Greek wool rugs. Every corner of the ceiling had a blue hand carved rosette cornice with a larger diamond-shaped carving in the center of the ceiling. The remainder of the ceiling had hand-carved filigreed wooden slats spaced apart. It was beautiful and impressive.

Lesley asked, "How large is this room?"

"The house has fourteen rooms and two large separate storage closets. All the main rooms are six meters by six meters (20 feet by 20 feet). The foyer is six meters by eighteen meters (20 feet by 60 feet). The two doors in the corners on the back wall lead to kitchens, but we use one for storage. Above those kitchens are storage rooms used as clothes closets, with racks for shoes, hats, and places to hang clothing. There is no room on the other side of the rear foyer's bottom rear wall. Two closets upstairs extend from one to the other above the foyer wall. There are two Greek Ionic columns outside supporting them."

George asked Christopher, "How do you heat this home?"

Christopher explained, "The outside walls are solid stone sixty-one centimeters thick (24 inches). The house is cool in the summer and warm in the winter, but we don't heat all the rooms. You will notice all the rooms have fireplaces. On the front of the building on the second floor there is a large balcony the width of the building. It is a nice place to sit and see down and across the valley. When we go upstairs we will go onto the balcony. Come, we will look in all the rooms. Three rooms are not used. In some of the rooms the cornices, wooden slates, and the center ceiling carvings are gone. In the two kitchens the entire finished ceilings were removed. My mother remembers the removed ceilings and this home as a young girl, but of course I never saw the ceilings. Either the Italians or Albanians removed them. I don't think the Germans would have bothered. My mother cries sometimes when she thinks of it. There are three furnished bedrooms. We use only two bedrooms. My parents use one, and my brother and I share one room. The three bedrooms and the sitting room have hand-knotted Greek wool rugs. The rugs were hidden from the intruders; they are very old but in good condition. Your room is for guests."

George said, "That was clever to hide them. I'm sure they would have been taken. Where is your brother?"

"He is in Greece working."

"Lesley said, "The carpets are beautiful."

While finishing the tour of the home, Sophia joined them. She said to George, "Your grandparents slept in your bedroom. In fact, your mother was born there."

George took Lesley in his arms and gave her a warm hug. This was one of the highlights of this trip. In a strange country, with all the wars and tragedies that took place, and eighty-two years after his mother's birth, he couldn't ever imagine sleeping in the same bedroom. A few tears flowed slowly.

Sophia, breaking the spell, said, "Dinner is ready. Are you ready to eat?"

Christopher said, "Yes. We have seen all the rooms except the kitchen."

George said, "This is a beautiful home. I'm happy that someone in the family lives here. Someday someone in the family will make whatever repairs it needs."

Sophia said, "All the family moved-mainly to Greece, some to Italy and America, and even a few to Australia after the war of 1912. You are the first of that family to visit, even from Greece. My father and mother stayed.

They didn't want to abandon the property. There were difficult times, but here we are hoping for the best. With my son in Greece earning money it looks promising. I'm sorry you won't get to see him."

"Me too. Please tell him hello. I'm excited to tell my family about this family home."

Sophia said, "Let's go to the kitchen before everything gets cold."

They went to a large kitchen that contained two large tables. The aroma was tantalizing, and the setting was inviting. The meal consisted of squash, okra, and cucumbers-a welcome break from the usual victuals. The family had grown the vegetables in their own garden.

After the meal they retired to the sitting room, and their past and present lives unfolded. Christopher worked in a nearby village taking care of the water supply, the oldest son was a diesel mechanic, Sophia worked in the agricultural fields, and Kostas worked with cement. All these jobs were selected by the government. Citizens had no choice as to vocations.

Coffee and watermelon were served along with Kostas' homemade tsipouro and wine. It was a pleasant evening. Eventually as the night passed they retired to their bedrooms. The visitors melted into the bed whispering about George's mother and the Doulas family.

Almost a hundred years old

George, Vassilis, and Aunt Stravoula's family

Chapter XXV

Because of the home's thick stone walls, Lesley and George awoke without the sounds of barking dogs, braying of sheep, goats or donkeys, or the honks of cars, even though they were in the middle of the village. It took them a moment to realize where they were and also when looking at the magnificence of the room.

The morning was bright with a few cumulus clouds. After a breakfast of eggs, bread, yogurt, and coffee, Christopher said he would take them on a tour of the grounds and the village. They went outside and saw the family vegetable gardens, fruit trees, and grape arbors. There were some vegetables and grapes yet to be harvested. There was at least a half acre of land in the rear and a quarter acre in front, all of it within a high stone wall; George captured it on film.

Christopher said, "Can you walk up the mountain? I have something to show you."

Lesley asked, "How far up the mountain?"

"Not that far."

Walking up the rocky path Christopher said, "My father was a Partisan for three years living and fighting high on this mountain and most of the others around here. He was young and strong. He also fought in Serbia, Tirana, and Argirocastro during the occupation of the Italians and the Germans. They lived with little food and old weapons, but they killed a lot of enemies and caused disruptions. He has shrapnel wounds in his left leg; it was never removed. The younger villagers respect him for his participation. They are aware of the sacrifices the Partisans made. Kostas does not exploit or say much about those days, but when asked about that time, his only remark is, 'I did what I had to do.' He is a good father."

George thought of his Uncle Sotir married to Aunt Evanthia. Kostas, like Sotir, is a reticent man. George wondered if they had fought side by side.

Following Christopher to a large leveled area, they approached the ruins of a Greek Orthodox Church. The walls were mostly in partial ruins and the roof had collapsed. The partial standing walls showed minimal evidence of faded icons. Where the altar should have been there was a heap of stones. On the last standing supporting column the most visible remains of an icon presented itself. It had the remnants of a blue robed body. It was difficult to imagine what the church had looked like, but you knew it had to have been beautiful. To one side of the ruins there stood a bell tower with a large bell hanging at the top. Molded on the inside of the bell was his mother's family name; Doulas.

George asked Christopher, "Can I ring the bell?"

"Yes."

George grabbed the hanging rope and pulled. The bell had a rich middle-tone ring. Not too high or too deep. It reverberated; sending a chill up George, and when it quieted George rang it again. Feeling satisfied, he let go of the rope.

George asked Christopher, "What if I rang it again?"

He replied, "It would have meant that someone in the village had died."

With a surprise look on his face, George was glad he didn't ring it again and he could only say, "Oh!"

Christopher informed George, "Your grandmother's family built this church. In fact, I was told they built five churches. Her father was the priest for this church, the small chapels, and the village. He moved to America just before the Italians invaded in 1939. I was also told that he was a spokesman for the village when the Turks ruled here. Eventually the Albanian government destroyed the church, as they did many churches. The bell was secretly buried in 1939 and was put back up when we became democratic recently."

Lesley, after hearing the translating, "That's amazing."

George said, "I met my great grandfather when I was little. I believe I was seven or eight. He always wore his religious robe. He had also studied to be a medical doctor. When he moved to America he became a librarian at the Greek theological school near Boston. He did not want to take on church duties. Boston is the city where I was born. I was also told that there are no relatives from that family living in Albania. They all moved to other countries. I know only the ones who moved to America. My grandmother told me they were the richest family in Morista. She also told me they were large landholders, exporters, importers, doctors, judges, and priests. Thank you for sharing the story about the bell and my family. It was sad and beautiful. There are chills running up my spine."

Christopher said, "Your grandmother's home has been replaced. It was large also, but boys destroyed the original building. It was vacant for many years. When we go down the mountain I can show you where it was. I remember it from when I was a young boy. It was in ruins then. The family living there now is not a relative of yours."

Christopher continued, "There is a doctor in Athens that who promised money to rebuild the church. I don't know his name."

George knew that a relative in Athens was a millionaire and that he was a doctor. Could that be the same donor doctor?

George took many pictures. Walking down the path they came upon an elderly woman dressed in black. George asked if he could take her picture. She didn't mind. She asked why he was in the village. He explained that his mother was from here. Of course, this required more information. Explaining his family she told George that she knew his mother and grandmother. George's grandmother was ninety-seven, and this woman, walking up the mountain with no problem was very spry. He asked her name and said he would ask his mother if she remembered her. George's grandmother was very ill when he left and had problems with her mind. He figured she wouldn't remember.

George said, "Well, that was interesting. Did you see how healthy she looked?"

Christopher said, "She is the oldest woman here. She is amazing. Close to one hundred, but I don't know exactly."

Continuing on, George told Christopher that he wanted to take a picture of the village from the same spot his great uncle had before the 1920s.

Christopher said, "Good. I'll see you when you return. I hope you find the spot."

George and Lesley left Christopher and walked along a narrow trail that George thought it might lead to the same area. Walking along the narrow path they met an elderly lady dressed all in black who was saddling up her donkey. As they brushed past her they greeted each other and the woman asked where they were from and who they were they visiting and invited them in for coffee, but George explained that he wanted to take a particular photo and they had to leave the village. So on they went. Some buildings that had been constructed recently blocked the way, so George did the best he could.

On the return trip the woman was still with her donkey. She stopped George and Lesley and invited them in again, as her house was next to the trail. She was very persistent, so George politely accepted, but told her they couldn't stay long, as someone was coming with a car to give them a ride.

In the sitting room of this quaint and stone home George spotted a photograph on the wall that looked familiar. Shortly after George and Lesley sat, the lady excused herself and left to make coffee. George got up to look at the picture.

He said, "Lesley, I know this couple. They are relatives. I have been to their home, and that picture had to be taken in America, where they met and married." George was stunned. Why would this woman have this picture?

The woman returned with preserves and coffee and George said, "I know those people in that picture. The woman is Sophia and the man is George. They lived in America, but both have passed away. I'm curious as to how you know them."

"That woman is my cousin. Now I have to ask you how you know them."

George said, "Your cousin? She's the sister of my great Aunt Eleni's husband."

"What! Dimitri Contas?"

"Yes, my great aunt was married to Dimitri."

"I am a Contas. Our family lived in this village. They all moved away but me. I married a man from Glifada."

"Glifada, that's where my family lives, do you know the Stamos family?"

"I am a Stamos, my name is Enkalada Stamos, and I am seventy-seven. I've been a widow for a long time."

George and Enkalada worked out the logistics and found out that she had married one of George's grandfather's brother's sons. That made her George's aunt. For being seventy-seven she was in great shape.

"That's amazing. We are family-connected. My name is George Stamos, and this is my wife, Lesley. We live in America and we are visiting here for the first time. Do you know Dimitri's daughters Martha and Libby?"

"Yes, we used to write, but I lost their address and they haven't written in a long time."

"Libby passed away, but Martha is well. Give me your address, and when I get home I'll have her write to you. She is my godmother."

"That would be wonderful. So we are related. Too bad you have to leave. You can stay here any time you want."

"We were staying with Sophia Papajanis. She is a distant cousin. My mother was born in their home but moved to America when she was ten. Before we leave, do you mind if I take your picture? "

"No, you can send one to my cousin in America and one to me."

Time was moving on, and Lesley reminded George that they should leave. They had to return to Glifada to re-supply and it was getting late.

George said, "This was such a delightful surprise to meet you and to know I have an aunt in this village. I'm thankful we stopped for coffee, but I'm saddened that we have to leave. We are returning to America next week, and we have many relatives to say good-bye to. I will write you when I get home to America and send you your picture."

They kissed good-bye and walked back to Sophia's home. Lesley said,

"Can you believe that? The world is a small place sometimes. What if we hadn't stopped for coffee? This entire day has been very interesting."

George was quiet, thinking about Aunt Enkalada, the bell, and the church. "You're right, very interesting. This entire trip has been interesting. So many stories to tell."

When they arrived at the house the front door was opened; they walked in saying hello. Christopher came out of the sitting room and asked if all went well. The family was wondering what took you so long.

They entered the room and saw Alex sitting there. George said, "We met Enkalada Stamos and she invited us in for coffee after I took a picture of the village. She was married to a family relative. She is my great aunt. The whole thing was interesting. I'm sorry we took so long. Alex, I'm surprised that you are here. How did you find us?"

"I asked where the Americans were staying. Villagers know what's going on that is different, and you two are different. Just teasing. I went to Kassandra and talked to Fevronia. She explained the home. How could one miss this home? I came to give you a ride to Glifada. Are you ready to go now or do you want to spend more time here?"

George asked Lesley, "Are you ready to go? I am."

"Sure. I don't like leaving after one day, everyone is so beautiful and accommodating, but we have so much to do and not much time to do it. You can tell them we're leaving while I get our things." She left the last of the surprise gift bag.

George explained their itinerary and that they loved the home, sleeping in that special room and that leaving was difficult. He told the family they hoped to return someday and visit longer.

Lesley returned as George was still talking. She said, "Please tell them I want to thank them for their hospitality, and tell Christopher thanks for taking the time for the tour of the house and the church. We hope to see them again sometime."

George translated the message, and Sophia came over and hugged Lesley and George with tears in her eyes and kissed them a few times. Christopher shook hands and kissed them also. Kostas shook hands and kissed Lesley. With that done they said, "Good-bye."

The ride to Glifada was quiet as George looked at the home from the road until the home disappeared. Alex left them at the bottom of the hill; Lesley and George walked up the mountain unescorted for the first time. The sun was getting lower in the west as they opened the gate and knocked on the door. Violetta opened the door with a surprise look.

"Kalispera (good afternoon). Are you alone?"

"Yes, but it's no problem. Alex drove us home from Morista and dropped us off. He said his car couldn't make it up on this side of the mountain and asked if that was all right. Lesley and I liked walking up together. How is everyone?"

"Everyone is fine. We expected you today, but we didn't know when. Vassilis will be home soon. He is in the village visiting his sister. Did you have a nice time?"

George said, "We had a fantastic time. So many stories to tell."

"Would you like some café?"

"We'd love some, Lesley do you want café?"

"Yes, George. I understood what she said. I must be learning more Greek."

"Good, now you can translate for me."

"Yeah, right."

It wasn't long before Vassilis returned home to find his guests. He joined them for coffee, and George had to relate all that had happened. In the meantime Lesley joined Violetta and Aunt Amalia to help with dinner. George knew that the language of cooking was international and that she would be fine without him translating.

Dinner was served with Nicholas at Lesley's side. During dinner the lights went out two times. After the second time they had to eat by candlelight. Violetta said the lights were going off every night, sometimes returning, and other times they stayed off all night. Sitting in the candlelit room after dinner they decided to sit on the porch. Everyone but Amalia went out and listened and watched lights of more truck columns.

Vassilis said, "Actually the lights in the village have been doing that for a while. While you have been here they have been on, but it started again yesterday. You can see lights across the valley while we sit in the dark."

George said, "Maybe something is wrong with the village transformer."

Vassilis said, "Maybe. What are your plans the last few days?"

"Tomorrow we want to visit Argirocastro and say our good-byes. That should take two days and two nights. Then we'll return here on Tuesday and leave on Wednesday. We can leave later in the day. We will probably stay one night in Ioannina. We need to get a ride to Argirocastro. Maybe Lesley and I will go down and hire a taxi."

"What! No, I'll get a taxi and come back and get you."

"I thought you would say something like that. You're the taxi man."

With the night passing away Violetta said, "When you get to the city you had better drink a lot of water. Many tears will be flowing."

As she said that, Lesley and Violetta had watery eyes already. They all kissed each other good-night and went to their rooms.

Lying in bed Lesley said, "It will be difficult leaving this family. They live so far away, and they need so much help. I feel like I've known them all my life. You cannot help but love them for who they are." Lesley sobbed quietly with George's arm gently holding her, as they fell asleep.

Church interior with destroyed altar

Family church bell

Foyer in family home

Chapter XXVI

Waking up, Lesley and George realized that today was going to be a tiring day. Saying good-bye was not going to be easy. Being separated by the ocean, their work schedules and other commitments, would make a day or weekend trip unrealistic.

Soon after breakfast Vassilis returned with a taxi. With their overnight satchel the three arrived in Argirocastro and Spiros' apartment. The family was there except Aleko. Spiros and Rezarta were pleased to see them again, and Artioli put his arms up for George. He picked him up and gave him a big hug; Artioli laughed and gave George a wet kiss on the cheek. Vassilis left for work and told them he would see them on Tuesday.

Rezarta said, "Aleko is going to take you to Aunt Penelope's home today. When are you returning to Glifada?"

Lesley said, "Tuesday, but not too late"

"So two days here. Good. Aunt Penelope invited all of us for dinner tonight. Aunt Evanthia will be there. Tomorrow we are invited to Olympia and Kostas' home for dinner. It will afford you to see everyone to say good-bye. What do you want to do today?"

George said, "I would like to walk and see more of the city. Does that sound good to you Lesley?"

"Yes, it would be nice to get some exercise."

Rezarta asked, "Spiros, do you want to go out? They would like to walk some, and I would like to stay home with Artioli."

Spiros said, "Good, I need to get out. It is a beautiful day. Where do you want to go?"

George said, "Maybe walk the main avenue, see some of the side streets, get an ice cream, coffee, or a cold drink. We could take Artioli. I bet he would like an ice cream."

Rezarta asked, "Do you think it would be too much to take him?"

Lesley said, "No, I'm sure he would like it, especially something to drink or an ice cream."

Rezarta said, "I'll make us a small lunch first. I was able to buy some spinach from a street vendor, so I made spanakopita."

The rest of the morning George and Lesley told them of their visit to Kassandra. Having to translate for Spiros took time. After lunch they got ready to go out. Artioli was excited that he was going.

As it was Sunday the city had many people out sitting on benches, families strolling pushing baby carriages, and couples walking and enjoying the day. George wondered how many were working and getting paid? Many noticed Lesley and George in their American clothes. More than one male would say hello in English. The woman would just look and smile.

They found the ice cream shop and purchased cones. Artioli received a small one with a few paper napkins.

Lesley said, "They have napkins but no toilet paper."

Spiros said, "They probably got a new shipment from Greece."

Walking on a side street George spotted the young man who belonged to the Peace Corps. When George was just about to say something to attract his attention he also saw George. He walked across the street and greeted the group.

He said in English, "It is good to see you and your wife again. I thought that maybe you had left. I am on my way to a meet some friends. When are you leaving?"

"This is my cousin Spiros, meet John. We are here for two more days. We're leaving here Wednesday."

"Do you have time tomorrow to get together? I would like for you and your wife to meet my sponsored family. Remember, she is a doctor. Your wife and her being in the sciences would probably have a little in common.

I'm sure their conversations about Albania would be interesting. They also are democrats and speak English."

George said to Spiros, "Spiros, I would like to see John tomorrow. Would you like to do that?"

"Maybe. There will be someone to go with you tomorrow whenever you wish, but it might not be me."

George explained that the family always accompanied his wife and him whenever they went out. Spiros just said, 'Someone will go with us.' "So what time and where can we meet?"

"They are being very protective of you. Good for them. Times are difficult here. We could meet at the end of this street and the main avenue. How about ten o'clock?"

"Sounds good to me. Okay, I'll see you tomorrow morning. Good-bye."

Lesley said, "Fancy meeting him again. I would like to talk to an Albanian woman doctor."

They spent another hour or so walking and resting on one of the empty benches. Seeing that the afternoon was passing and that Artioli was getting tired, George put him on his shoulder, and they headed home. When they arrived home Rezarta was lying down, and Aleko was having coffee.

Aleko said, "Kalispera (good afternoon), did you have a good time?" Artioli hugged his father's legs.

George said, "Yes, we had a good walk and refreshments, and we met that Peace Corps man. Lesley and I want to see him tomorrow so we can meet the family who sponsors him. The woman is a doctor."

Lesley said, "Maybe Rezarta will want to go."

Spiros said, "They are to meet not too far from here. We'll ask Rezarta if she wants to go."

Rezarta, coming out of the bedroom and overhearing the conversation said, "I would like meet her. What time?"

George said, "Ten o'clock, Spiros knows the street corner. Do you know the street corner?"

Aleko said, "We'll discuss that issue later. We should get ready to go to Aunt Penelope's home."

George said, "Sounds good, that way we can spend more time there."

After refreshing themselves they squeezed into the car and headed up the mountain. When they arrived, Aunt Penelope's entire family was there already and everyone was busy doing something. Aunt Evanthia had not arrived yet.

They were served preserves and drinks. George sat next to his Aunt Penelope. She held his hand, and they talked about his visit and his leaving. She seemed to be in a saddened state, as her eyes were reddened.

Softly she said, "You must realize how happy I am to have seen you. Your father used to write and tell us about your sister Eli and you. Please tell her I send my love."

She paused and whispered, "I will not be here the next time you return. I have trouble with my heart." With that statement she squeezed George's hand.

George, puzzled as to what to say swallowed hard and said, "Thia (aunt) Penelope I love you very much. My wife and I are very happy to be in your home, and I am greatly honored to be able to hold your hand and look into your eyes. I only wish I could have visited Albania before now."

George held back his tears and put his arm around her and kissed her. Lesley watched with tears, knowing that something intimate was said, and those nearby quieted and watched. The moment was solemn and treasured. The spell was broken as Uncle Sotir, Aunt Evanthia, and young beautiful Sophia entered the room.

The room became alive again with everyone greeting the newly arrived guests. Conversations were mixed, but everyone talked to Lesley and George about their leaving and saying they were hopeful for their return. George told them that he would return but that he didn't know when. Probably the next year, but he didn't want to commit to an exact time. Of course Lesley would return if their free time schedules coincided.

As they were talking a telephone rang. George and Lesley were surprised. This was one of the families privileged enough to have a phone. George wished that he would have seen their name in the book of 388 numbers. He was aware that Penelope's daughter Margarita, and Emir, the husband, were economists, and that maybe they had been connected to the upper echelon of the communist party. Well, that party was no longer in control, but connections to the party were still in existence. What their position was for democracy, George didn't know.

Aunt Evanthia was somewhat cheery, but her cheer seemed to be controlled. She told Lesley and George that they must return some day. Sotir was his quiet self, telling them he was happy to have met them and that he hoped for their return. Sophia was attending with drinks. She finally announced that dinner was to be served. Two tables were set to accommodate the fifteen diners. The dinner was plentiful, with lamb and beef for meat, vegetables consisting of carrots, string beans, eggplant and spinach, the usual tomato onion salad, beer, water, tsipouro, wine, and Fanta for drinks. There were so many toasts to George and Lesley that all the guests' glasses had to be refilled many times; there were many laughs and tears. Lesley received compliments for the toilet paper, which brought laughs. Someone said they saw toilet paper in one store and that was good because they needed to re-supply. That brought many laughs, even from little Artioli.

Lesley said, "I've run out of stock."

When the subject returned to the Americans leaving, sadness entered the space. Everybody took turns expressing their feelings and their thanks for George and Lesley's arrival. Tears flowed as from a fountain, but the fountain was unheard from those sitting next to it.

George rose from his seat unexpectedly, which came as a surprise, as everyone looked in wonderment. He said, "I want to thank all of you for your generous words and expressions of love. Lesley and I are very happy that we are here and that we had the opportunity to sit and talk with all of you. It is time to be joyous for this occasion and for the times we spent together. I can only say thank you, we love you, and we shall return."

That brought cheers in Greek, Albanian, and English. It changed the mood, and the atmosphere was now merry. George sat down and Lesley gave him a kiss. She knew that what he had just said had been well-received.

Hours had passed, the sun had set, and it was time to say good-night and leave. Kisses, handshakes, and good-byes were delivered, and the company dispersed into the night. George felt that one of the final days in Albania was satisfying. Aleko arrived for the ride home.

The ride to the apartment was quiet until Spiros said, "George, I want you to know that your arrival here has brought the family together. It's not that we don't love one another, but our lives are busy, and we don't go out of our way to connect. Thanks for that. And please return. That will guarantee more family gatherings."

Artioli had fallen asleep. Aleko carried him upstairs and put him in his bed. They sat and talked about the evening. Rezarta mentioned that all had gone well, but that Aunt Evanthia seemed somewhat cold in her emotions. Spiros remarked that she shows very little emotion and that she is the distant one in the family. "She has always been like that, maybe because she is the youngest one among her brothers and sisters." He went on to say that at least she attends family gatherings.

George said, "Aunt Penelope said she is sick. She told me it was her heart. I assume she has the same disease that runs in the family. Five of her siblings died early in life from heart problems. Of course, she is seventy-three and older than the ones who died. I'm very happy that I got to meet her. Aunt Stavroula is seventy-two, and she is not feeling well either. They both seemed like very nice ladies. Evanthia is sixty-seven and is very lively in her steps and walks erect. She seems like a nice lady, but different."

Spiros said, "Yes, the two older aunts are both pleasant. I already said something about Evanthia. It's not that I don't like her, but I could never get close to her, and others in the family feel the same way."

Rezarta was tired and went to bed. Soon everyone decided to retire also. George and Lesley knew that their time in Albania was coming to a close. Only two full days left. Lesley cuddled up to George as they fell asleep.

Chapter XXVII

In the morning the household was somewhat solemn. Aleko had gone to work early, telling Rezarta that he would be home to take George and Lesley back to Glifada after their early dinner at Olympia's. Rezarta reminded him that they were to meet the Peace Corps man at ten o'clock and that she was going to go, as she wanted to meet the female doctor. It would probably be midday when they would return. Maybe he should come home about then.

"I'll come around three and take them to Olympia's," he said.

After breakfast George and Lesley showered separately. Artioli was playing with George, Lesley having finished dressing, walked into the kitchen. Spiros was playing solitaire. Rezarta was sitting looking out the kitchen window.

Artioli looked at Lesley and said, "I want to marry Lesley."

Everybody turned to Artioli with a surprised expression, except Lesley. She didn't know what he had said. Everybody wondered what had brought that on. Rezarta told Lesley what Artioli had said. A large smile overtook her face. With that, everyone laughed softly.

Rezarta asked, "When do want to do that?"

"When I get big."

Lesley replied through a translator, "I'm already married."

George said, "She is married to me."

Artioli shrugged his shoulders and said, "She can marry me." With that he left the room to get toys.

No one understood what had brought that on. Maybe it was because Lesley was dressed in a beautiful dress and looked very pretty. Rezarta couldn't wait to tell Aleko. George said he was going to tell little Nicholas in Glifada. Maybe they both would fight over her when they got older. With that everyone laughed. It was nearing ten o'clock, the time to meet the Peace Corps man and the doctor. Spiros was staying home with Casanova Artioli.

The three walked to the meeting place and saw John talking to a young man. As the group was approaching, the two men were saying good-bye, and the man turned around and walked away.

"Hi John, nice to see you again," George said. This is Rezarta; she is married to my cousin, and she speaks English. She is a teacher here. My wife Lesley is excited to meet the doctor. You did say she spoke English."

"Yes, but unfortunately she had to go to the hospital on an emergency call. She sends her apology. She didn't know when she would free."

Lesley said, "I understand. Tell her I met Rezarta's doctor and he lacked medical equipment. He asked for help. I'm sure the hospital is in need also. When I return home I'm going to try and send donated supplies. Can I have her address, and a telephone number?"

Retrieving her address book, paper, and a pen they swapped addresses. Lesley said, "Well that ends that. We are leaving later today to go back to the village, and we are scheduled for a dinner here. We're leaving for Greece on Wednesday. If and when we return, we can meet her. Tell her I was looking forward to meeting her."

John suggested having a coffee and a dessert. Everyone agreed. Not too far from where they met there was a small coffee shop that sold baked goods. Rezarta knew the place but hadn't been there in a long while. She was satisfied, because she didn't want to walk too far.

The shop was quaint and decorated with prints of Albanian people dressed in various folkloric clothes. One print reminded George of a photograph of his great- grandfather wearing knee-high leather boots and blousy pants; that photographic image was now in his possession. Everyone had coffee and a baked pastry; George paid. The conversation went to John. Interestingly, everyone spoke English.

Lesley asked, "John. Where are you from?"

"Indiana."

"How long have you been in Albania?"

"About four months. I arrived in June. There were twenty-one volunteers. We had an intense ten-week course in learning the language and about Albanian customs. Each of us was placed with a family. It has been very interesting."

Rezarta asked, "What do you do here, and do you find our country very different?"

"I'm here to teach English. And, oh yes, very different, especially with the shortage of goods, food, etcetera. It is nothing like home. The countryside and the Ionian and Adriatic Seas are beautiful. I've been to Saranda and Butrint. As for the language, living with a family makes it easier. I make mistakes of course. They correct me, so now I am getting more fluent. You can try me out if you want."

"No, I don't want to test you. Besides, practicing my English is better for me. What changes here did you find the most different?"

"Your toilets. In America every home has a sitting flush toilet, except maybe in the rural back-country or when camping. I was told that the only flush toilet in Albania is here in Gjirokaster, (Argirocastro) in Enver Hoxha's home. Not even the hotels have them."

Rezarta replied, "I've never seen one except on television. Maybe some day I will have one."

John asked Rezarta, "Are you a Greek-Albanian? What does your name represent?"

"No, I am Albanian. I learned Greek by being married to one, and I learned English in school. My name means Golden Shine,"

George said, "How beautiful! You do very well speaking Greek and translating in English to Lesley."

"Thank you."

Lesley said, "Golden Shine! I love your name."

John asked George, "What village does your family live in?"

"I have relatives in Glifada, Kassandra, Morista, Tirana, and here. I was also told that there are some in Fier, Vlora, and Permet, and maybe

more in other places. I have only been here and the three villages. We will
not get to visit those other places. Maybe next time. It has been wonderful
visiting just these. It took me over two years of trying to get here. I couldn't
get a visa, but I am here and I'm thankful for that."

Lesley said, "Amen to that."

They sat watching pedestrians and finishing their pastries. George
asked if anybody wanted anything else. They all said no.

Not knowing what else to do in Argirocastro, George said, "We should
go home. We have to get ready for our last dinner here. Rezarta should rest
some. She's having her baby next month. She didn't want to walk too far
today, so we can't walk around. I guess we had better go. It was great seeing
you. We have your address here, and you have ours. Please keep in touch.
I want to know how things go for you. Thanks for trying to introduce us
to your doctor sponsor. She must be a good person."

John replied, "I'll write. Have a safe trip home. Good-bye everyone."

With that they walked home. Artioli was happy to see his mom and
Spiros was playing solitaire. Rezarta went to the bedroom to lie down.
George and Lesley wanted to freshen up and relax before a joyous and
difficult night.

Aleko returned home as everyone was preparing for the dinner. He
showered and dressed in clean clothes. By then everyone was prepared to
leave. Artioli was excited and hung on to George. They got into the car
and drove to Olympia's home. It was a short walk, but Aleko didn't want
Rezarta to have to walk both ways. Rezarta also decided she wanted to
go to Glifada for the ride and to say good-bye there; they would drop off
Spiros and Artioli at the apartment on the way.

When they arrived at Kostas and Olympia's, Kostas opened the door.
As usual, George entered first, with Lesley behind him. They were greeted
by Kostas and Olympia's daughter and husband, Zoietsa, and George,
as well as Margarita, Anthula, and Dimitri. Olympia walked out of the
kitchen. The greetings and the kisses seemed to take forever. Finally they
managed to settle down for preserves and drinks. Everybody asked George
and Lesley where they had traveled and whom they had visited. When the
subject of conversation turned to Lesley and George's departing, the tears

and sobs seemed to overtake the situation. Even little Artioli cried, for he realized that George and Lesley were leaving.

George decided he needed to say something, "This is a beautiful family gathering. I would like for us to be celebrating a happy occasion. Tears are beautiful also, but I would like for us to cheer and celebrate our arrival and meeting all of you. We will return and write and make phone calls when you get telephones (that brought a few laughs). It is not a departure forever. Lesley and I are looking forward to our return. We might be a little bit older then, but it will be another exhilarating visit. We'll have these present memories to talk about. And your country will be in a better situation. Time is on your hands, and it will improve."

Olympia announced that dinner would be served. This broke the spell, and they went to eat a fabulous meal, cooked by the family's favorite cook. There were a few different items on the table beside the usual, including sausages, sardines, and pasta. Olympia had made spanakopita-like pie using corn meal and squash. Everything was tasty and plentiful. Wine was served, along with coffee, tsipouro, Heineken beer, and Fanta for the young ones.

When the group finished eating they decided to take their drinks and go outside to the long upstairs porch. It was a warm evening. George sat down on a couch, with Lesley on one side and Anthula on the other. Anthula put her arm around George and left it there.

George apologized to Margarita, Anthula, and Dimitri for not visiting their homes. "There were so many places and travels to the villages, and then back here, it became impossible. I did tell Vassilis to tell you of our commitments whenever he sees you. He did inform me that you would be here today."

Margarita replied, "I understand. You can visit when you return. Maybe my husband will be home. You can then meet your cousin."

The family gave gifts to George and Lesley. Olympia gave Lesley some hand-made crocheted doilies, Margarita gave George a wooden plaque etched with an Albanian scene, Kostas gave George a brass shoe horn, and Anthula gave an embossed hand-made cotton handkerchief. Rezarta handed George a large crocheted doily with raised rosettes. Artioli gave kisses. All the presents were unexpected but well received.

When leaving, as they kissed good-bye, George gave the Kostas' family and Margarita and the children fifty American dollars each. He also reminded Anthula about the dictionaries. No one looked at the amount. They just said thank you. He would give Spiros and his family money later. He would leave all the remaining leks and drachmas with Vassilis but keep a few drachmas for travel to Ioannina where he could go to a bank and draw money with their credit card. Albania's banks had not yet established credit cards, and George's family had no knowledge of them.

Leaving was difficult, but they managed to drop off Spiros and Artioli. Aleko went quickly up to get George's and Lesley's luggage.

While George was giving Spiros his money he said, "Vassilis told me I am the oldest man in the family. He claimed that made me the Patriarch. Because I live in America and you are the oldest man living here you are the Patriarch."

Spiros, kissing George, said, "Thank you." His face had a wide accepting grin.

Artioli didn't want George to leave, for he realized that George was going far away. He stood on the front steps with Spiros, calling George's name, waiving and sobbing as they drove away.

It was still light when they arrived at Glifada, but the sun was lower in the sky. Aleko asked George, "Do you mind if we leave? I don't want to leave Rezarta alone in the car."

"No, not at all. We're okay. I want to thank both of you for your hospitality and your generosity and for allowing us to stay in your home and taking us touring in the city. You know we love you both. Have a safe and happy childbirth."

Lesley said, "We can't say enough to thank you. My love to both of you. I'll write and keep in touch."

Rezarta said, "I love you both. Mirupafshim, mirupafshim."

George said, "Rezarta, I don't understand what you are saying?"

With the sun sparkling off a tear, she said, "That means good-bye in Albanian. I wanted to say it in my language. Mirupafshim."

Lesley and George repeated the word. George gave them money and some for Artioli and their new arrival. Rezarta and Aleko waived while driving away. As Lesley and George climbed the mountain they repeated the word for good-bye: mirupafshim. They walked quietly hand in hand with tears in their eyes as the colors in the western sky were forming on the few cumulus clouds.

Vassilis and Violetta were waiting for George and Lesley to arrive. When they knocked on the door and Vassilis saw them alone he said, "This is the second time you walked up the mountain alone."

George said, "I was not alone, Lesley was with me."

With a smile Vassilis said, "You know what I mean."

"Just teasing. Rezarta and Aleko drove us home, and Aleko didn't want to leave her alone while he walked with us. I wouldn't leave her either. We're okay, and it is still light out. No problem."

Vassilis said, "How did it go, seeing the relatives?"

"Everything went well, but there were a lot of sad faces and too many tears. We received some beautiful hand-made small gifts. Aunt Evanthia told Olympia that she was coming to the dinner, but she never arrived. I hope nothing happened.

Vassilis nodded his head sideways, "I'm not surprised."

"It is difficult to leave, but we had a marvelous time. Now we pack and spend the day here tomorrow."

Violetta asked if anybody wanted coffee. Everyone said yes. Lesley followed Violetta into the kitchen. Aunt Amalia and Nicholas were finishing their dinner. Nicholas loudly said Lesley's name. Amalia told him to be quiet and eat. Violetta carried the cups of coffee on a tray to the men on the front porch, and Lesley and Violetta sat with them, holding their coffees in their hands.

Vassilis said, "Thomas and Alex are going to take you to Kakavia. They'll drop by early tomorrow to see what time."

George said, "Lesley and I discussed the time. We thought that three to four o'clock would be a good time to leave. We would get a hotel for the night and find a place to eat. That way we could spend most of the day here,"

Violetta asked, "Do you want something to eat?"

Lesley and George both said they were not hungry. They sat there relating their stay in Argirocastro, and how much everyone was so generous and giving, considering the state of the country. In the meantime, Nicholas came out and sat on Lesley's lap until Aunt Amalia came out and told him it was bed time. Reluctantly he went inside.

Vassilis said, "Your arrival here brought some of the family together. As in most families there are disagreements. This family is no different. Some have not seen each other for some time, or they don't talk to each other. There are some in Argirocastro that you didn't meet, and no one mentioned them. In this village that has not happened. We all get along."

George said, "I'm sorry to hear that, but I understand. Maybe we can meet those others when we return."

Violetta said, "Aunt Evanthia has a daughter in Argirocastro who married a blind musician. Now Evanthia won't talk to her, and the daughter has two daughters. The daughter is a nice lady. We see her once in a while, but not too often. Her daughters are beautiful. They are teenagers now. No one in the family understands Evanthia."

George said, "That's too bad. She tried to help me to get here. It is too complicated for me to comprehend. Family politics, it's everywhere."

With the night passing, and the lights in the village flickering twice, it was time to retire. Lesley and George went to sleep for their last night in Albania,

Chapter XXVIII

The village roosters greeted the American visitors with vigor. Although there had been recent rain showers, today was clear and sunny. Violetta had coffee ready, as well as fried dough, buttered eggs, milk, coffee, bread, salami, feta, honey, and yogurt. Aunt Amalia greeted them with kisses and a wide smile. George had only dough and coffee. Lesley ate a hearty meal. Nicholas was outside playing.

Violetta said, "Vassilis is at work, but he will be home later. George, eat some more."

"I'm sorry. I'm not too hungry this morning, but I'll have another cup of coffee."

No one said anything. Yesterday and last night had been very difficult emotionally. George felt drained thinking of his departure, leaving his family so far away in a country that was desperately poor. Their meat was rationed, but they gave George and Lesley their share. They had little money, but they did their best to provide. The family was aware of his sadness because of leaving, which made them sadder. George did his best to hold up, but he found it difficult.

Alex arrived after breakfast to find out what time he was to drive to Kakavia. George and Lesley agreed that they wanted to leave at three. Alex said he wanted to show them the lake which serves as a reservoir on the other side of the valley.

"It's a short drive from here. There is large village above the lake. You can see the night lights from here. Would you like to go?"

George, thinking that it might break his thoughts about leaving, said, "Lesley, would you like to do that?"

"Sounds interesting, as long as we don't take too long. I have a little more preparation to do."

George said, "We can go, but we can't stay too long."

Alex said, "We can go right now."

Alex told Violetta where they were going and that they would return soon. With that, Alex said that his car was on the other side of the ravine. They walked quickly on a direct trail to Alex's car and rode down a rough and bumpy so-called road.

As they headed south they approached a paved road that was in better condition than the main highway. It switch-backed up a mountain, passing a large lake, and a section that was tree-lined. The view was spectacular. George took some photos, and they continued further. Alex drove into a large village and parked in the main plaza. There were men sitting, smoking, and talking everywhere; fewer women were seen. Alex told them this is a Turkish village.

George said, "I want to take some pictures. What is this place called?"

"Libohovo."

There was a teenager sitting on a donkey. George pointed his camera, and the boy gave him an approving nod. As he went to take his picture the boy smiled and gave George the peace sign and a wide grin. There was a line of men squatting against a wall. Some smiled, some just looked as the camera clicked; a couple of men waived. Alex took them to a large oak tree in the plaza that stood beside a flowing stream. He said it came from a spring and the water was good to drink. The water was clear, but there was trash in the stream.

Alex tried to buy cold drinks in two places, but there was only coffee available. He said, "All these men have no jobs. They come here to talk and see friends. Albania is in tough times."

George said, "I hope it doesn't last too long. It is poor enough here already."

After walking through the plaza they decided that it was time to go home. As Alex was proceeding down the mountain the car's oil light came on. George told him to stop. Alex checked the level of the oil in the motor and saw that it was full. George told Alex that maybe the sensor that tells if you have oil is faulty. Alex drove to his parking place near his grandmother's home.

Alex said, "I'll see you at three on the road. Thanks for taking the ride."

George, "Thank you, and keep an eye on your oil, and see about getting that part fixed. We'll stop quickly to see your grandmother and say good-bye. Bye."

Alex drove down the mountain bouncing over the rough road. George and Lesley walked the short distance to Aunt Ana's. Thomas was harvesting grapes and Ana was crocheting. They greeted each other, and George told them that Alex had taken them to Libohovo and that he would meet them at three to take them to Kakavia.

George told his aunt how good she looked and how happy he was to have met her. She left to make coffee after thanking him and giving him a kiss. She returned with preserves and coffee. They visited for a short time and said that they had to leave to pack.

Thomas said, "I'm going to Kakavia with you. Vassilis has to work, but he will see you off."

George said, "Good. We'll see you then. Good-bye thia, take care of yourself. I love you."

Lesley said good-bye and kissed Aunt Ana. George reached in his pocket and gave her some money. She thanked him, and they kissed good-bye. They departed and walked across the ravine, seeing the village from this view point for the last time. Nicholas and Violetta were on the porch to greet them. It was past noontime, and Vassilis had returned home. Eleni, Vassilis' sister had arrived.

Vassilis said, "You arrived alone again."

George said, "We came from Aunt Ana's home; it's only across the way. Vassilis, can I see you privately?"

They walked into George's bedroom. George said, reaching into his pocket, "Vassilis, I want to give you the leks, some drachmas, and American dollars to give to Eleni and to Aunt Ollga and Theodore, and also Aunt Evanthia. Divide it up equally or whatever you think is best. I'm giving you and your family American money. Don't say no. You have been very generous, and we thank you."

Vassilis accepted the money and said, "Thank you. I'll do as you wanted."

With the guests and family sitting, everyone tried to get comfortable. Violetta changed into a red dress (depicting love) and brought the baby out for George and Lesley to see again. They took turns holding him. There was no sobbing, but everyone had tears; Aunt Amalia joined the group tearfully. It wasn't long before Thomas and Spiros arrived. Alex went and got Spiros, as he wanted to be there. Nicholas stood next to Lesley as he went in and out of the house many times. Lesley decided to get George's camera and take a group picture. George took some also. The conversations finally led to thanks for everything from George and Lesley, and the family wished them safe travel and thanked them for traveling to their homes and to Albania.

During these conversations Nicholas came into the house smoking a cigarette. Where he got it no one had a clue, but Spiros took it away from him. Nicholas had no reaction. When he went out people laughed softly, so he couldn't hear them.

Vassilis said, "Can you believe my son?"

That seemed to break the ice, but by then it was time to walk down the mountain for the last time. Amalia would stay with Nicholas; he said he didn't want to go. Violetta and Lesley walked together with their arms around each other. Eleni held George's hand. Thomas carried George's bag, and Spiros carried Lesley's. Vassilis carried the baby, and he and Spiros led the way. They walked in this manner all the way to the bottom.

Alex was not at the bottom of the hill. Thomas mentioned that he had to buy gas. They waited about thirty minutes, but everyone was patient. George explored the area looking at the flowers and plants. Vassilis said one was chicory and another was oregano. George found a woody mushroom similar to those in New England.

Thomas spotted the red Audi. When Alex stopped he said he'd had trouble finding gas. Everyone was glad he did. Everyone kissed except Thomas. Vassilis hugged and kissed George fervently. George could see that he was holding back tears. Everyone else was crying. George and Thomas got into the back of the car, and Lesley was told to sit in the front, and off they went, waving and blowing kisses.

Alex played Greek music on his tape player. The music was soothing to the soul and calmed the situation. Thomas put his hand over George's hand and moved his hand with the music. When they reached the border crossing George, Lesley and Thomas got out. Lesley gave Alex twenty dollars. George gave Alex fifty dollars and the same amount to his father. They kissed Alex good-bye and passed through the Albanian custom's to have their passports stamped. Thomas carried their luggage through the gates and spoke to the Albanian officers. When they approached the Greek gate there were many Albanians crowding the gate, trying to get into Greece.

The Greek official was chaining the gate because they were not letting any more Albanians through. One of the officials spotted Lesley and motioned her through, which was surprising, and George flashed his passport. They got through easily, but when Thomas tried they stopped him. He told them he was helping his relatives, and he wanted to make sure they hired a taxi or got on a bus. George told the official that Thomas was his cousin. Reluctantly they let him through. Lesley and George got their passports stamped, and they were now officially in Greece.

Thomas went outside and saw a taxi. He asked George, "Do you want to take a taxi or a bus? You will have to wait for the bus."

"We want a taxi."

Thomas approached the taxi and returned. "He will take you for five thousand drachmas ($30.00)," he said.

They got into the taxi, thanked Thomas, and said good-bye. The taxi took off and went down the paved road. They could see Thomas disappearing into the building. There were two men in the taxi who lived in Albania. The driver was Theo, and his companion was Michael. They lived in a village called Goranxi. They knew Vassilis and Thomas, and Michael's wife worked with Vassilis. George thought, "What a small world.

Or had the family made arrangements for them to be there assuring that we would have a safe ride to Ioannina?"

The ride was enjoyable and not too fast, and the conversations were interesting. Before long they arrived in Ioannina, a large Greek city. George told them to take them to a class B hotel. They left them at the Palladion, got paid, and drove away.

George and Lesley showered together and went out to see the city. After walking a few streets and viewing the shops they saw an interesting looking restaurant that served home-style Greek dishes. They entered and ordered food. Sitting there, Lesley spotted the two taxi drivers across the street. George went out and hailed them to come for beers. They gladly accepted.

George and Lesley ordered chicken lemon soup, trout, eggplant, okra, salad and one half liter Heineken beer each. The meal came with bread. They told the Albanians to order what they wanted. They ordered stuffed green peppers, trout, orzo, salad, and Heinekens. Everyone had another beer.

The Albanians, knowing that this couple spoke English, asked that they say the names of all the food dishes in English; they repeated the names. The owner of the restaurant listened and laughed. The entire cost was 6200 drachmas ($45.00). The Albanians offered to take them to their hotel, but George refused, saying they wanted to walk. The men departed, and the owner approached George and thanked him for buying their meals. He was aware that they were Greeks who lived in Albania, and he was also aware of the troubled situation encompassing Albania.

Lesley and George started walking toward Lake Pamvotida, as they had decided to take a ferry ride, but it began to sprinkle. The sprinkle was brief, but they turned toward the hotel. As they passed the same restaurant the owner came out, and seeing George's camera he asked George to take a picture of him. He removed his apron and then he put it back on as he stood in the doorway. When he finished George took his picture, He gave his business card and asked for a photograph. George said he would mail him one. They returned to the hotel, watched some TV, went to bed early, and made love.

Boy on donkey

Soviet tractor

Greek restaurant and owner

Libohovo jobless men

Spiros, George, and Thomas

Two friendly Libohovo men

Chapter XXIX

The next morning after a continental breakfast at the hotel, George and Lesley went to the bank for money and hired a taxi to Metsovo. There was an old monastery, Saint Nicholas, that they wanted to visit. It had been built in the 1300s, and the walls were decorated with beautiful icons. The monastery was abandon in 1700, and travelers used it for shelter. They had fires inside the building, and over the centuries soot coated the icons. A visitor removed some soot and found the underlying icons in perfect condition. The monastery was restored in 1960.

They tried to get plane reservation to Athens. The flights were all booked, but they could get plane reservations from Preveza. The trip would be similar to George's arrival, but in reverse. They returned to their hotel to rest. They spent the evening on the lake having a dinner of octopus, calamari, pilaf, salad, and they split a liter of beer.

After another continental breakfast the next morning they walked to the old Turkish fort on a hill overlooking the lake. The fort had been used when the Goths attacked the city, in the year 551. It was manned under the Ottoman Turkish ruler, Ali Pasha, 1743-1822. In a museum on site were costumes of Turks and Greeks, ancient artifacts, old paintings, and old Epirus music for sale. George purchased a set of Epirus music. They returned to their favorite restaurant for a light lunch, shopped, and George purchased two icons.

They returned to their hotel and checked out, took a bus to Preveza, arrived at 3:20 p.m., got a hotel room, and then booked a flight to Athens for the next day; they wouldn't have to pay until they picked up their tickets.

George and Lesley went strolling along the waterfront until 6 p.m. They met an English tourist who advised them to visit a good fish restaurant that had vats of wine. They arrived at the restaurant at 7:30 p.m. and had a meal of small sardine-size red fish, rice, greens, salad, feta, Kalamata olives, bread, and one half liter of white wine. It cost 2600 drachmas ($17.00).

When they had arrived in Preveza it appeared to George and Lesley that the town was deserted, but after their meal they decided to go for a stroll, and it seemed to them that the town's entire population had decided to join them. They went to a quaint coffee shop and paid 900 drachmas ($6.00) for two coffees and kataifis (baklava-type using shredded wheat instead of philo dough). They returned to their hotel to prepare for their trip to Athens.

When they arose, at 7:00 a.m., there was no hot water, and there was much more noise than there had been the villages. George, wanting more drachmas, said they need to go to a bank. Walking the main street Lesley saw a bank that opened at 8:00 a.m. They entered, but they had to wait until 8:30 a.m. to exchange money. With more money, they purchased their tickets for 96000 drachmas ($32.00 each) for a flight to Athens that left at 1:25 p.m.

George saw a restaurant with a sign advertising eggs, toast, juice, and Nescafe coffee for 700 drachmas, less than $5.00. They told the waitress they wanted only plain toast. The toast came with a slice of cheese and a slice of ham. After breakfast they toured the city's center, went to the airport, and flew to Athens. Boarding was easy, and the flight seemed quick.

In Athens their taxi driver located a decent hotel within walking distance of the center of the city. Having had a busy morning and the flight, they decided to take it easy for the rest of the day. They could shower with hot water, change clothes, rest, and have dinner in the Plaka (Athen's famous area of restaurants and shops). They had two full days to tour the city.

Sitting in a restaurant after dusk, they had an excellent night-time view of the lit Acropolis. They had a wonderful Greek meal with all the fixings. Arm-in-arm they walked the narrow Plaka streets with all the Greeks and tourists.

The next two days they visited the tourist areas and hiked up the Acropolis, walked through the Parthenon, toured the Dionysus Theater, visited Omonia Square, walked to Syntagma square to see the Parliament building and watched the changing of the guards in front of the tomb of the Unknown Soldier. They viewed two museums, explored the ancient Agra, and completing their religious duty they entered the Orthodox Cathedral and lit candles. The weather cooperated, as the days were sunny and not too hot. To top this off they ate in a different restaurant for every meal.

George was proud of his Greek heritage, and he now felt more Greek than ever. Lesley could sense his feelings, and she was happy that they had been able to visit family in Albania, and also to see parts of Greece. Before they knew it, it was the 29th of September and time to go home.

Mirupafshim!

PART TWO

Chapter XXX

George was sitting in seat 16L, non-smoking, next to a sixty-two year old Italian man and his wife. They were returning to their native village east of Rome, called Pescaria. They now lived in Southbridge, Massachusetts. It is September 6, 1994; at 5:43 p.m. and George is alone as Lesley could not make the return trip to Albania.

The plane's engines roared and it is in takeoff mode at 5:46 p.m. In a matter of seconds it was lift-off. George sitting next to a window seat saw autos, different colored roof tops, and people playing baseball in a park, and then the plane entered into a light overcast.

George was flying on Alitalia airlines to Rome then to Athens, and then a flight on Olympic Airlines to Iaoninna, Greece. The plane had gained altitude, above were some spotty clouds, and the plane should be leveling off soon. The sky was clearing with the dark blue Atlantic below and the lighter blue sky above. His Greek-Albanian family was looking forward to his return.

When George went through the arched metal detector at the airport it sounded the alarm. He had to remove his belt which had a large buckle. After showing his boarding pass to enter the plane he was intercepted by two men dressed in suits and ties in the jet way; George approached the men and stopped. One man asked for his passport, the other man asked where he was going, for how long, and what George did for work. George looked at them straight in the eyes and answered their questions. George told them he was going to Albania for about a month and he was a retired electronic researcher. The man holding his passport explained to George that if he had over ten thousand dollars it had to be declared by law. He then asked George how much money he had in his possession. George told him he had seven hundred and fifty dollars in cash and a credit card. The man told George that he could proceed.

Some of the passengers asked George what was that confrontation all about. George explained to them the circumstances that had transpired. They said they had never seen customs or any officials there before and they were surprised by the confrontation. George had never seen that before either, but he had nothing to hide or fear.

During the overnight flight George and the Italian couple exchanged their itineraries. When the couple heard that George was going to Albania they inquired about the country as they knew little about Albania and were totally unaware of its problems. As George briefly explained its past history, and what he had experienced on his last visit with the family, and also the country's predicament, the lady reached into her pocketbook and handed George ten dollars and told George to give it to a child. George was reluctant to take the money, but the woman was persistent. George took the money and told her he would honor her request and thanked her. When going their separate ways in the Roman airport they hugged and kissed good-bye.

George departed Rome after a seven hour stopover and then took a flight to Athens. He arrived in Athens in two hours. George went to a bank at the airport and exchanged American dollars for drachmas (Greek money). The exchange rate was 239 drachmas for one dollar. He taxied to the domestic airport and boarded the flight to Iaoninna and arrived in two and half hours. On the domestic flight his seat companion was a five year old cute Greek girl with deep blue eyes and black curly hair. He helped her with her seat belt. She was quiet but she smiled after he finished.

On arrival in Iaoninna George taxied to the Hotel Palladin where he stayed on his last visit, checked in, stored his luggage in the room, and walked to the HBH Restaurant. The same restaurant when he ate with Lesley and the two Albanian men on their return to Greece. As George was looking at the menu the owner recognized George. They exchanged hellos.

George had a tasty meal of orzo (rice shaped pasta), roasted eggplant, lamb, feta and olives, and bread with a glass of ouzo. The cost was 1650 Greek drachmas ($6.90). George took pictures of the owner and the owner paid for George's beer.

George returned to his hotel room and went to bed. He had not slept since he left America, almost two days. George knew that he needed a good night's sleep. He had told the desk clerk to give him a wake-up call at 8:30 a.m. He had a disturbing sleep waking up a few times during the night. He was aware that it will take him a few days to adjust to the jet lag and to adjust to being in Albania again.

He awoke at 7:30 a.m. and called the desk clerk that he did not need the wake-up call. He showered, dressed, and went to eat breakfast in the hotel. He ordered coffee, orange juice, bread that came with a thin slice of cheese, and a thin slice of cake, the cost was 1200 drachmas ($5.02). George sat next to a married couple living in Belfast. They exchanged their travel itineraries. The couple was interested in George's travel to Albania. He explained the conditions in Albania on his last visit, and that he was told that some things had improved. After breakfast George shopped in a market and bought grapes and nectarines to snack on the way to the border. He went to a school supply shop, because he forgot to bring any pens. George purchased three pens as he wanted to keep notes about his travels.

George returned to the hotel, paid his bill and hired a taxi for the hour ride to Kakavia. The driver was quiet, pleasant, and smiled a lot. George shared his grapes and nectarines; the grapes were green, with seeds, and very sweet.

Approximately two miles from the custom building at Kakavia (the border crossing) three Greek soldiers stopped the taxi and asked George for his passport. After seeing his passport they said he could continue. There were many soldiers on the road as the taxi proceeded, and then they saw a long line of trucks stopped up ahead. A Greek policeman stopped the taxi and told them they could not proceed any further. If George wanted to enter into Albania he had to walk the rest of the way. George could see that there was room for the taxi to drive to the custom's building, but he didn't want to argue with the policeman. George paid the driver 7,000 drachmas ($29.29) and walked one thousand feet to the custom's building.

There were many people mingling inside and outside the Greek custom's building. With his passport in his hands and held so everyone could see it was not Greek or Albanian, George passed through the crowd, approached the desk, and handed it to the official behind the counter. The official seeing that it was an American passport stamped George's passport and told George that he could enter into Albania, but be careful; there are some problems between Albania and Greece. George thought no wonder there was a traffic situation and all those people mingling. George went through the gate and entered the no-man passage way. There were three people walking towards the Greek custom gate. He was the only one walking to enter Albania.

George entered the shabby Albanian custom's office and handed his passport to a different official than on his last visit. He asked George where he was going and who he was staying with. George told him. There was a woman standing in the office and she spoke up and said she knew Vassilis Stamos when George mentioned his name. The official stamped George's passport with a smile on his face. This encounter was friendlier than George's last entrance.

At the same time George was having his passport checked in the office a Dutchman was also having his passport checked and they seemed to be giving him some trouble asking many questions. They also made him pay fifteen hundred drachmas ($6.27) to enter. They never asked George for any money.

Entering Albania there were about fifty persons standing at the gate trying to go to Greece. The Albanian policemen were physically pushing them to leave. This created a large commotion and anger from many individuals. Similar to the Greek border, the Albanian border was stacked with many trucks, cars, men, women, police, and soldiers.

George had written to Vassilis and told of his arrival time. Vassilis had written back and acknowledged the timing of George's arrival. George arrived at the border at 10:30 a.m., an hour earlier than expected, so he knew he had about an hour wait.

George was approached by many individuals saying, "Taxi, taxi."

George firmly replied, "No, no, no." They finally left him alone.

Similar to his first visit George was approached by a young man of twenty-three years. He said in English to George, "I see that you refused to hire a taxi many times. Are you waiting for someone?"

George replied, "Yes, my relatives. Why is it so crowded with all these people and taxis? What's going on? By the way how do know I speak English?

"I saw your passport in your hands and I knew it wasn't Albanian or Greek because of the color. I assumed you spoke English."

The man explained that Greece and Albania were having political problems. No one seemed to be able to leave or enter either country. Luckily, George had no problem with an American passport. He felt fortunate.

George and the young man conversed for thirty minutes, mostly about America, when George decided to walk to one of the many vendors to get a drink. The young man was kind enough to carry George's valise. George paid for two sodas. After finishing the soda George decided he better go back to the gate so the family could find him among the crowd.

Approaching the gate George saw Spiros, Aleko, Rezarta, and Artioli. After all the kissing and greetings they told George that Aunt Evanthia, Aunt Penelope, Vassilis, Violetta, Eleni, and Olympia were there, but they didn't know where. Aleko took George's luggage and walked to their newer car, a yellow Ford Escort. Rezarta and Spiros left to find the family. They returned and said they couldn't find them, so everyone got into the Ford and went down the hill towards the village of Glifada. When they reached the main road they saw soldiers on trucks with rifles and hauling artillery cannons heading south. The family told George that the two countries were having trouble, but they wouldn't elaborate.

Arriving at Glifada, Spiros stayed with the car and everyone else walked up the mountain towards Vassilis' home. When they arrived at the house Aunt Amalia was sitting on the porch with the two boys. After George kissed and hugged her she giggled quietly and went into the kitchen. It wasn't a long time after that when Violetta and Vassilis returned along with Olympia and Eleni. Knowing that George would be with Violetta and Vassilis, Aleko, Rezarta, and Olympia said they had to go, but would see George soon.

Eleni explained, "When we arrived at the border we looked for you, and when we didn't see you we were afraid that you went with one of the taxi divers, and they are known to be bad persons. But we also knew that you had been there because when we checked with the custom officials to see if a George Stamos had been there, the official said an American man about forty years old with a mustache and the initials of GS had passed through customs and went away in a taxi. We are happy that you are in Glifada and you arrived safely."

George said, "I'm happy to be safely here also."

Violetta and Eleni went into the kitchen to prepare a lunch. George, Vassilis and Nicholas sat on the porch as Alex had gone inside with his mother. Eleni served the men their coffees.

During food preparations, Aunt Ollga, the aunt that lived in the village, visited briefly with her two sons and one son's wife with her two children. Two other family members dropped by just to say hello, as did Ziko Goritsas, the science teacher who spoke some English. After the visitors brief visits they returned to their home, except for Eleni. Of course, drinks and preserves had been served to everyone.

It wasn't long after the visitors left that Violetta came out to the porch and said, "I've prepared lunch. Please come in to eat."

Violetta and Eleni had prepared a handsome looking lunch. George could see that this meal was plentiful, no rationing of meat or bread. Violetta served okra, rice, beef, bread, yogurt, apples, peaches, wine, and last but not least, watermelon. Like on his last visit to Albania George inspired another cheer for the watermelon growers.

George noticed that because the food was plentiful the family did not have to apologize for lack of anything. After finishing eating and sitting at the table, Violetta and Eleni asked George if wanted to visit the new church in the village.

George asked, "You have a church here?"

Eleni answered, "Yes. It was an old chapel, but was closed by Enver Hoxha. The village people wanted a church here again, so some villagers supplied what they could to open it as a church. It is beautiful."

George being surprised about hearing of a church in the village said, "I would love to see it. When can we go?"

Violetta said, "Let's go now. It will only take a few minutes to get there. I'll go get the key." She went to her bedroom and returned with the key. Why Violetta had a key George did not ask.

It only took a few minutes to walk to the church. It was off to one side of the village and down the mountain some, and not near any home. That is why the villagers kept the church locked. The church's dimensions were approximately sixteen feet by twenty feet. There were some small windows on two sides, and with enough light inside they entered. The walls were decorated with small framed icons, and a small altar was at one end of the building. Behind the altar there were more framed icons. George left some drachmas where they had candles and said a prayer. When George had finished they went outside and Violetta locked the door. The returned walk home was solemn. George felt elated that the village had a church again.

When they returned home they were told that Kristos had made a brief visit with his daughter and granddaughter, but they had to leave for Agyrokastro. George told Violetta that he would like to have a cup of sketos coffee and sit on the porch. Eleni and Vassilis joined George with Violetta going in and out catering to George's needs.

Sitting on the porch and viewing the surroundings, George spent the rest of the afternoon relaxing and asking about the family. He was happy that he had returned and sitting there he felt like he was home again. They asked George about Lesley and his family, and he in return asked about everyone in Albania. Vassilis told George that he now had his own business and was making twenty dollars a day. George understood that Vassilis was doing quite well for an Albanian worker. The afternoon seemed to slip away as the sun was on its way across the ocean to America. And after a few cups of coffee Violetta said dinner was ready.

George noticed again that the food was varied and plentiful because

Violetta served salad, liver with potatoes, a leafy green vegetable, Amstel beer, and fruit with yogurt. With the sun set, and George feeling tired and sleepy, and his need to adjust to the jet lag, he felt that he required a good night's sleep as he would be busy with visiting and adjusting from being away from home without Lesley. He had found out that calling Lesley would still be a hassle as the phone situation had not changed.

After dinner, Eleni returned home. Vassilis and George were sitting at the kitchen table when George said, "I'm getting sleepy. I need to go to bed."

Goodnights were said. George retired to his bedroom falling asleep immediately.

Chapter XXXI

A rooster decided it was time for George to wake up in the morning. After shaving and a light breakfast George decided he wanted to stay in the village and relax.

He was told that Eleni had gone to Argirocastro early in the morning to sell milk. She returned at 9:00 a.m. Violetta walked to Morista with her donkey loaded with wheat to have it milled. She returned after lunch, so Aunt Amalia had to cook for the family and their guest. Vassilis had left early in the morning and returned with two friends after lunch. One friend was the other friend's brother-in-law who spoke some English. This in-law wanted to practice his English with George.

Vassilis friend's son who was five years old said he has a serious hearing loss, and the boy did not talk. George told the father, "If you could go to America you should take the boy to Massachusetts General Hospital in Boston. They are worldly known for hearing problems."

The father said, "I have taken my son to Athens, and an ear doctor informed me about that hospital. I am trying to save money so we can travel there." After a two hour visit Vassilis left with his friends.

Three families from Argirocastro came to visit after Vassilis had left, but they came at different times. As one family left another arrived. It seemed that it was arranged that way, but it wasn't. George was kept busy, but he enjoyed the visitors because he didn't have to travel or leave the village.

A second cousin of George, with his wife who visited, had a young boy, eleven years old with them. His name was Stephano. On George's last visit to Albania George had given Stephano a one dollar bill and Stephano gave George one lek. The family had been to Greece this past August and Stephano was baptized at a Greek church. Someone videoed the event and the family had purchased the tape. They brought the tape with them and they wanted George and the family to watch the tape. This family was very proud of the baptism. A Greek family in Greece sponsored the baptism paying for new clothes for Stephano and for the meal afterwards. It seemed that many Greek-Albanians went to Greece for this event as Greek citizens wanted to help them; they knew that the northern Greek families in Albania had been closed to religion and they had little money.

Vassilis returned home in time to view the tape. When the second cousin and his family left, Vassilis asked George if he wanted to take a walk through the village, but not visit any home. George thought that it would be a good idea. On their walk George had spotted a box turtle, and Vassilis showed George many medicinal plants, including oregano which grew, it seemed, everywhere. George knew that's why Greeks cooked with oregano.

Returning home, Theodore, who lived where George's father had lived, visited. He was having trouble getting a visa to work in Greece and now he was having money problems. He told George that many family members were having the same problems. Theodore also told George that there was friction between the governments of Albania and Greece, but when George asked why, Theodore wouldn't elaborate.

George remembered the day he arrived in Albania and saw the soldiers on the main road. He didn't push Theodore for more information. George thought I'll ask Vassilis sometime later. When Theodore was leaving, George gave him some money. Theodore didn't want to take it.

George said, "It's for your children." Theodore was thankful, but shy.

After another night in the village George got up at 6:00 a.m. When he walked into the kitchen Vassilis was surprised to see him so early in the morning.

Vassilis asked, "Why are you up so early?"

George said, "I had a good night's rest. Where is Violetta?"

Vassilis said, "She is selling milk in Argirocastro with Eleni and buying food."

George thought how busy the women are. They do many chores while taking care of the home, children, always serving guests with drinks, preserves or fruits, and catering to the men. Aunt Amalia took care of the two boys: Alex two years old and Nicholas six years old, while Vassilis was at work and Violetta did her chores.

Little Nicholas played ball with George, watched sheep and cows eating grass on the valley floor, watched Albanian and some Greek television, and saw a portion of Snow White (Turkish production). George thought that the movie was very amusing.

Emir and his daughter, Suela, arrived to take George to see Aunt Penelope in Argirocastro. The aunt was sickly but still alive. Emir's son, Emir, now sixteen years old was with the car. George said good-bye as Emir carried George's overnight bag.

Walking down the mountain-side Emir said to George, "I'm your Negro."

It wasn't said in a derogatory tone, but it surprised George. George asked, "What do you mean by that?"

Emir said, "Well, I've been reading about American history and about your slavery days, and I'm your slave carrying your bag, and you are an American."

Emir chuckled. George gave no response, but he thought at least they can now read about the outside world.

They arrived at the house and George noticed a new garage built at street level with the garage roof leveled to the first floor of the home that was built on a knoll. There was a spacious patio on the garage roof with an iron fence surrounding the patio. Uncle Taki had made the fence. It was quite fancy.

Aunt Penelope kissed and held George tightly and cried. She was very happy to see him again. When George was leaving on his last visit she thought she would never see him again. She had lost weight and was having heart problems. Containing her emotions she asked many questions about George and Lesley and his sister Eli and her family.

George had brought a picture taken in 1931 of two men dressed in military clothes. He had found it after Vlassi had died. He wanted to know if any of the aunts or the family would recognize who they were.

Aunt Penelope looked at the photo, paused, and said, "I think it's my oldest brother, Spiros. The other man could be a friend, or cousin Demetrius Stamos' son, Dimitri. (Dimitri moved to Boston and sold hot chestnuts and peanuts at the corner of Stuart and Washington Streets). George used to see him there when he was a young boy, but he never knew who he was until his father mentioned him that night when Vlassi talked about his family in Albania.

George said, "I'll show it to Aunt Evanthia and when I return to Glifada, I'll show it to Aunt Ollga. When I was thirteen I thought my father told me that they were his brothers, but I don't remember exactly."

There was a knock on the front door and Suela went to answer. Suela had turned eighteen and had learned some English, so she talked to George in English as best she could. She had invited a friend who spoke English well. It seemed that this friend belonged to an English speaking club and it was comprised of all girls. The girl's name was Valetta. She was pretty, dainty, blonde with scarlet cheeks and bright black eyes. Valetta wanted to meet Suela's relative, an American. George thought she was a charming young lady.

Mid-afternoon Aunt Evanthia arrived after a lunch of meat and vegetables, and varied fruits: apples, nectarines, peaches, and grapes. George thought again about the food situation on his last visit. It was good to see the abundant supply of food, but jobs were still not available in Albania and now Greece was experiencing the same phenomenon.

Emir had a telephone, one of the few in Argirocastro, so George called Lesley. He told her that all is well in Albania and she replied by saying she was well and missed George. They were happy to talk and George said he would call again when he got a chance. She sent her love to the family.

George showed Aunt Evanthia the picture. She thought it was their brother, Spiros. So there was some agreement there. She didn't have any idea who the other person was.

The conversation turned to Greece's closing the Albanian border and that America does not give any money to Albania, and the Albanians have no jobs or money. Greece also reduced aid and the importation of materials and the family didn't understand Greece's position. They also told George that their president was a fascist, and someone in the government got two years for balloting infractions. They didn't explain all the details so George couldn't quite understand the total situation, but the fact was that the family was disappointed with their government.

Aunt Penelope changed the subject and started talking about their father, Vangeli Stamos. Aunt Penelope said he was a respected man and had been given the role as the mayor of Glifada. It was not an elected position, but he was the spokesman to the Turkish authorities when they were in power, and to the Albanian government concerning the village and any villager's difficulties. The family was very proud of him even though he worked as a shepherd and never made a lot of money. George wished he could have met his grandparents.

Olympia and Kristos arrived, and Emir made a suggestion that it being a nice day outside that the group should take a walk. Everyone but Aunt Penelope, Aunt Evanthia, and Olympia wanted to go. Uncle Taki and Margarita (daughter), and the son were not at home, so the five of them went out and walked down to the main avenue all the way to the road going to Tirana and then to a bar to have a drink. Along the way Emir stopped to talk to two friends. One friend, during the introductions, said he was an electrician and he made ten dollars a week. The other man was a retired military officer, but he never said what he was paid. There was some small talk about the Albanian-Greek problem, but not in depth, so George still didn't understand the situation.

The electrician turned to George and asked, "Would you move to Albania and live here forever?"

George told the man, "I would not do that because of my family in America."

In response the man said, "You pass the test!"

George didn't quite know what the object of the answer was, but he left it alone. The two friends departed together, and Emir and the group entered a bar. The young girls had sodas and the men had beer. They sat at tables outside as the interior of the bar was dark, and the sun was starting to set, and George said it would be romantic to have candles. Emir went inside and came out with two candles. Kristos mentioned that George's wife should be here if he felt romantic. That brought laughs. The conversation was light, funny stories were told, and then they decided to go home before the sun went below the horizon.

The next day Kristos returned to Aunt Penelope's home late morning as George was going to spend the night at his home. Suela said she wanted to go with them. The three of them walked to Kristos's home, sight seeing on the way.

When they arrived, Olympia had a made a great lunch: really a feast of pumpkin pita, egg lemon soup with lamb, okra, roasted eggplant, bread, sweet cinnamon rice with milk, and a soda called Koca Cola. It was made in Albania. After lunch Suela walked home, and Kristos and George went for a walk to the ancient fort. Along the way they visited a tourist hotel. A suite for one night with a shower and a large bed cost 3500 leks, a room with a shower cost 2500 leks, and a room with no shower cost 2000 leks, and all rooms came with a continental breakfast. The lek was inflated so that 800 leks was equal to one US dollar.

After a spirited greeting, on the return trip to Kristos's home, they met Spiros walking along the main avenue. Spiros asked George, "When are you going to visit and stay over?"

George said, "Probably in a few days. I'll let you know when, but right now I'm visiting with the aunts here in the city."

George and Kristos resumed walking after saying good-bye to Spiros. Arriving at Kristos's home Olympia greeted George warmly and said that Aunt Penelope had sent a message that George was invited tomorrow at her home.

George enjoyed another great meal by Olympia. George was given a room with a comfortable bed for the night, a place to shower, some tsipouro to drink, and of course, friendly conversations. George noticed that because more food was available, the family was more relaxed. It took the strain away for hosting the oldest male relative, and the only one from America. Their merry attitudes and happy facial expressions were quite noticeable. George was happy for them.

Chapter XXXII

George awoke at 5:00 a.m., but hearing no one stirring he laid in bed for another hour. He got up when he heard Olympia and Kristos talking about Eleni and Violetta coming to their home with milk from Glifada. George went downstairs and was drinking his morning coffee when the ladies arrived with the milk. Eleni poured the milk into liter Koca Cola bottles, and as she was finishing filling the bottles, a number of ladies and one man came to buy some milk. After it was all sold the three of them started to count the money and there seemed to be some confusion as they seemed to raise their voices. George ignored the situation, but thought it was very amusing. Eleni and Violetta settled whatever the problem was and they sat there laughing. Violetta gave Olympia and Eleni their share of the money and then the two ladies left for their homes in Glifada, kissing George good-bye.

After breakfast, Olympia, Kristos, and George walked to Aunt Penelope's home. The day was warm and sunny and there were many people walking the streets. George noticed that the people were not as thin as before, but there still were many males loitering about. George enjoyed the pleasant walk.

When they arrived at the house, Aunt Penelope and Uncle Taki, Suela, and cousin Vangeli and his daughter Fevronia from Kassandra were there. What a pleasant surprise for George.

With everyone greeting each other with kisses, Fevronia spoke in

English to George, "It is so nice to see you again George. My family wants to invite you to Kassandra tomorrow. It is my birthday and I will turn twenty-three. Can you come?"

George replied, "It would be an honor to attend. I'll have to make arrangements to get there."

Fevronia said, "That should not be a problem as someone in the family will help you. Once you're there we will take care of your transportation needs. Good. That is settled. We have to go, so we will see you tomorrow."

They said their good-byes, gave kisses, and left. Suela also had to leave. Aunt Penelope served everyone rice cooked with milk and cinnamon, and drinks. The morning was spent listening to Greek music, talking about the family, and discussing the news on the TV.

The discussion turned to the Greek-Albanian problem again. It seemed that the family blamed Greece. They told George it is Greece that had closed the border, it is Greece that won't allow Greeks or Albanians from Albania to cross over for work, and it is Greece that won't allow supplies to enter Albania. George understood the family's position, but what caused Greece to react that way.

During that conversation, Suela returned home with her friend Valetta, the girl that spoke English. They joined in the conversation and the older folks talked about what it was like during World War II. They said the Italians soldiers who occupied the country seemed to be alright, but when the Germans came, they were cruel and harsh to everyone. It didn't matter how old you were.

Suela changed the subject and started talking about hiking clubs. She said that there were many before the fall of communism. It seemed that none existed anymore because people were interested in jobs and earning money to buy food. They have no time for relaxing. The family also thought that during Enver Hoxha's regime their living conditions were number one in the world. As it was, they realized that during and after the fall of communism they were far behind the rest of Europe and the modern world. The country needed to grow and catch up. They knew it would take time, and they were not too pleased with their present president.

It was early afternoon when Aunt Evanthia arrived and wanted George to go to her home, which was a short walk. George was going to spend the night. When Aunt Evanthia and George arrived at her home there was a young girl named Kontilya visiting. She had long black hair, large eyes that were bright, and olive skin. She had a pleasant smile and face. She was Albanian and lived close by. She spoke perfect English with a very slight accent only noticeable on certain words and she wanted to meet George. She announced that it was her eighteenth birthday and she came to visit because she wanted to invite George and Aunt Evanthia and Uncle Sotir to her birthday party. As it was, she only stayed a few moments as she had to return home for party preparations. George thought two birthday parties in a row and this one today should be interesting, and why did this young girl seem so anxious to want to meet him?

Uncle Sotir greeted George with a firm handshake, and Aunt Evanthia's Turkish friends from next door came by. George had met them on his large visit. Aunt Evanthia served lamb meatballs, bread, yogurt, watermelon, and beer. After eating, the group went outside. It was hot and sunny. George thought of the one time he was there and the son was drunk and caused a problem. It was very quiet on this visit.

A handsome young man of eighteen entered the gate. He was tall, thin, black hair, black eyes, shoulders straight, and a gentle face. He was the nephew of the Turkish couple who visited the last time George was there.

There was quite a discussion between the uncle and the nephew. The nephew was blaming the Greeks for the problems of the economic situation, and the uncle was blaming the Albanians. It was said that Albania had forty percent unemployment, and the Greek situation was causing many problems for Albanians as there is work in Greece, and the Albanians want to work. During the argument the two men were laughing. No one else entered into the discussion. George was amused at the friendly interaction between the two, and he learned a bit more about what was going on. Because they spoke in Albanian, the conversation had to be translated.

Finally, time was moving on and Aunt Evanthia said if they were going to the party, they better leave. The party, it seemed, was taking place late afternoon. The Turkish family and the young man left after saying good-bye.

George's uncle and aunt walked through a residential area with beautiful old style stone houses with oak and beech trees lining the street. They arrived shortly and entered Kontilya's home. George was introduced to Kontilya's parents, her sister and three girl friends. The girls were all closely aged, sixteen to eighteen, and they belonged to an English speaking club. George now understood why they wanted him there. He never thought of being invited to an eighteen year old birthday party, and especially in Albania. What a treat. Two of the girls were of Greek descent and one was Albanian. Kontilya was Albanian also.

The family offered cake, cold drinks, and a fruit salad, which was very tasty. When George finished with his cake and salad the conversation turned to George as the girls politely addressed him with questions.

The girls were excited to have a conversation with an American and a relative of Aunt Evanthia. None of the girls had met any American, so this was a first in many respects. They asked questions about Boston, Michael Jackson, New York, and they wanted to know all about George and his wife. What does he do for work, and what does his wife do? They also told some funny jokes. George thought about how they were all very respectful young ladies. No one interrupted anyone, and they listened intently when George spoke. The English dialogue went over the heads of the rest of the guests, but the girls paid no attention. Not that they purposely ignored the rest of the family and guests, but this was such a treat for them, they wanted to get the most out of it. The parents and the mature guests talked to themselves.

While the English speaking group was having an interesting dialogue, two more young girls arrived. As it turned out they were sisters. One was a second year student at the university in Tirana, and the other sister was a year younger and a pianist. Of course, they spoke English. In the meantime, George's aunt and uncle wanted to go home. When the girls heard that, they begged for George to stay.

One of the girls said, "I will walk with you when you leave as I live in that direction."

George said, "I'll stay a little longer after I talk to my Aunt Evanthia."

The younger girls talked about the high school they went to, and the disrespect of the young boys toward girls. George knew that they seemed to be among the brightest among their class, and he felt sure that all of them would be accepted to the university when they applied. The older sister told George about the university. She told George the competition to enter the university was very competitive.

George stayed another thirty to forty minutes longer and then he decided to leave. As he stood up the entire group also stood up. Everyone was surprised because there action was unified. George told them it was ESP. George thanked them for the invitation and it was such a pleasure to meet such pretty and bright young ladies, and who all spoke English so well. He wished them success in whatever they do. Kontilya and the one that said she would walk with George left with him.

As they were walking, a group of young boys, eight to ten years old yelled at the girls. 'English! English!' This showed George the disrespect that the girls talked about. In English George loudly told the boys to stop. Surprisingly they did. The girls thanked him.

The girls told George that they have some difficulties when walking alone, but rape attacks are not heard of. None of them have boyfriends or even thoughts of having one. School is too important and parents do no allow it. They also said that divorce is shameful in their country. George thought about America and Europe in general.

When they reached close enough to the aunt's home, George told them he could go the rest of the way by himself. He thanked them again and said he had a marvelous time. Off they went talking English.

After arriving at Aunt Evanthia's home, about a half a hour later, Rezarta, Areti (from Tirana), Artioli, and little baby Ana visited. The baby is twenty to twenty-three months old and says a few words. They wanted George to visit. He told them that he would visit in two days after visiting his aunt in Kassandra. They visited about an hour.

Aunt Evanthia had prepared a late dinner. Sotir's nephew and a fifteen year old girl joined the family for dinner. George felt full, so he ate very little. The nephew drank tsipouro and George drank beer. The nephew kept filling George's glass. Finally George had enough.

The guests left and the aunt and uncle retired. George slept in the living room on a thin mattress placed on the sofa. It was comfortable enough that he fell asleep quickly. Maybe it was the beer.

Chapter XXXIII

George woke up to a quiet household. Luckily he had some napkins as Aunt Evanthia had no toilet paper. His impression is that she has little money and toilet paper is not important when you can use… George didn't know what.

After a light breakfast George showered. Sometimes a sponge bath was the norm, but Aunt Evanthia had a normal shower head. He had to prepare to go to Aunt Stavroula's home in Kassandra for another birthday party. George had brought from America a few English-Greek dictionaries, so he was prepared to give something to Fevronia.

Outside of Aunt Evanthia's home sat a fairly new Mercedes with Zahari behind the wheel. He is the oldest son of Aunt Stavroula, and the father of Konstandia. The car was polished, comfortable, and large. With good-byes said, Zahari drove George to Kassandra. George felt like an ambassador sitting in this beautiful automobile. The last time of his visit to Albania, he rode in junky-looking vehicles. What a contrast!

The Mercedes and its passengers arrived safely in Kassandra. The household was busy with preparations, and Aunt Stavroula was happy to see George. Soon after, cousin Margarita and her husband Emir, Aunt Stavroula's seven grandchildren, and two of the children's mothers arrived. The celebration was to take place late in the afternoon. Everyone sat down and ate various prepared dishes.

After the meal and many drinks, George said, "If there is enough time before the party I would like to take a walk."

Vangeli, the father said, "I would like to do that."

Fevronia, Konstandia, and Alki (8 years old) said, almost in unison, "I want to go."

On their walk around the village Vangeli told George that he should see their newly renovated church. The village people named it Saint Paraskevi. Not like the church in Glifada, it wasn't locked and it was larger. On entering the church, George saw many religious framed photos and framed icons on all the walls. After everyone blessed themselves, Fevronia and George lit candles, Vangeli and George left money, and George took pictures. When they were leaving the church everyone drank water from a hose that was attached on the outside of the church.

George inquired while they were drinking, "Do you think we have enough time to walk to Morista and make a short visit at my cousin Sophia and her husband Kostas's home?

Fevronia said, "We have enough time as long as we don't stay too long."

As it was, Fevronia wanted her father to see the inside of the large home. When they arrived Sophia was home with her older son, Spiro. George hadn't met him on his last visit; he was in Greece working. Christopher and Uncle Kostas were in Agyrocastro. Spiro was shorter and eight years older than his brother, he had a full crop of white hair, and his face resembled George's uncle in America.

George greeted his cousin Sophia and introduced his relatives, Vangeli and Alki; Sophia remembered the girls. George told Sophia that they couldn't stay long as Fevronia was having a birthday party later this afternoon. He would try to visit Sophia when he got a chance as he was occupied visiting his father's family, so it was a short visit. When they departed Vangeli decided that they should walk to Zahari's restaurant which was located in Morista.

Konstandia, as in 1992, sang softly as she walked. George loved to hear her as she has a beautiful voice. She either walks beside George or very close. When they first met two years ago she was very shy, but that changed slowly.

While walking down the hillside she told George that she had quit school and will not finish her last year, and she hates math. George told her he would do her lessons if she mailed them. She laughed. Konstandia will turn eighteen in October, and George thought how more beautiful she is.

When they arrived at the restaurant, Zahari was surprised that they had walked all the way to Morista and then to his restaurant. Actually it wasn't that far. He had spotted them walking down the hill from Sophia's home. Zahari fed everyone lamb chops and French fries topped with oregano. George and Vangeli had a beer and tsipouro; the younger ones drank Albania's Koca Cola.

George's cousin Theodore, from Glifada, was driving a truck when he spotted George and his entourage entering the restaurant. He turned around and joined them for a drink and then he had to leave. They stayed another fifteen minutes after their meal and then left for Kassandra. Zahari said he would drive them there, but George said he wanted to walk. Everyone agreed.

On their way, along the road, Konstandia put her arm over George's shoulder and sang quietly. Arriving at the house, Greek Dropoli music was playing on the radio. Fevronia, Konstandia, and little five year old Andromaki decided to dance. When they finished dancing Konstandia sat beside George.

Talking to George, Konstandia said, "I do not like school, and I want to marry a man from Dropoli and have children. I can read and write, so that's enough."

George understood her position and why. What did Albania offer young men and young women at this time? He wished her well for whatever she did, and he thought that she will not have a hard time finding a man with her singing and her good looks.

Fevronia joined the conversation during Konstandia's telling George what she wanted. Fevronia said, "I want to get married and work in the house raising a family and cooking and cleaning and all that goes with marriage. I do not understand the ways of American women. They go to clubs, smoke, and drink. Divorce is not the Albanian way. I would not marry an American-Greek because I would be afraid of divorce, and I do not want to live alone, but I would like to visit America. I would go if I had a sponsor."

George replied, "American marriages don't all end in divorce. It is about a fifty-fifty chance, but I understand your position. If you need a sponsor I will sponsor you. Just let me know." She smiled at the offer.

Vangeli wanted to talk about Albania and its own problems. He spoke up and said, "Our President, Sali Berisha was the doctor for Enver Hoxha. People have claimed that he does not like Greeks or Greece. He stopped the teachers in our local schools from teaching the Greek language, but the teachers demonstrated and he backed down. They call him the communist dictator claiming to be a democrat. He changed the color of his tie from red to blue. Others say he is a fascist. The residents of Dropoli have fear of the Albanians and the Albanian police, and the Greek women in the villages are afraid of the Albanian men. Some claim that they enter homes and steal. If you are walking the streets wearing gold someone would probably accost you and steal the gold."

Fevronia said, "We would like to have some gold, but it is a dream."

Konstandia said, "To be married and have a gold ring is also a dream."

Fevronia ended the conversation by saying, "We don't know anyone in the entire family that has gold."

It was time for the party. A big cake was brought out with candles, and a table was prepared with all kind of foods and drinks. Everyone sang happy birthday to Fevronia as she blew out the candles. She was given gifts along with George's English-Greek dictionary. It was a joyous occasion.

With the family discussing George's itinerary it was decided that tomorrow Zahari will drive George to Aunt Penelope's home. He will return to pick up George for a family outing in Saranda on Sunday (Saranda is a seaside resort on the Adriatic Sea one mile across from the island of Corfu).

George's thoughts drifted to Aunt Stavroula and Vangeli's wife, Dorothea, having medical problems related to their hearts. The aunt's problem was more serious. George assumed that without proper medical attention, and soon, he might not see her again on another visit to Albania.

George also knew that she knew it. There wasn't much he could do but advise her to change some of her eating habits, and try to see a doctor in Greece. With the problem of travel to Greece, that was now out of the question. If Lesley was there she probably would have had more influence on a diet change than what George prescribed. As it was, George did the best he could.

The next morning George woke up early hearing, dogs, roosters, cars and trucks. He dozed off until hearing voices in the kitchen. After eating a light breakfast George took photos of the young ones and gave them ten drachmas each. They smiled with glee. George prepared to leave Kassandra, and feeling like a gypsy, he said his good-byes and thank you.

Vangeli, Fevronia, Alki, and George walked to Morista for George to get a ride to Aunt Penelope's home. Vangeli carried George's bag, and Alki wanted to carry his camera. Alki was mesmerized when he first saw the camera, so George let him, telling Alki to be very careful. Everyone was solemn. They did not want George to leave, but they understood his position.

Zahari was supposed to drive George to Argirocastro, but when they arrived at the restaurant Zahari said he was too busy, but his friend, using the Mercedes, would take George to Argirocastro. Zahari gave George a fresh loaf of bread, telling George they were made in German ovens at the local bakery. Dorothea had given George a dozen fresh eggs and peaches. George wanted to sit and have fresh eggs with fresh bread, coffee, and top it off with peaches, but as it was he had to leave with this friend and the three family members; eight year old Alki wanted to go so he could be with George.

The road had little traffic and the ride seemed to go quickly. When they arrived at Aunt Penelope's home George said thank you and good-bye to the driver and got out. The Mercedes drove away as George waved. Zahari had told George that he would pick him up 8:00 a.m. on Sunday for a trip to Saranda for a family picnic. That was in three more days.

The aunt and uncle were home watching the news on television. The station was reporting about the cholera in Romania, Turkey, Russia, and in Tirana, the capital of Albania. George thought, I guess I won't go there.

Suela and her brother were playing with a soccer ball on the veranda. After greeting his aunt and uncle, George went out to the veranda and joined them. A scoring game was set up for one goal. Suela got the first goal, so that ended the game.

Suela said, "I would like to play soccer in school, but girls are not allowed to play. We are home because all the schools have been delayed three days because of no books. There are no books in the villages either."

George replied, "A few days off gives you time to do what you want."

Emir said, "There isn't much to do, so I rather be in school." Suela moved her head sideways in agreement.

Aunt Penelope served George's favorite dish; bean soup with salad. The drink was Albanian Koca Cola. She told George that it was mountain peasant food.

George said, "Well, I guess I'm a mountain peasant." She laughed.

Later in the day George said, "Maybe we could walk to Spiros' home."

Suela said, "They are probably resting or sleeping (siesta time practiced in Albania and Greece)."

George didn't know if Spiros knew he was going to be at Emir's home. Suela tried to call a friend of Spiros who had a phone that lived in an apartment above Spiros, but she had trouble getting a connection. It was obvious that the phone service hadn't changed all that much.

After trying a couple of hours later, Suela finally got through to the neighbor. Rezarta returned the call after the neighbor told her about the call. She had been out shopping for food. It wasn't long after when Aleko arrived with Rezarta and the baby girl. George left soon after, and Aleko drove to his home. On entering the apartment Spiros was happy to see George as well as Artioli.

George could sense that the family was happy to see him, but Rezarta said kind of sternly, "How come you haven't visited before."

George replied, "My visit plans have not been planned too much in advance and I'm trying to see everyone. It is difficult because there is friction between the families. I have no friction, so it is hard to please everyone; I'm doing the best I can."

Spiros and Rezarta agreed that there is a problem. Rezarta said, "Yes. This one visits this one, and that one won't talk to this one, and so on. It is a mess. At least you can talk to everyone, like me."

George said, "I haven't heard anyone say anything bad about you."

Spiros said to George, "There is jealously among the family. Vassilis makes twenty dollars a day, Margarita makes eighty dollars a month and no one knows what Emir makes, but they seem to have more money than anyone else. Some are getting rich, and money and poverty are one of the problems between the families."

George thought money will change people, especially if someone has plenty and they don't; a world problem. He also thought that twenty dollars a day does not make anyone rich, but maybe in Albania.

George wanted to change the subject and said, "Zahari is going to pick me up and take me to Saranda on Sunday."

Rezarta said, "Why don't you go with Aleko?"

George said, "I've already made plans and I cannot change them as it would not be the best thing to do."

Everyone agreed, but Aleko said, "We could go on our own tomorrow." Aleko continued and said firmly, "Yes. We will go after our midday rest."

That settled that. George spent the rest of the day relaxing, playing with Artioli and holding little Ana, conversing with Spiros, Aleko, Rezarta, and Julietta (Spiros' daughter who was living up north when George visited two years ago). She's staying with her father. Spiros' sister Areti returned to Tirana.

George was having a good time and feeling very comfortable. George always enjoyed their company. After a generous dinner meal, some coffee, tsipouro, and conversations, George said, "I didn't have too much sleep last night and now I feel tired. I think I need to go to bed earlier than usual. Hope you don't mind."

Spiros said, "No. No. Go to bed and rest."

George retired and fell to sleep quickly. During the night an electrical storm with blasting thunder rolls woke him up a few times, but overall he felt good the next morning. Of course, the dogs in the city have early revelry and when one starts they all join in.

With a cup of coffee in his hands he went out to the small balcony and watched people below going to work or wherever they were going. A few were on donkeys; a man was galloping on his horse. George also noticed that some of the people were much heavier, indicating that they have more food. George thought that they seem to make a little more money, but items are somewhat more expensive. It was interesting for George to see the change. He was enjoying the activities when Spiros joined him.

Spiros said, "Aleko and Rezarta have to go to work today. She will be back in an hour. Aleko said he will come home early, and Julietta will mind the children, and maybe my sister will return."

Spiros and George decide to go out for a walk on the main avenue. They went into a small quaint shop, sat, and had a cup of coffee. After drinking their coffee they went out and started walking again when Spiros spotted Aleko who was on his way to get Rezarta. Aleko saw his father the same time and turned around to get his father and George. George and Spiros got in the car, and Aleko drove and picked up Rezarta. Instead of going straight home Aleko decided to drive to the ancient fort, but when they arrived it was closed. Aleko wanted to go in and have a beer in the fort's interior snack bar, but he decided to return home to have something to eat.

After a light snack and siesta time of about two hours everyone piled into the car except Spiros, Julietta, and the baby. They left for Saranda at 4:00 p.m.

Before leaving, Spiros said, "My sister might not be able to visit. Have a great time."

The ride to Saranda was picturesque driving up and over a rocky-filled mountain pass. The lower hills were verdant with grass and flowers. The high peaks were bare of vegetation except grass in sheltered areas. There were many switchbacks, and the rock formations were stunning being able to see anticlines and synclines stratifications of various colors. After going down the mountain there were small villages and farmlands, a crystal clear river, and finally a view of the Adriatic Sea. The sea spread its deep blue color in every direction. The views were spectacular. George was able to take many pictures on the way.

They arrived at Saranda in two hours which gave them time to stroll around and enjoy the warm salt air. They sat on a large rock and put their feet in the warm water. George took one picture as the sun was settling to light up the east shore of America. They sat and watched until the sun disappeared.

It was decided to stroll to a shop to get soft drinks. On the way to a shop George heard two adults speaking English. He stopped and asked if they were Americans. They said that they are American missionaries from Mississippi. He and his wife and two children had been there for almost two years. It was a brief encounter while Aleko got the drinks. After the missionaries departed Aleko told George it was time to go home. The ride home was quiet, Artioli fell asleep, the great views disappeared, and only lonely lights were visible.

Arriving home, everyone was tired and it didn't take long for everyone to say goodnight and retire to their beds. It had been a very busy and rewarding day.

English speaking girls

Chapter XXXIV

George once again heard the revelry of the dogs. He could never imagine having to hear it permanently. He thought of his home in New Hampshire and how quiet his neighborhood is.

He left the bedroom to find everyone up. Rezarta gave him his coffee, and George went out to the balcony and watched women down below getting water. He thought of the time when it seemed that everyone was getting water when Rezarta was pregnant. It seemed so long ago. As it was, Rezarta had to go down again to get water, so George went with her. He also brought his camera. There were not as many ladies getting water, so George was able to take her picture filling her jar.

Returning upstairs, Rezarta left for work carrying baby Ana. She told George she had to go for about two hours even though school was not in session. Aleko had to leave for work, and Julietta was packing her things. She was moving back in with her husband.

Spiros had told George that the husband does not want children and Julietta does. He doesn't treat her well, and that the mother-in-law runs the household. Spiros said his daughter had married into a difficult situation. She returns to see her father about the difficulties she has to live with, but he encourages her to keep trying. George had empathy for her, understanding the Albanian position on divorce, although it might be her only way out.

George wanted to spend the day relaxing. He told them he didn't want to visit anyone and that maybe just going out walking would be all he wanted to do. He was enjoying his visit with them and he didn't want them to feel that they had to entertain him. Just being there with them was enough for him. With all the visits and going from place to place, he was having a satisfying visit, but sometimes a person just wants to relax, and today was that day. Besides, he had more days in Albania to make visits.

The family honored George's request, and for the family they could also relax and do whatever they had to do. George and Spiros went out for their usual coffee and walk.

Walking the main avenue they could not help but notice numerous police, soldiers loitering about the main avenue and on the road to Tirana, police cars everywhere, and policemen wearing different uniforms depicting police from different cities.

George asked Spiros, "Why are there so many police, and why all the red banners?"

Spiros answered, "President Berisha is visiting tomorrow."

The main avenue had many Albanian flags and large red banners along the side of the road as far as the eyes could see up the avenue. Some of the banners had the President's name and some had slogans. George always took his camera on these walks and when he started to take photos, Spiros told him to stop as Spiros was afraid of the police and soldiers, but mainly the police.

George asked, "What are you afraid of?"

Spiros replied, "They might arrest you."

George said, "Why would they do that? First of all, they don't know who I am, and with this camera they'll think I am an Albanian photographic journalist as my appearance is like everyone else here or even a foreign photographer. So far, I have taken pictures of the policemen looking at me and they don't even look away or make any gestures for me to stop. Also the President isn't here. He arrives tomorrow, so I am no threat to him. Governments usually don't stop journalist or foreign photographers, besides I'm not photographing anything secret or military. So, you stand over there and I'll keep shooting, if the police arrest me call the American embassy and Lesley, and bring me food and a gun to the station." George was smiling when he said that last remark.

Spiros didn't appreciate that last remark, so George told him to relax, not to worry, and just watch. Spiros walked to the sidewalk and waited.

As George was taken pictures, a truck full of soldiers sitting in the back drove by slowly. George took a picture and then waved at the soldiers. One soldier waved back and smiled. This surprised George, as he never expected for any soldier to wave back.

After George got the photographs he wanted he walked over to Spiros and told him he had enough photographs.

George said, "Did you see that soldier wave at me?"

"Yes. You are lucky they didn't arrest you."

"Well they didn't."

They returned home from their walk and George started playing with Artioli, which excited Artioli. Aleko and Rezarta were home and Spiros told them of George's photographing the police and soldiers.

Spiros said, "I was afraid they would arrest George, but they didn't. I kept watching them, but they seemed to ignore him, which really surprised me. I can't believe it."

Aleko, said, "We don't like the police. We are forced to pay for everything, passports, visas, if there are five people in a car, and other business activities. The Greek minority cannot become police or officers in the military. Even on our passports we are considered Greeks not Albanian (similar to when Russia put Jew on a Jewish person's Russian passport instead of putting Russian). This situation in Albania has not changed yet, even though we are supposed to be a democratic country. When we elect a new president that might change."

The only remark that George could entertain to reply to that statement was, "In time my friends, in time."

The day seemed to go by peacefully: eating, talking, and resting at night. Tomorrow they were scheduled to go to Zahari's restaurant at noon time. George and the family were looking forward to that visit as George told them he liked the food. No one was interested in the President's visit tomorrow.

Another early morning for everyone, only the baby was asleep. On the television news station they were announcing that the President of Albania will be in Argirocastro today. Luckily the family was going to Zahari's restaurant. George knew the cities streets would be crowded with police, soldiers and citizens on-lookers, and he had no desire to watch, like the family.

At noontime, six of them (two were children) piled into the car and drove to Zahari's. When they arrived there were many new autos and security men in uniforms and some in suits standing about.

Before exiting the car Spiros said, "Be careful. They are officials."

No one else said anything. George could see that the family was nervous, except Aleko. He said, "So what?"

When we walked into the restaurant there were ten government officials sitting at one table, somewhat casually dressed. They paid no attention to the family as they grouped to one table.

Zahari came over and said, "Hello. It is so nice to see you all. Order what you want. I'll be back with the menus."

As they were ordering, the officials departed and two of them said 'hello' as they passed by the family. The family responded with 'hellos.' I could see the tension dissolve from everyone especially Spiros after the officials exited. The family ate, drank, and had a good time with Zahari sitting with them for a spell.

While Zahari was sitting at the table he started talking about going to Saranda tomorrow. Rezarta said, "I want to go if there is room for me. The rest of my family will stay home."

Zahari said, "There is plenty of room. There are three cars going, so that is no problem. I will arrive in the morning for George and you."

With the arrangements settled, Spiros paid for the meal. During the drive back to the city Aleko spotted cousin Eleni and a lady with cows entering the grassy fields across from Glifada. Aleko blew his horn and everyone waved. Eleni waved back.

By the time they returned to the city, the streets were empty of the police and the soldiers. Only the flags and banners reminded them that the President had been there, and the street scenes were back to normal. They returned to the apartment and were settling in when Aunt Evanthia knocked on the door.

After the hellos, she asked George, "I'm going to visit my daughter in Fier. Do you want to go? I do not want to go by bus. We could go by taxi, but it would cost one hundred dollars and the driver would have to stay with us and eat. We could go by bus, but it would take too long."

George said, "I could pay for the trip."

Aleko spoke up and said, "If I can get the time off I will drive you there and we can return the same day. The gas will not cost that much. It would be fun and George could see more of the country."

Aunt Evanthia said she would like to go this coming week, maybe Wednesday or Thursday. George told her that he was scheduled to go to the villages and visit Morista and Kassandra for his last visits before he leaves Albania on the twenty-sixth of September. George told her that maybe Thursday would be the best day.

Aleko said, "That would give me time to ask for the day off. It should be no problem."

Aunt Evanthia left with a smile on her face. Spiros and George decided to take one of their walks again. It was mid-afternoon and George asked Spiros, "Spiros, are the men exchanging money on the street today?"

Spiros said, "They are there every day. Why?"

"I would like to change some money for leks. I would like to have some when I go to Saranda and Fier."

Spiros said, "Let's go now. I'm sure they will still be there."

Walking up the avenue they could see twenty to thirty men bunched together in the same spot. Spiros saw a man he knew (called a Kambists) and approached him with George at his side. As usual there were policemen standing to the side. George didn't feel anxious as before. The man asked Spiros in Albanian, "How much do you want to exchange and what kind of money do you have?"

Spiros turned to George with the same question. George said, "I want to change fifty American dollars for leks."

The man gave George forty-five hundred leks which was actually worth forty-five thousand leks. Being that the inflation rate was eight hundred leks to the dollar. Rezarta had told him the value of money was confusing. For George, he thought to himself, everything in this country is confusing, but for George he just exchanged fifty American dollars.

When George and Spiros returned home, Dimitri, the Greek man that lived upstairs with his daughter Eli, came down and gave George one and a half liters of home-made wine. Dimitri knew George's great grandfather when he was a little boy; Dimitri had lived in Morista. He had told George that he knew where his great grandfather had lived, but some people had built a new home as the original home had been destroyed by the local boys. It was Dimitri's daughter who would come down and bring tidbits of food when George was there. She was middle aged and unmarried. Rezarta told George she was looking for a husband. George smiled. George opened the wine for supper.

The next morning George got up hearing his alarm clock; the dogs. He knew Zahari would arrive between seven or eight this morning. Everyone else was up. Rezarta was feeding the baby cereal, Spiros and Aleko were quietly drinking coffee, and Artioli was having his milk and cereal. It didn't take long before Aleko got coffee for George.

Zahari knocked on the door about an hour later. Rezarta and George were ready. Artioli cried when he saw his mother and George leaving. Aleko quieted Artioli by saying we'll go out for ice cream.

Zahari drove to Kassandra to go with the other cars. The families packed into three, two year old shiny Mercedes. Zahari's car was model 3000, and the other two were models 2400. George thought what a fancy entourage. George asked Zahari how much he paid for his car. He said five thousand dollars (US). George did not tell Zahari how much they cost in America (Aleko told him later that they are stolen vehicles and the government doesn't say anything). George thought how else are they going to get new cars?

George did not tell Zahari that he had been to Saranda a few days ago. Zahari was telling him how beautiful it was, and George did not want to spoil his cousin's trip. Of course, George made comments as they drove up and over the mountains. Rezarta said nothing either.

Along the way, they had to slow down to pass some soldiers working on the road. George spotted the same soldier that had waved back at him.

George waved again and the soldier recognizing George returned the wave. What a coincidence and a treat for George and maybe for the soldier.

George had been in Albania for ten days and the Albanian television (they spoke only Albanian) had been talking about the Greek problem every day. Talking to whomever was in his presence; it seemed to George that it was turning more dangerous. When he asked about the situation, no one seemed to have any answers except everything is okay. George thought that if a war is about to break out, he wanted out of Albania. With Greece's belonging to NATO, and they being equipped by the Americans, and also three times the population of Albania, he thought that the Greek soldiers would come streaming through the border not too far from where he was staying, even if it was in Agyrocastro. George knew he had to pay more attention to the situation because he did not want to be in Albania if there was going to be a war. As it was, in the villages or in the city, life seemed to be normal and the citizens were doing their normal activities. No one seemed to be troubled by the news.

George knew that the ride to Saranda would take a couple of hours, so George thought that maybe he would ask Zahari if he knew what the problem was between Albania and Greece. It would also help pass the time.

George asked Zahari, "Do you know what the problem is between Greece and Albania?"

Zahari replied, "Yes. I've been following it closely because I live close to the border and I see all the soldiers and guns pass by my restaurant."

George asked, "I don't want to stay here if the two countries go to war. Do you mind telling me what you know?"

Zahari replied, "No. Not at all. It is a long story, but I'll tell what I know. It all started last April."

George asked, "This year?"

"Yes. There is an Albanian military post on the Greek border called Episkopi in Greek, Peshkepi in Albanian. It was attacked by unknown gunmen, and two Albanian soldiers were killed and three wounded. Albania said it was done by Greek soldiers and the attackers were speaking Greek. Of course, Greece denied any involvement."

Zahari paused, "A week later Albanian police carried out searches, seizures and arrest without warrants in the Greek occupied southern Albania. The arresting persons were in civilian clothes and refused to identify themselves. It was said that they were Albanian secret police called, 'SHIK.' The Greek newspaper, Omonia, in Saranda was searched without a warrant, and other Omonia offices were searched. From what I understand many items were confiscated without the proper Albanian authority. The stories and problems get very confusing. According to reports, the Albanians are still using past communist laws and present day laws, which conflict with one another. Anyhow, the authorities arrested five men connected to the newspaper, Omonia, and another man. It seemed that illegal interrogations and the use of force, and of course, poor detention conditions were used against the men. About a month later fifty-five or fifty-six witnesses were arrested, and this was done illegally. There are many problems with these detentions. The Greeks say that these five Omonia men were arrested because they are ethnic minority activists. The newspaper writes about the Greek minority land in Albania and it wants it to go back to Greece."

Zahari continued after going through switchbacks, "When the trial proceeded in August there were many irregularities in the court proceedings. Too many for me to elaborate here, but it came to be a real tragedy. The reality is that the defendants were deprived of their basic legal rights. The final conclusion was that all five men connected to the newspaper were found guilty on all accounts on September 7th. When did you arrive in Albania?"

George said, "I arrived on the ninth of September."

Zahari said, "That's two days before you arrived. The Greek government reacted to the arrest and trial, and that is why they closed the border. The sixth man arrested was convicted yesterday and was only charged for illegally carrying a weapon. The Greek government also has deported thousands of illegal Albanians in their country starting in 1993, and it has intensified its deporting in August because of the trial, and of course, it continues on this day. And another factor in this situation, Greece is deporting Albanians with legal immigration papers to work in Greece as well. This is illegal. Beside all that, there are many problems between the Greek minority and Albania. It would take days to tell you all about it, but I'm sure it will improve in time with democracy improving, which will take many years."

George said, "No wonder there are problems here. That's an interesting story and I'm glad that I asked you about it. No one else seemed to want to tell me or they didn't know enough. I can't believe they didn't know. And about democracy in America, it didn't happen very quickly. It took well over one hundred years. Anyhow, is there anything going on between the two governments?"

Zahari answered, "Well, I don't see more Albanian soldiers arriving at the border, so that's a good sign. Someone told me that he thought that the two governments, with outside official help, are talking. I wouldn't worry if I was you."

George said, "That's a relief. Thanks for telling me what you know. By the way, I'm looking forward to our visit to Saranda today."

Zahari said, "Before we go to the resort, I'm going to take you to an old Greek and Roman ruins aside a beautiful lake. You will really enjoy it."

Andromaki and Alki

Chapter XXXV

decorative flourish

The approach to the ancient ruins was on a two lane dirt road passing through large olive groves. The olive trees were large, foliaged with green leaves and olives, and they spread their wide branches like oak trees. George thought how beautiful they appeared. He thought of all the olives and oil he had used all his life. He was happy to be so close to them now in his life.

With Rezarta, Konstandia, Fevronia, Zahari, and George going to the ruins, the remainder of the group went to the seaside somewhere. The Greek-Roman ruins, called Butrint, were now situated surrounded by farm land. In ancient times the area was in the Roman Province of Dalmatia in the south west part of Illyria. The ruins were founded in 4000 B.C.

There was a Greek-Albanian man from Dropoli that not only was the care taker, but he knew the history of Butrint. When Zahari approached him he told the caretaker that George was his cousin and he was visiting from America. The man told Zahari he spoke English, Greek, Albanian, and Italian. When Zahari introduced the rest of the family, the caretaker spoke in English.

George said, "I speak Greek, so you can use that language."

He replied, "I want to speak English. That way I can practice. We don't get many Americans here. I don't want to lose the language. I'll relate the story in Greek and English for everyone. My name is Peter."

With that said, Peter began the tour, "These ruins were built in 4000

B.C. It had a basilica, gymnasium, baths, theatre, aqueduct, and heated water to kill diseases. It is eleven hectares (four and a quarter acres) in size, and has been destroyed by time, war, and earth quakes. It had been occupied by the Romans, Venetians, and Greeks. It was excavated in the 1930s and after the Second World War by the Italians, France, and the University of Texas. The many statues that were here are in Italy. The tile on the gymnasium is outstanding and in great condition. In ancient times the area was guarded by a fort on the outlet of a nearby large lake."

As Peter talked, everyone walked listening intently while also viewing the remaining stone walls, some rooms, and the remaining tiled floors. The group walked through the remaining ruins of the basilica and the gymnasium. Remarks were made as to all the souls that walked here before all of us. It was a beautiful area and the ruins were fantastic. Peter was a wonderful guide. It wasn't a long tour, but enough, so that it was very satisfying. George appreciated the tour and that Zahari thought to take him there. There was a small entrance fee, and Zahari paid for that, but George gave Peter a generous tip.

After the tour, everyone got in the car and Zahari drove to where everyone else was picnicking on the sand aside the sea. There was plenty of food and the entire family from Kassandra, except for Aunt Stavroula and Dorothea were there. The kids were playing soccer ball on the beach, the adults were drinking beer and soft drinks and eating roasted lamb, potatoes, salad, cooked greens, fruits, and especially watermelon. The family was having a good time telling stories. Before long the afternoon was slipping away. No one wanted to go home, but there was work tomorrow, and they wanted to drive home in the daylight. The family gathered the kids and themselves and piled into their Mercedes. With Zahari in the lead car, off they went. It was a wonderful time and one that George and all the others would never forget.

On the return trip taking George and Rezarta to her home, Fevronia and Konstandia told Zahari that they wanted to ride in the car to Argirocastro. Most of the conversations were about Butrint. They all had been there before, except George of course, but they did say that it had been a while since they were last there, and that they seemed to get more out it on this trip. It made them remember that their homeland had a long history going back thousands of years. George could feel their pride.

George had to return to Argirocastro to prepare for his stay in Morista and Kassandra, his belongings were at Rezarta's. The ride seemed to go quickly and they were in Argirocastro before dark. Zahari said good-bye along with the girls and left Rezarta and George at the apartment front door. Rezarta and George thanked him and walked up the stairs. Spiros, Aleko, and especially Artioli, were happy to see them return.

While George was collecting his belongings, Rezarta told him that even though it was late, he should rest for a half hour or so before Aleko takes him to Morista. George thought that was a good idea.

Resting the half hour, Aleko and George left for Morista. When they arrived there was still some daylight, but the sun was at its lowest in the sky before it set. George got out of the car, said good-bye to Aleko and walked up the hill, and by chance, he met his cousin Sophia on the road. They were both surprised to have met that way. She had gone out to buy bread before the bakery closed.

Sophia entered her home with George. Kostas and the oldest son Spiro with his two daughters, Leonora and Demo, and Spiro's brother, Christopher, were there. The family greeted George warmly. Spiro had returned from Greece because of the Greek-Albanian problem.

After Sophia served dinner, and the night was passing on, George had told them that he had a long day going to Saranda and he needed to retire. Saying good-night, Christopher led George to the same room as he and Lesley had slept in on their last visit to Albania. George admired the wooden ceiling beams as he dozed off to sleep thinking of the wonderful day and of Lesley. George thought that when he gets a chance he must call her.

The night went quickly as George slept very quietly in that thick-walled home. No dogs or vehicles to wake him up. After a light breakfast and two cups of coffee, a man from the village visited. His name was Demetri Tolis.

Greeting George, Demetri told George that he had many cousins living in the Boston area. Demetri asked George about his family here in Albania and in America. Going through each others family's genealogy, George and Demetri found out that Demetri's grandmother was George's aunt, Aunt Urania, George's father's sister that had passed away in the 1960s. The aunt would have been seventy-five tomorrow. What a coincidence.

George thought of the time he visited Morista in 1992. He found out that he had an aunt whose name was Enkalada. She had married his father's relative who had lived there after their marriage. George wondered who else lived in the village that was related to him.

George wanted to see this aunt. The one he met by accident on his last visit with Lesley; the lady with the donkey. George told Sophia that he was going to Enkalada's home for a short visit. He left the house and knocked on the aunt's door and Aunt Enkalada answered. She was very surprised to see George. He kissed her and told her he was here in the village for a short visit, and like his last visit in 1992, he could only stay a little while. With that said, he apologized.

Aunt Enkalada left the room and returned with coffee and preserves. When she sat down, she asked George, "Do you think you could get a picture of my cousin's son, Michael?"

George said, "He lives in California and I am not in touch with him, only with his aunt. Have you written to his aunt, your other cousin? I gave you her address two years ago."

She replied, "I have, but she doesn't write very often."

George said, "She is old and very sick. She probably has difficulty writing. She is not in good shape as you are. All I can do is write to her, but I can't promise you anything. She lives many miles from where I live."

The aunt said, "Do the best you can. I am in my eighties now."

George said, "You look very healthy. Do you still take care of your sheep in the fields?"

"Yes."

George said, "I'm sure you are in better shape than most women your age living in America. I can't stay long, so unfortunately I have to go. It was nice seeing you again. I am leaving Albania soon, so I don't think I can return to see you. You take care of yourself and say hello to your family. I love you. Good-bye."

Aunt Enkalada hugged George which seemed like eternity. When she let go of George he took the opportunity to leave. Walking through the rain, he thought about her life style, her jet black hair with hardly any grey, she still didn't need eye glasses, and she had just returned from the fields working her sheep in the cold rain. He thought it must be that Mediterranean diet.

George returned to Sophia's home. She had prepared a small lunch of vegetables of which most came from her garden. George was thinking, as he ate, that he was returning to America soon, and he was wondering when he would return to Albania. At least, Albania was in a somewhat better position than on his last visit.

Sitting and enjoying his meal, Fevronia had arrived to take George to Kassandra. Of course, Sophia told Fevronia to sit and eat. Fevronia said she was not hungry, but that did not satisfy Sophia, so Fevronia sat and had a small plate of food and a glass of Koca Cola.

An hour later, George kissed Sophia, Kostas and the rest of the family good-bye. Fevronia and George left for Kassandra. The rain showers had stopped enough for them to walk untouched by rain drops, albeit Fevronia had brought umbrellas.

When George and Fevronia left Morista it was siesta time. If George had stayed, he would have been asked if he wanted to lie down. The men would nap for a half hour to an hour; George had never seen the women nap, unless they are very old.

In the villages, there is little motion or noise during siesta time, except the occasional braying of a donkey, maybe the barking of a dog, sometimes a rooster crowing, a parent yelling names of children, the mooing of a passing cow, or sheep or goats talking to each other. It gives you the chance to hear birds sing and chirp. Except for people noises, it reminded George of the forest in the northern woods of New Hampshire and northern Maine.

As George and Fevronia walked towards Kassandra they could see the highway below and the buildings next to the road. There were six eighteen wheelers parked at Zahari's restaurant, just like a truck stop in America. There was some moving traffic of a few eighteen wheelers, two buses, three cars, one van, and a couple of light trucks all heading either to the south or north. George and Fevronia asked each other if that maybe the borders had opened up.

Watching the traffic, George's thoughts went to the Albanian driver's habits. They blow their horn for everything: passing a car, people walking aside the road, when seeing a car wanting to enter a road, on corners or turns on mountain roads.

George and Fevronia arrived as the family was watching the news. Kissing the family, George sat and watched. There was talk of America sending soldiers to Haiti, Albania still has cholera, and six people had died from the disease. The UN was talking about the Greek and Albania problem, and it seemed that the two countries were starting to talk. That was a positive sign.

Fevronia's mother, Dorothea, is quite ill. George checked her pulse and it was very rapid. He pleaded his case again about her diet, that she needed to lose weight and to exercise. She listened, but what she really needed, was for her to see a doctor. Vangeli told George that he did not trust the doctors in Argirocastro. The hospital did not have modern equipment, and the only place to go was to go to Greece. The family was stuck between a rock and a hard place. Hopefully, the situation would change soon.

Sophia's son, Spiro, arrived to take George to Spiro's home which was practically on the edge of Kassandra, so the walk to his home was not far.

George met his daughters again. Areti, who is sixteen, had been going to school in Ioannina, Greece, and working in Patras, Greece, but because of the closing of the border, she had been stopped twice trying to go. It was now settled that tomorrow she could enter Greece and go to school, but for workers it was still closed. The family had their fingers crossed. Their other daughter, Demo, who is twelve year old, goes to school in Morista. Their son Dimitri is five. Meeting Spiro's wife Eli, who was not too tall, pretty with blonde hair and dark blue eyes, and a great smile, told George she was very happy to meet him.

She asked George, "Do you want coffee?"

"Yes. Make it sketos. Thank you."

When she left to make the coffee Spiro said, "It is very frustrating for me and my wife and for my daughter, Areti. She is a good student and misses going to school. I hope this is not another false alarm."

Eli returned with the coffee and preserves. After George and Spiro drank their coffee, Spiro said, "George, would you like to see my truck?"

George said, "Sure."

They went behind the home and sitting there was this old rusted Chinese truck. On the side of the driver's door there was this large painted and faded star. The truck needed a paint job, but the tires were in good shape, and when Spiro put the key in, it huffed and puffed but turned over.

Spiro said, "I paid fifty dollars (US) for it. I can use it to haul things and make money."

George said, "I have never seen a Chinese truck before. I assume it was made in the 1960s?"

"No. It was made in the 1950s."

George said, "Well, it is in good shape for being that old."

Spiro and George returned to the house after Spiro showed George his garden. Most of it had been harvested, but George could see that it was a large garden. Spiro claimed he had gotten a good crop, and it was still producing food.

George spent a good part of the afternoon at Spiro's home. Finally, Fevronia and Konstandia arrived to take George back to their house. Finishing his tsipouro, George thanked Spiro and Eli for their hospitality. On departing George gave Spiro forty thousand leks ($50 US). Spiro and Eli thanked him and they all kissed good-bye.

Returning to Stavroula's home a friend of Zahari's called Tomas, came and visited with the family. He wanted to meet George. During the conversation, Tomas said, "I own the bakery in Morista."

George said, "I've had bread made there. I really like the taste of the wheat. How is the bakery doing?"

Tomas replied, "The bakery does well, but I've had some problems. It had a fire once. It was arson. I pay a man one hundred dollars (US) a month for security. The ovens are German as well as the dough mixers, and all the bread pans. I worked in Greece to make the money to buy the equipment."

George asked, "Why do you think someone set it on fire?"

Tomas said, "Jealousy, pure jealousy."

Tomas told George and the family that he had to leave and go back to work. He said he was happy to have met George, and when George leaves to go back to America, stop by for some bread. With that he went out the door.

Sitting at the kitchen table, Fevronia helped George figure out his remaining days in Albania; a stay here, a stay there, and a stay somewhere else. George was leaving on the twenty-sixth.

George said, "I'm leaving Albania, but going to the Aegean Sea to see Margarita and her three daughters, their son, and their father. I didn't meet the father when I was here the last time. He was in Greece working. They live on the island of Skiathos. It will be a nice change for me, as I have not been to any islands in Greece. Besides, I love the sea. Too bad you cannot go. I would take you and whoever wanted to go."

Fevronia said, "I would love that."

George said, "I want you to do whatever you can for your mother. When you are able to go to Greece take your mother to a doctor or to a hospital. She needs to be on medicine and a diet."

Fevronia replied, "My father wants to do that. We are just waiting for the opportunity to go."

George said, "It's good to hear that Fevronia. I'm so happy to see you and all your family again. I feel like I've known you all my life. I hope the best for all of you. I'm giving you some money. Do not say no. Use it for whatever you or what the family needs. If I can be of service or if you need anything, let me know in America. Don't be bashful. I love you all. I better quit before I cry." He gave her American dollars.

Fevronia kissed George on the cheeks and on the lips. With that said they went into the front room and sat with the family and talked the night away.

During the night there was thunder and lightning. George slept well through most of it. Morning came and George knew another day had passed, and the time to leave Albania was getting near. George had his sketos coffee and then packed his belongings.

George, Fevronia, and Vangeli walked with George down the mountain to meet Aleko at 10:00 a.m. The girls had tears, and George felt sad. When they arrived at the parking lot, they saw Aleko and Artioli. They approached his car and said their hellos and good-byes.

Aleko said, "I arrived here early"

The ride to Argirocastro was very musical. Aleko played on his cassette, 'Papa Was a Rolling Stone.' The band playing was a European band.

George asked, "What is the name of the musical band?"

Aleko said, "I don't know. I was taping music off the radio when this song came on."

George said, "It is a good version of the original."

The song was still playing, as Aleko had repeated it. Passing a cemetery in Argirocastro, Aleko pointed toward the cemetery, turned the music down, and said, "Mama."

George said in English, "Respect."

Aleko repeated the word, "Respect."

Surprisingly, Aleko drove to Rezarta's school. She had asked Aleko to bring George because she wanted him to visit the school while she was working. Rezarta seeing the car from her window came out and greeted George. Aleko stayed with the car as Rezarta, Artioli, and George went inside.

The building was large and made of bricks. From the outside it looked like any school in America. Rezarta took George on a tour of the rooms, and she introduced him to the teachers in their rooms. There were no school children. George was amazed as they visited room to room. George decided to take photos of one classroom, as the rest looked the same. The furniture was old and in poor condition. All the rooms looked stark and gloomy; not enticing for educating children. It reminded George of movies depicting the settling of the far west when a one room building was used for a school and only the bare necessities were available.

Rezarta took George to the director's office as she wanted him to meet her boss. The director was a man. He was wearing a suit with a tie and white shirt. He met George with a pleasant smile and hand shake. George, Artioli, and Rezarta sat down, and George and the director discussed the conditions of the school and of the educational system.

The director said, "The government is expected to buy books and material so we can open the school soon. I can't do anything but wait."

George briefly explained the American school system and all the money spent on books and materials. The director listened and told George that maybe some day Albanian schools will be like the Americans. The director had a favorable future for the country.

George said, "I hope so too. Do you think I can get I can take a photo of you?"

The director responded, "I would like a picture of all the teachers." He got on the PA system and told the teachers to come from their rooms and meet outside.

George, with some reluctance from a few teachers, took photos of the entire staff with the director. The director was very firm with the teachers to have their pictures taken. It made George feel uncomfortable, so he tried to be patient with the teachers, but there was nothing he could do about some of their discomfort. There were about thirty teachers and all were women.

George thanked the teachers and the director. He told the director, "I'll send you a copy of the picture."

Rezarta went back to work, and Aleko took George to Aunt Penelope's home. George greeted his aunt and uncle. While George was showering the rest of the family came home. They all sat and had lunch together.

After lunch, Suela sat with George and talked about her school and America. She is intelligent and is in school learning Italian and English. She showed George her Italian-English language book. George perused it and found that it had many English grammar mistakes. It reminded George of the last time he was in Albania when he saw Anthoula's English book.

George said, "When I get a chance I'll send you an Italian-English grammar and dictionary book not printed in Albania. I can probably get it in Greece."

Suela said, "Thank you. They cannot be found here in any store. I attend a special school and my parents spend $6.00 (US) a month for my schooling. I know they are looking out for my future. When I get older I would like to go to America."

George said, "Well, if I can be of any help let me know."

Rezarta arrived at Aunt Penelope's home later in the afternoon, but alone. Aunt Penelope asked where Aleko was.

Rezarta said, "He dropped me off. Julietta and Aleko do not like to visit here, and I don't ask why." George thought of the family friction. The aunt didn't push the issue.

George and Rezarta said good-bye to the family and walked to Aunt Evanthia's home. They visited for a couple of hours and left. George had to promise the aunts that he would return to visit before he leaves for America.

Walking to Rezarta's home she stopped and bought chicken. She said she paid two dollars. George didn't know if she meant leks or dollars, but she said it was too much for one kilo (2.2 lbs). George did not want to ask about the money spent, but he knew she would talk about prices sometimes in dollars.

Spiros and Artioli were sitting in the kitchen when they arrived. Artioli was happy to see his mother and George. Rezarta went upstairs to get the baby from Eli, the baby sitter. Little Ana was a quiet baby who hardly ever cried. Eli came down with Rezarta to visit.

George said to Eli, "I have a cousin who is a Tolis. That is your last name, so that makes us family."

Eli laughed with a big smile on her face. Just about then her father knocked on the door. He's from Morista and he knew my cousin Sophia. He likes to tell stories and most are funny. They visited for an hour and returned upstairs.

Rezarta went into the kitchen to prepare dinner. Aleko arrived home later than usual, so Rezarta waited for Aleko to return before she served dinner. The chicken was delicious, along with rest of the food. Eli came down with bean soup. George said it was one of his favorite foods. Everyone laughed because it was considered peasant food. The night passed and everyone retired to their beds around mid-night. George was excited about tomorrow as he was going to Fier.

Chapter XXXVI

The next morning, Aleko and George drove to Aunt Evanthia's home for the trip to Fier. Her oldest daughter and three grandchildren lived there. Aunt Evanthia was very happy that she was going. She sat in the rear and got comfortable. Aleko blew his horn and went down the mountain.

George wanted to take in the sights as he hadn't been beyond the restaurant next to the reservoir. When they drove by the restaurant and the lake, the lake was dry. There was very little traffic on the main highway, as far as George was concerned.

Watching the scenery, George saw a green-house that was used for growing tomato plants. The two-lane highway had poplar trees in many areas along the sides of the road. There are people walking and riding donkeys, and a few persons on horses pulling small buck-boards. George saw many agricultural farms with men and women turning over the fields with very large hoe blades and wooden plows pulled by a donkey, a horse, or an ox. A few times George saw a woman in the front of the plow and a man in back. At one point they drove past an old oil field that looked like it was mostly shut down, but there was a strong aroma of oil in the air. George did see a few wells pumping oil, but most wells were just idle. The equipment and structures were soiled with dirty oil. Nothing looked sparkling or clean, and George could see small pools of oil on the ground.

Driving on, Aleko pointed out that in this particular town they were passing through sat the Ali Pasha's fort and home overlooking a river in the valley. It brought back George's memory of his seeing the Pasha's fort in Ioannina, Greece. In the hill country, George could see the hillsides terraced for farming. As for the condition of the road, George compared it to a back country road in northern Maine.

After two hours of driving, Aleko stopped at a small country-looking store for drinks. At one point Aunt Evanthia needed to get out the car as she felt car sick. The needed stop gave her time to recoup. They continued on and finally arrived in Fier. George looked around and thought that the city was dusty and dirty. He thought that it should be rebuilt to modern standards.

Aleko drove to a five storied apartment building that looked like it was built in the 1800s. George could see the shoddy work. George's aunt said it was twelve years old. It was hard to believe. Her daughter lived on the first floor in a small apartment. The kitchen was smaller that Rezarta's.

Aunt Evanthia's daughter's name was Ollga. George thought, another Ollga in the family. Ollga's oldest daughter was Sophia. George had met her on his last visit in 1992 at Aunt Evanthia's home.

George said in English, "Hello."

She said to George, "I have not been practicing my English, so it will be good to talk to you again."

George said, "I brought you an English-Greek dictionary. I promised it when I was here last. I didn't forget. I'm glad I finally saw you, so I can give it to you."

Sophia said, "I forgot all about it. Thank you so much. I will put it to good use."

George was introduced to Ollga's three other children, two girls, one sixteen and the other eleven respectfully, and one boy of eight. The youngest girl had a serious eye problem. She could not see well and needed an operation, but she can't go to Greece for help. The young boy spent most of the time outside playing. He was extremely shy.

Ollga's husband is in Skiathos, Greece, working as an electrician. He cannot return home because he would not be able to reenter Greece and then return to work. He has been gone for three months, and he is hopefully expected to return home for Christmas.

Ollga served a meal. The two younger children did not eat with them. Ollga gave her mother, George, and Aleko one piece of meat on their plates along with potatoes and salad. It was apparent that food was not abundant in this home. Both George and Aleko didn't eat the meat, but Aunt Evanthia ate hers. George and Aleko ate some salad as to not insult Ollga. They both told Ollga that they were not hungry. George felt sad for her living conditions. If he only knew he would have had Aleko stop to buy food.

After the meal, George was sitting in a position so that he could see into the kitchen. The young son had come home long after the meal, but remained elusive in the kitchen. Ollga was preparing her son a plate of food. On the plate she had put one of the pieces of meat with a few potatoes. George cried internally.

Trying to avoid the situation George turned towards Sophia and asked Sophia, "What are you doing with your life?"

Sophia replied, "I'm attending the university. My major is history and geography. I hope to get a job, but maybe I'll have to go to Greece for work. That is, if the problem between Albania and Greece is resolved."

Aunt Evanthia was happy to see her daughter and her grandchildren. The family sat and talked for a while until Aleko spoke up and said, "We better leave. I want to be home before dark, and who knows what will happen on the roads. You never know what to expect." Aunt Evanthia agreed.

George said to Ollga, "Thank you for the meal. It was nice to meet my cousin and your children. I hope to see you again. Please say hello to your husband. I hope that you can get your daughter to a doctor soon."

To Sophia he said, "Do well in school. I'm sure you will get a job."

With that said, and as the group was leaving, George passed to Sophia an American one hundred dollar bill. She took it with a huge grin on her face.

On the way home everyone was quiet. No one said anything about the meal. Aunt Evanthia seemed to be satisfied with every thing. As they drove home, the scenery was the same, except George had spotted some children in the fields tending a flock of turkeys, a herd of goats and sheep, and two men with pigs. Most people stared at the car as they passed.

At once place there were police standing in the middle of the road, what seemed to be nowhere in particular. They moved over as Aleko drove by them. Aleko told George that there are also so-called financial police looking for contrabands. As it turned out, at one point they stopped Aleko and were about to check the car. Aleko told them he was taking his American cousin back to Argirocastro. They left him alone.

Aleko said, "If you were not in the car they would have made me pay something. That's why I said you were an American. When you're driving, the police will yell at you to stop, and when you stop they ask for money. If you don't give them any or refuse, they take you to the station."

Driving further, a solitary policeman standing at the side of the road with his hand up yelled at Aleko to stop. Aleko stepped on the gas pedal and kept on going.

Aleko said, "He doesn't have a car, and he is all alone, so why should I stop? All he wants is money, and I don't want to give the police money for nothing. I work hard for my money, besides I won't be going that way for who knows how long."

George laughed. He was happy that the police didn't chase them like they would have in America. As they were approaching Argirocastro there were a few policemen standing aside the road, one of the policemen held up his hand for Aleko to stop; Aleko did.

The officer approached the car and said, "A man was shot outside a new savings bank, robbed the bank of a lot of money, but he was shot and killed. This is just a routine check."

After looking at every one in the car the policeman said, "You can proceed."

Taking Aunt Evanthia home first, George said to Aunt Evanthia, "I'll see you again. It was nice meeting your family."

She replied with a kiss, "Thank you."

Aleko driving home said, "Can you imagine a robbery here, and a bank?"

George said, "It happens in America all the time."

Walking in the apartment, they were met by Rezarta, Spiros and Artioli. With the television news covering the bank robbery, Rezarta immediately asked, "Are you hungry?"

Aleko said firmly, "Yes."

As Rezarta prepared something to eat, Spiros, Aleko and George watched the news. Besides covering the bank robbery they talked about the Democratic Party of Albania. It had just made a motion to remove President Sali Berisha. The Party said that he is an ex-communist and still acts as one.

There are six parties in the Albanian parliament: Agriculture, Labor, Socialist Democratic, Republican, and two smaller separate Democratic Parties. The major Democratic Party is quite large with over five hundred members. George didn't understand how the other two democratic groups identified itself.

Today is September the twenty-third. The time for George's departure from Albania is really getting close. George woke up at 8:00 a.m., it was the latest time he had awoken since his arrival in Albania. He thought to himself that maybe the stress of leaving had made him tired.

Eli, from upstairs, sent down cookies and a pastry made with philo dough, and she said they were for George. Eli had polio when she was young. It left her with a deformed leg and foot which gave her a drastic limp. She is about thirty-five to forty years old with a pleasant personality and a pleasant face. She has never been married.

Spiros said, "George, our cousin Georgiana who lives in Devitsian called and wants you to visit. Do you remember her?"

"Yes. I visited them briefly the last time I was here."

Spiros said, "I don't want to go, but Aleko said he would drive you there today, and he will stay with you. Do you want to go?"

"I suppose I could go just to say hello."

Today was going to be a busy day for George, with a trip to Devitsian, to Aunt Penelope's home, maybe Olympia's home, and who knows where else.

Aleko and George arrived in Devitsian mid-morning and met Georgiana, her husband, Demi, and her three daughters. The oldest daughter, Valeri, is married; the middle one, Zoiesta is twenty-one and single; and Irini who is fifteen, is very pretty, has a deep sexy voice, and is learning English. George had brought an English-Greek dictionary with him and gave it to Irini. George had remembered that he said he would give her one on his last visit to Albania. Luckily, he gave her his last one. She was very pleased.

Georgiana's home was quite large with a second floor. The yard had a large garden with fruit trees, grapes, and vegetables. Demi had been working in Greece, but he had to return to Albania. He was outside working on the first process to make tsipouro. George and Aleko toured the garden, drank tsipouro, and ate some boiled eggs, and salad.

George said, "It is so nice to see you all. You'll have to forgive me, but I can't stay too long as I have to see my Aunt Penelope today, and maybe Aunt Evanthia. I am leaving Albania on the twenty-sixth and there are many relatives to see before I leave. I will be in Glifada on my last day. George kissed them all good-bye and departed.

Aleko drove home. Spiros had gone out, and Artioli and Ana were upstairs with Eli. Rezarta had gone to work. She was securing the building and would be there for six hours. Rezarta had prepared two large size fried fish, small balls of mashed potatoes, sliced tomato placed in rows with onions cut into ringlets.

Aleko said, "Rezarta is a beautiful woman."

George agreed, "We are eating in Rezarta's restaurant."

Aleko continued, "My mother was a beautiful woman also. She had a big heart. She died in Aunt Penelope's arms of brain cancer. I love little Ana, but my father is so, so."

George was surprised to hear the last remark, but he didn't say anything. George knew that Spiros drank a lot.

Aleko said, "Artioli is a problem child. Rezarta agrees. I want to show you pictures of my mother and me when I was younger."

Aleko returned with a scrap book. He showed pictures of his mother and father, Julietta, and himself when they were teenagers, and a picture of when he was in the army. Aleko is balding, but he had lots of hair in the army.

Aleko said, "When I was in the army I drove tanks. I have to leave now, but Julietta will come here. We don't want you to be alone."

Julietta arrived about two minutes after he left. Also, Dimitri knocked on the door and said, "George lets go up to the roof. I want you to meet someone. Bring your camera. I want you to take some pictures."

George obliged and walked up to the roof with Dimitri. In the meantime Eli had brought the two children down to Julietta, who was visiting, and went up to the roof to be with her father. Dimitri introduced George to a retired policeman. His name was Omar and he was born in Albania, albeit, his heritage was Turkish. Omar was shorter than George with a robust body. He had grey thin hair, brown eyes, and a firm handshake. There was something about him that George liked. As it turned out, it was his personality.

After taken photos, surprisingly Omar said to George, "I want to take you to that building over there for a drink." He pointed to the police headquarters, which you could see from the rooftop. He did not invite Dimitri. George assumed because he was a Greek, and it was okay to take George because he was an American.

Omar said, "It is a private club for the police. Even though I am retired I can go there and bring guests."

George said, "It would be a pleasure. I can go for a short while as I have to go to my aunt's home." George thought about all the negative comments his family said about the Albanian police. George thought this should be very interesting.

George felt at ease on entering the building. There were many men in fancy decorated uniforms and some with fancy epaulets on their shoulders, men in plain clothes, and junior police walking about and sitting at tables drinking. Omar ordered beer and tsipouro. As it was, Omar could speak English. He introduced George to a few officers. Some could speak English also. Of course, Omar told his fellow officers that George was his American friend who lived in America. They spent about a half hour talking mostly about America and their police. It turned out to be a positive meeting.

They left the club and returned to the apartment building. Omar told

George that he enjoyed his visit and if George returns to Albania to make sure he visits him again.

Aleko and Rezarta had returned home and were surprised when they were told of George's visit to the police headquarters.

Aleko asked George, "What was it like."

George said, "Very interesting. I had a good time and I met many policemen. So, if you get arrested call me."

Aleko said, "Yeah, right. If you're ready I'll take you to see Penelope now, but we rather have you stay here with us."

George replied, "I need to go there because my large valise is there, and while I'm there I can clean up and change clothes, besides I want to see my aunt. It will be my last day in Argirocastro."

Aleko said, "Okay, I'll drop you off at her house. On Sunday we'll go to Glifada to see you before you leave and I'll drive you to Kakavia on Monday."

George, Rezarta, and Aleko arrived at Aunt Penelope's home. She was the only one home. Only George and Rezarta went inside.

George said to Aleko, "Why don't you go inside with me?"

Aleko said, "I have to stay with the car."

George said, "Okay." George thought about the family friction.

Butrint and guide

Chapter XXXVII

A fter George changed into clean clothes and made a collect call to Lesley, Uncle Taki, Margarita, Emir and her two children arrived. They were all happy to see George as well as George was happy to see them. George sat and visited and talked about his stay in Albania, and all the relatives he got to visit.

George said, "Today I want to see Olympia and her family, Aunt Evanthia, and of course, I wanted to see you. I will try to get that all in today. Tomorrow I'll go to Glifada and spend my last night there. You know I leave on Monday. Aleko said he would drive me to Glifada and to Kakavia. He drove me here today. I asked him to come inside today, but he said no."

There were no remarks made from anyone after that last comment. Only Aunt Penelope made a negative head gesture. A half hour after George's arrival, a meal of vegetables and fish were served. With drinks in their hands the family made many toasts for George's arrival and for a safe trip to America.

George said, "I'll return after I make the rounds today. It will be nice to spend my last night in Argirocastro here with you."

Suela, Margarita, and Emir went with George to Olympia's home. They were met at the door by Olympia and her ten year old granddaughter. After Olympia served her drinks and preserves, and along with Kristos the group relaxed on the front porch.

Olympia said, "Aunt Evanthia will either come here or go to Penelope's home to see you."

George replied, "It's too bad that there is friction among the family. If there was no problem everyone could get together and enjoy each other. Anyhow, I can't do anything about it. What I do notice mostly, beyond the families problems, are the problems in the country."

Kristos said, "Yes, there are many problems, but at least there was no violence when the communist government was over-thrown, it was done somewhat passively. Rather than kill officials or set fires, the populace destroyed materialistic properties such as factories, or items related to communism. I think the most devastated property I saw destroyed was the statue of Enver Hoxha here in Argirocastro. It felt like a new beginning."

Emir said, "Because of the destruction, many jobs were lost. The factories were operated and supervised by the communist's, so there was no one to take their place, and of course, no one wanted to work under them again. The average person does not have the background or education to replace them. The young people in college will have to take over."

George said, "And that will take time."

George spent a few hours with the family relaxing and having a good time. He gave the granddaughter an American dime and a dollar, and four thousand leks ($50 US).

She said to George, "I will keep the dime and dollar and spend the leks."

The family laughed. As the afternoon was slipping away, Emir said, "It doesn't seem that Aunt Evanthia is coming here. Maybe we ought to go back to the house."

With that said, George kissed everyone good-bye, and thanked them for everything. He gave money to Olympia, and with tears flowing, out the door they went.

Returning to Aunt Penelope's home, George inquired if Aunt Evanthia had come. Penelope said, "Not yet."

Sitting with his aunt, she said, "George, there are many problems between our families. Evanthia has another daughter who lives here in the city, but she never sees her. The daughter married a blind musician, and they have children."

George replied, "She never told me about that daughter."

Penelope continued, "Evanthea doesn't speak with our family in Kassandra. Spiros' children don't speak to me or my family. Anyhow, I personally have no problem with anyone and I pray for everyone. Besides, being the oldest person in the family it hurts me to see this problem."

George said, "I can understand your position."

Penelope continued, "Without mentioning any names, they want you to stay in their home only for your money. Of course, many want you to stay because they love you and you live so far away, and they can't visit. Also, they respect you because you are the oldest man in the family, like the position I hold as a woman. They have told me that personally."

George said, "Very interesting. I'll dismiss the notion about my money. With three aunts and over a dozen cousins with their families, there is no way I could afford to give away my money to every person. I do the best I can. I do know that Spiros and his family won't let me pay for anything, and Aunt Stavroula's family likes me and I can tell they do not look for money, although I leave some anyhow."

Aunt Penelope said, "Some have told me of your generosity. Thanks for doing the best you can. I know it must cost a lot of money to travel here, and of course your expenses back home. I'm very happy that you have come to Albania twice."

George thought of what Penelope said the last time in 1992 (of not being here whenever George returns). At least she is still alive, but she is sicklier, as is Aunt Stavroula.

George spent another meal of abundance at the aunt's home. The night seemed to pass quickly with everyone talking about George's visit and his impending leave of Argirocastro tomorrow and Albania on Monday. It was a sad ending of the day. It rained during the night washing away the words of sadness.

The household awoke early, and breakfast was ready when George appeared from his bedroom. The mood had turned to pleasantness and well wishes for George's travels. Not long after breakfast, Rezarta appeared to take George to Glifada; Aleko was waiting outside. With many kisses, hugs, and tears, George with his valise in his hands departed his aunt's home.

George asked Aleko if he would stop at Aunt Evanthia's home before going to Glifada. When they arrived and knocked on the door no one answered. There was nothing else to do but go to Glifada. George thought that maybe his aunt will be there in Glifada. She knew the day he was leaving. As it was, when they arrived in Glifada there was no sight of her.

Aleko walked up the hill with George; Rezarta stayed with the car. Vassilis, Violetta, and Aunt Amalia were happy to see George. Nicholas shook George's hand and returned to the yard to play. Violetta served coffee to everyone, and to George he received his sketos coffee.

It wasn't long after George arrived when Fevronia and Vangeli arrived with five years old, Andromaki. Fevronia had on a stunning black dress with white printed flowers. She looked very beautiful. Vangeli had brought a bottle of his tsipouro for George.

Vangeli said, "When you have a drink, you will think of me."

George thanked him. Just about then, Violetta came screaming out of the kitchen with Amalia behind her. Vassilis and Vangeli both asked her what the matter was.

Violetta said, "There's a snake in the kitchen."

Fevronia hearing Violetta describing the snake to Vassilis said to George, "It is a cobra. It is a poisonous snake."

Vassilis told Fevronia, with little Andromaki, to leave the house immediately as Vangeli went rushing outside. Vangeli returned with a shovel and went into the kitchen. George followed him, as he was curious but cautious; George was not afraid of snakes.

The two of them looked around to see where the snake was and how the snake got into the house. Vangeli saw a small hole in the chimney a few feet above the floor. The snake was in the hole and appeared to be exiting. Using the shovel Vangeli got him out of the hole and struck it, killing it with one blow. The snake was a foot long.

Vangeli said to George, "This is a small one. They grow to one meter. There might be a nest in the chimney."

Vassilis went outside and prepared cement. Vangeli lit a small fire to smoke-out any snakes that might be there. No more snakes appeared, so Vangeli patched the hole. With no more snakes in the house everyone went back inside relieved. George thought, what an exciting way to start the day off.

Not soon after that incident, little Andromaki announced to everyone in her high pitched voice, "George is my husband and not a friend."

Everyone looked at each and thought what brought that on. George looked at her with a smile.

She then said, "George you should be my mother's husband because my father is gone and you have a moustache like my father. You don't tell the truth, but you are my husband." Insulting – why? A child's remark!

Everyone laughed, and Andromaki turned around and left to play with Nicholas as if nothing had happened.

With the household back to normal after the snake excitement and Andromaki's remarks, Violetta announced that food was on the table. She served: sausages, chicken, lamb, sardines, eggs, potatoes, tomato salad, and green onions with olives, bread, wine, beer, sodas, watermelon, two kinds of grapes, and fresh walnuts in the shell.

It was a feast that lasted for two hours. When it was time for Vangeli and Fevronia to go home, Fevronia said to George, "I want you to return when I get married."

George said, "I'll do that. Please kiss your grandmother and tell her I love her, and I hope she and your mother can go to Greece for medical help.

Vangeli and Fevronia kissed everyone good-bye and went out the door heading for their walk to Kassandra. Little Andromaki walking in front of Vangeli turned around and peeped in her high voice, "Kalinikta (goodnight)." It was still very bright out. George knew he would miss that family.

George and Vassilis decided to walk up the hill to where their grandparents had lived. Aunt Ollga, her son Theodore and his wife Mariana were the only ones home. The children were playing at a friend's home. Receiving a joyous welcome, Vassilis and George were invited in for drinks and, of course, preserves.

George said, "I would like to have coffee."

Finishing their coffees, Mariana said to George, "Turn your cup upside down on the plate, and turn it clockwise a full three times. I will read your fortune. My aunt taught me how to read the grounds on the inside of the cup."

Reading George's cup she said, "George, you will have lots of money, and you will visit three more homes before you leave Albania. You will have safe travels, and when you arrive home in America, you will receive three kisses."

George thought that was interesting. The money, kisses, and safe travel sounded good. He thought of the homes he wanted to visit before he leaves.

George kissed them good-bye and said to Vassilis, "Let's go see cousin Thomas."

Vassilis and George walked to Thomas's home. Thomas's mother, Aunt Ana had passed away in 1993. Thomas, his wife, Bereta, and their son, Alex, were still living in the house. Alex was not home, but Bereta and Thomas were there. Thomas was surprised to see George.

Thomas said, "I've been busy trying to make money in Argirocastro. I get home very late in the day. A couple of times I went to Vassilis's home to see if you were there, but you were visiting somewhere. So, now you are leaving. I'm happy to at least see you today. I can't stay long here now as I have to leave for Argirocastro. Alex is picking me up. At least have a drink. What do you want?"

George said, "A nice glass of water."

Vassilis said, "Me too."

After drinking a few sips, Thomas said, "I have to go now. Have a safe trip and please return again with your wife."

George and Vassilis decided to leave also. They said good-bye to Thomas and Bereta and walked back to Vassilis' home. George thought to himself, that is home number one, after his visit with Mariana.

Violetta served a fulfilling dinner. With Aunt Amalia and the boys in bed, George, Violetta, and Vassilis sat on the porch and watched the lights of Glifada go off and on, and also view the lights of traffic on the highway down below. They talked about George's visit and his return trip to Albania. The night air cooled and the stars were showing their brilliant glory as the family turned in for the night.

It seems that the entire household awoke at the same time the next morning. Today, being a Sunday and the last full day for George in Albania, he asked Violetta, "Do they have a Sunday service here in the church today?"

Violetta said, "No. There is no priest available today."

During coffee George's thoughts went to what the day would bring. He wanted to make a visit to Eleni's. Vassilis told George he would go with him after breakfast.

Visiting Eleni, George asked her, "How are you and your daughter doing?"

Eleni responded, "My daughter is doing fine. Since I saw you two years ago, I get to go to Tirana and see her and my grandchildren. I'm feeling less depressed, and as you know, I sell milk and that gives me extra money."

George said, "I'm happy to hear that. You have a glow about you that shows your happiness. I leave tomorrow, but I'm going to Skiathos to see your brother and his family. Then I leave for America."

Eleni said, "Please give them my love, and to Lesley."

George said, "I have to go back to the house and plan my last day. Here is some money. Buy something for your grandchildren. I hope to see you again, but I don't know when."

With a beautiful smile on her face George kissed her good-bye and walked out the door. Returning to Vassilis's home George thought to himself, that's home number two.

Sitting on the porch drinking coffee, Vangeli and Fevronia appeared. To George's surprise they said they came to take him to Kassandra if he had the time.

Vangeli said, "We borrowed Zahari's Mercedes. My mother wants to see you once more. Can you come?"

George said, "Sure. Why not?"

The drive to Kassandra went quickly. The visit was pleasant, and Aunt Stavroula was happy to see George again. Fevronia gave George hand-made crocheted doilies and small pillow cases that she had made. George told her that they were beautiful.

Fevronia said, "I have lost my job because some of the children can go to Greece for school now and the schools in the villages are closed."

George said, "Maybe something will come your way, or you will marry soon and your husband will take care of you."

Fevronia had a big smile and said, "I have to find a man first."

After Dorothea served a light lunch, Vangeli said, "I have to return the car to Zahari. I'll take you back to Glifada now. Here are some grapes to eat on your way into Greece. Have a safe trip and please write when you get home. I'm glad you came to see my mother again. She is very happy you came."

George said his good-byes and off to Glifada they went. George knew that he would spend the rest of the day in Glifada. That was home visit number three.

George packed his belongings, and talked to Vassilis about seeing his brother, Vangeli and his family in Skiathos. George had not met Vangeli because he was working in Skiathos as were his two daughters on his last visit to Albania. George was excited about going to an island on the Aegean Sea, and seeing Vangeli, Margarita, and her three daughters and son. As the day passed on, Aunt Evanthia had not made a showing. Night approached, dinner was served, and the atmosphere turned solemn. Tomorrow, Aleko will arrive at 7:00 a.m. George wants to get to the Olympic Airline's office in Ioannina time enough to change his flight plans to America and fly to Skiathos. George had told Lesley of his change in plans and that he was going to Skiathos. He would let her know when he plans to fly into Boston. He hoped to stay for a week, if possible, in Skiathos. Lesley thought it was a good plan; she wished him well.

Night time seemed to pass quickly when the time to retire arrived. Dreams faded away as George did not need an alarm clock to wake up early. Village noises of roosters and dogs barking assisted him. It seemed that morning approached in a hurry.

Eating a small breakfast and having his last cup of sketos coffee in Albania, George was surprisingly visited by Eleni, and Olympia and

Kristos. Eleni, Violetta, and Olympia were going to Argirocastro by riding a bus to sell milk, and Kristos came along just to see George.

George kissed Aunt Amalia and said good-bye to Nicholas and Alex. Vassilis grabbed his large valise, and George with his carry-on hand bag walked down the hill with everyone else. When they arrived at the bottom the bus was waiting for the passengers. George and everyone kissed good-bye with tears. The bus pulled away as George saw his relatives waving from their seats. Soon after, Aleko, Rezarta, Artioli and Spiros arrived. George hugged and kissed Vassilis and thanked him for everything. Sadly, George got into the front seat and Aleko stepped on the gas pedal.

Driving on the gravel road up to the border crossing there were a few vehicles going down the hill with items packed on the roof and inside the car, an indication that the border was now open. The tension between Greece and Albania had subsided somewhat.

Aleko drove and parked as close as he could to the Albanian small ramshackle custom's office. There were many cars with Albanian license plates waiting to cross over to Greece. Only a few civilians loitering with luggage were at the Albanian gate.

George and everyone else got out of the car to say good-bye. George handed Rezarta all the leks and most of his drachmas he had and said, "Give some to Aunt Evanthia and keep some for you."

Inside the custom's building the official smiled and stamped George's passport. Rezarta and Aleko were allowed to pass through the gate with George after they said George was their relative and they wanted to make sure he passed through Greek customs.

There were many people at the Greek gate trying to pass through showing their red Albanian passports. The Greek official yelled at them to stand back. George had to push his way to the front, holding his blue American passport high in the air, so the official could spot it easily. The official saw the passport and allowed George to pass through, but he seemed to be angry that he had to let George pass through.

Once inside George had to go to the desk to have his passport signed. The man behind the counter was rude and unfriendly to George as he handed George the form to fill out.

After the official stamped his passport George said, "Ευχαριστούμε (thank you)." The official said nothing. George assumed that the official had to stamp his American passport, but he really didn't want to.

George went out and approached the fence where Aleko and Rezarta were standing and said to Rezarta and Aleko, "The Greek officials were unfriendly and seemed angry that they had to stamp my passport, but they did. This metal fence between us is like we're in a prison. It is hard to tell who is on the free side. Being that the world is one big place, and the earth is connected by water or dirt, with these separating metal fences, you would never know it. In America we hold up two fingers and say peace. I have to go now. Thanks again with love. I'll write when I arrive home. Love you. Good-bye."

Rezarta held up her two fingers and said, "Peace."

George did the same. He turned around and didn't look back as he boarded a bus for Ioannina; there were no taxis. George had to show his passport before he could pay his fare. The bus only had a few passengers, so George was able to sit alone.

Before the bus could drive away, the Greek police entered the bus and checked everyone's passport. All the passengers but George were Albanian. Seeing George's blue passport they didn't even check it. When the bus drove a mile or so it had to stop at a Greek soldier's check point. A few words were exchanged between the driver and one soldier. The soldier told the driver he could pass. A few minutes later the bus stopped again and three Albanian men got on, showing their red passports they paid their fare. They separated and sat by themselves.

As the bus drove away George's thoughts turned to what Albanian citizens want for themselves and Albania. First of all they want true democracy, they want jobs and to make a good living. They are not satisfied with their hospitals, their doctors, their government, their army, or their police. They realize that Enver Hoxha had them isolated from the rest of the world and that he falsely preached that they were better off than the rest of the world. The questions Albanians asked George: what is America like, what are the wages there, and what do items cost? George thought how unbelievable their life was and is.

George is now in Greece. Mirupafshim to Albania!

Family in Fier

EPILOGUE

In chronological order you will read important events, physically and morally, that took place in Albania following the years of Lesley and George Stamos's trips there. Albanian's government's cultural and moral changes slowly conformed to Europe's and the world's modern way of life, but of course, it took time, and many mistakes were made along the way.

To achieve these changes, Albania had to struggle through political predicaments, like the periodic changing of political parties, riots, anarchy, political thievery, and minority acceptance into their system. Albanian citizens and world countries knew for positive governmental changes to occur, and moral rightness, time was the only measures to look forward to.

Albania's past history of communism, totalitarianism, and isolationism from the rest of the world during Enver Hoxha's regime, gave them little to go on. They had to learn and change their government and their way of life to a new system. First of all, they had to learn how the rest of the world lived. Changing their complete way of life would not be an easy task. Albanian professionals and everyday citizens knew that the changes they wanted would take time and education to accomplish, but they wanted to initiate new procedures into their political system, and also bring their lifestyle to new standards.

*On April, 1994, almost two decades have past as I write, and not long after the fall of communism, there was the killing of two Albanian soldiers along the Albanian–Greek border. This created a major conflict between the two countries. Borders were closed between the two countries, and Greece broke immigration policies by expelling legal Albanian immigrants

285

from Greece. Greece also expelled Albanian-Greeks that were working throughout their country. During this period, Greece expelled 115,00 illegal Albanian immigrants between August and November, 1994, to put pressure on Albania due to the treatment of Greek members of an organization named 'Omonia' (located in the Greek-populated south of Albania) that were arrested for the killing.

The Albanian authorities arrested six Albanian-Greeks living in the Greek-speaking minority area in southern Albania. Only five were put on trial and sentenced.

An international committee: International Helsinki Federation for Human Rights (IHF) was formed to inspect the treatment of all concerned. The committee reported that Albania violated the conditions of the arrest, searches and seizures without warrants by persons in civilian clothes that were identified to be the Albanian secret police; The National Intelligence Service (Sherbimi Informativ Kombetar [SHIK]). The violations also included their treatment in jail, the lack of due process of the law, irregularities in court procedures, unqualified lawyers for the defendants, and many other legal breaches.

This same committee (IHF) cited Greece for the mistreatment of illegal Albanian deportees as a violation of specific articles under the International Covenant of Civil and Political Rights. Greece had to respect the rights of those deported.

On September 7, 1994, the Albanian court convicted, on all charges, five of the Albanian-Greeks arrested for the shooting of the Albanian soldiers. All defendants were given a sentence of 6-8 years. The Albanian Appeals Court reduced their sentences to 5-7 years on October 6, 1994. One defendant was released on December 24, 1994, by a presidential pardon. On February 8, 1995, the other four Omonia defendants were released.

With the treatment of the Omonia members, other minority issues came forth from the investigations of the Commission on Security and Cooperation in Europe (CSCE). These issues constituted areas in education, distribution of agrarian land, number of minority in the public sector (policemen or officers in the armed forces), minority political representation, the use of Greek symbols in the Greek minority sectors (Greek flag and Greek anthem), problems of the Autocephalous Orthodox Church, and intimidation of the minority.

To discuss all the issues above in depth would take volumes of discussion. Listed below are brief summaries of the conclusions and recommendations of these issues by the International Helsinki Federation for Human Rights, the Greek Helsinki Monitor, and reports of other NGOs of the problems discussed between August 15th and September 7, 1994. After 1993, the Greek minority and the Orthodox Church were subjected to discrimination.

1. Limitation of Greek schools in minority zoned areas.
2. Dismissal of minority from the civil sector.
3. For the minority Greek Orthodox Church to proceed with its work.
4. To allow Omonia to hold business as a political organization.
5. For Greece and Albania to work together on the issue of legal and illegal immigration policies.
6. Greece and Albania should have a positive dialogue to remove discrimination of minorities, and condemn groups or persons undermining their relationships.

* Greek Helsinki Monitor- September 1994

Mirupafshim {Good-bye} to the legal process and hello to the illegal confinement of Omonia members, and Mirupafshim to the hopes to settle the above problems. This was the only conclusion one could take to these problems in 1994.

****

The following information you're about to read concerning Albania in the 1990s is a sad state of affairs. In chronological sequence you will read historical events from 1992 to 2006. This history is concise, condensed, and to the point. As you read the following, remember that Albania had to learn to enter into the 21ˢᵗ Century from a dreadful political situation.

Albania held its first free election in over fifty years in 1992. The Democratic Party elected Sali Berisha as its first President for a term of five years, and Aleksander Meski became its Prime Minister. Because of the Democratic Party's economic policies, the economy became liberalized after over forty years of a communistic system. The financial system, endorsed by the government, was dominated by a Ponzi scheme funded by pyramid investment funds. There was no public bank or corporations to fund the money; the average Albanian invested in this scheme.

The pyramid came to an end in January, 1997. Because Albanians lost $1.2 billion, citizens took to the streets to protest. Believing the government was profiting from the scheme, the first protest took place January 16ᵗʰ in the south.

In the days that followed, protesters burned a cinema, a police station and a savings bank. During the last days of January, protests and violence erupted in Vlora (a southern coastal city), their police force were over whelmed, and clashes took place between police and protesters in downtown Tirana (the capital) at the same time.

A few days later a new opposition party was formed in the south. It was named: Forum for Democracy. Albanians were angry at their President because he and the government allowed the scheme to continue after warnings by the International Monetary Fund. Many citizens wanted the Democratic Party and the President to be removed, by force if necessary.

During the month of February thousands protested in Vlora, their police station was attacked by armed persons, the Vlora Democratic Party office was burned, and demonstrators blocked roads. Fifty Albanian Special Forces clashed with hundreds of protesters and throughout Albania chaos developed. The first person killed because of the chaos was buried in Vlora in February.

President Berisha promised to do all he could to resolve the problems. Students at the University in Vlora began a hunger strike in February and forty-six students at the University of Gjirokastra (Argirocastro) joined the

Vlora strike. They demanded that the Ponzi monies be returned and for the government to resign.

In March hundreds of prisoners were illegally freed, and hundreds of weapons seized. Vlora became the stronghold for protesters and gangs. In the beginning of March the Prime Minister, Aleksander Meski resigned and Bashkim Fino was appointed Prime Minister. Parliament then approved a chief of surgery to restore order. He ordered all schools closed and restrictions on the press. In the coastal city of Saranda the navy was attacked by masked persons, and a war ship was commandeered and thousands of weapons were confiscated. The day after, the army in Shkodra capitulated. About fifty soldiers joined the rebels and two Albanian Air Force pilots flew to Italy on Albanian planes. A SHIK branch in the south was attacked. One SHIK personal was taken hostage, six were burnt and two escaped. Riots were still erupting in the south, and also in a northeast border town bordering Kosovo.

In the middle of March, President Berisha announced a Government of National Reconciliation. Rumors spread that rebels were going to invade Tirana. Hundreds of individuals go to Tirana to protect it. A person named Franz Vranitski was appointed to restore order in the country replacing the chief of surgery and at the same time the chief of SHIK resigned. The port city of Durres was occupied by rebels. Parliament approved President Berisha's Government of National Reconciliation proclamation, and a massive peace rally was held in Tirana the next day. The government announced a National Mourning for all the victims of the rebellion, and following this announcement President Berisha declared amnesty and released fifty-one prisoners.

President Berisha also released Fatos Nano, the opposition leader from prison. Three days later a group called: Public Salvation Committee held a meeting and demanded for the President to resign. Greece talked about sending troops to Albania to protect the Greek minorities. President Berisha afraid of Greece's intervention called for Turkish military aid. Turkey informed Greece that if they invade, Turkey will invade Greece. The Greeks not wanting a war with Turkey had to capitulate.

The situation in Saranda and Gjirokastra still remained serious, gangs ruled and killings took place every day. The remainder of March was violent in areas across the country, but mainly in the south. Durres was retaken from the control of the rebels. People were killed in the towns of Kukes, Berat, Vlora, Levan, and Fier. During this ill period, Mother Theresa made a public statement praying for the government, its people, and for the country.

During the end of March the United Nations Security Council authorized a 7,000 man peace-force to go to Albania. It was called, 'Operation Alba', and it is being led by an Italian-led mission. In the Adriatic Sea an Italian naval vessel rammed and sunk an Albanian ship with refugees on board; eighty-two refugees died. The Albanian ship was controlled by a gang from Vlora. The Italian government sent condolences for the tragedy on March 31st. President Berisha and the Prime Minister also sent to the families of the tragedy their condolences.

In April, the resurrection continued, and in some areas local gangs clashed amongst themselves. Citizens were still being wounded and killed in major cities and towns. Violence and terror continued in the south during the entire month. Bombs and explosions occurred in Gjirokastra, at a University in Tirana, in Burrel, and in Berat. The UN peace troops entered Albania on April 15th. They were first deployed to the port city of Durres, and then to Vlora on April 21st. Schools reopened in the north. The month of May turned out to be violent throughout the month. Special Forces fought armed gangs, people are robbed and killed, a library was burned, a bridge was destroyed and another bridge was attacked, a warehouse exploded, a police car was attacked, and killings continue in Vlora.

May continued with bomb explosions resulting in citizens being killed or wounded. Parliamentary elections were held during the end of June with the Socialist Party winning the election. For the Democrats it was their largest defeat. Also on election day, a referendum was held voting to return to a Monarchy or to stay as a Republic. The Republic won with 65% of the vote. During May and June gangs continue to intimidate the public with fear and terror. Murders, robberies and the trafficking of drugs and weapons increased.

Sali Berisha resigned from the Presidency on July 24th; he served from 1992-1997. A Socialist government was formed with the election of Rexhep

Meidani as the President. Because of these results the insurgency ended as this meets the demands of the rebels. UN forces leave Albania on August 11, 1997.

To recover all the arms stolen and in the hands of the populous, the government offered money for any guns turned in. It was such an incentive many Albanians turned in their guns and collected money, thus many guns were taken off the street.

Mirupafshim to indiscriminate killings and anarchy.

*****

This next story is not so much about the country of Albania, but Albanians living on their border, and the somewhat involvement of Albania and those Albanians struggling to have a separate country.

Using arms stolen during the Albanian anarchy of 1997, Albanians in Kosovo received military arms and ammunition. Using these arms, the Kosovo war of 1998-1999 took place. The Albanian population living in Kosovo wanted a separate country free from Serbia; Kosovo borders north-east Albania.

During the Kosovo conflict NATO air forces were used against Serbian military, and American cruise missiles and airplanes were used to attack Serbian forces. Also, American Marines provided security as members of the Canadian Mounted Police in Kosovo.

Tens of thousand of refugees took refuge in Albania. The Kosovo Liberation Army (KLA) held their headquarters in an Albanian hotel located in Albania, and the north-east town of Kukes, Albania, held Serbian prisoners.

With the aid of NATO, and the arms received from Albania, persons of Albanian descendants living in Kosovo fought a brief war and won their freedom from Serbia, and it did not become another ethnic cleansing. Fortunately the conflict did not drag out, albeit it must be said that the country of Albania did not enter in the conflict.

Mirupafshim to another conflict in Europe.

*****

Albania tried to capitalize on its successes. In June 1999 Albania applied to join the European Union (EU). The EU responded that for Albania to be accepted political and economic changes must first occur in Albania. It is expected that Albania will join the Union in 2015.

Returning to relate what was happening in Albania after the Kosovo war, there were still many problems. There was rampart corruption, economic chaos, fraud, and changes of political governments following the problems created by the pyramid fiasco. It was not until the year of 2002 did some stability be achieved when the separate political parties finally worked out their differences.

During the communist regime, Greek education or the use of anything in Greek (language, books or newspapers) was limited to a so-called minority zone. The majority of these zones were in the southern part of Albania called Dropoli. If a few ethnic Albanians moved into one of the villages or towns, either through marriage or whatever this so-called minority zone was revoked.

This situation was still in existence many years after the fall of communism, the pyramid scheme, the Kosovo war, the changing of governments, and the recommendations of the International Helsinki Federation for Human Rights commission (IHF). This became a major problem between the new government and the minority Greeks. The Greeks wanted Greek language schools not only in the so-called minority zones, but in other non-Greek populated areas. In 2006 the government changed that policy and a Greek language university in Gjirokaster (Argirocastro) was established. Also, in the town of Himara a private Greek language school was opened.

Mirupafshim to discrimination.

*****

With better economic stability in Albania, roads were improved and paved. A modern custom's building and a paved road along with various shops were built at the border crossing of Kakavia; Greece also improved their custom's building.

Although somewhat crude, roads were improved in villages so at least vehicles could drive on them. Villagers do not have to walk up their mountain to get to their homes anymore.

Another major improvement was flush toilets. Under the communistic government control, only one flush toilet was in use in Gjirokastra (Argirocastro) at the home of Dictator Enver Hoxha. The city had a population of 35,000. Now there are many throughout the country, even in hotels.

Where debit or credit cards were not in use in the early 1990s, and there was no such thing as an ATM, as of 2010 there are ATMs and credit cards are in use. They are now accepted in every major city such as major hotels, supermarkets, and boutiques. In some shops cash is still preferred.

With all the modernizations put into place, of course cell phone services are in use throughout the country. Albania put into affect separate emergency phone numbers for police, medical, fire, and road police. How modern is that?

Mirupafshim to everything that had Albania living in the past. Of course, everyone knew it would take time, but Albania has joined the rest of the modern world. Congratulations.